MY STONE OF HOPE

To:

Susie Whitemore,

Thank you so much
for supporting our
work on behalf of
Haiti's children.

Best wishes,

Jean A.

MY STONE

JEAN-ROBERT CADET

with the assistance of Jim Luken

OF HOPE

FROM
HAITIAN
SLAVE CHILD
TO
ABOLITIONIST

UNIVERSITY OF TEXAS PRESS   AUSTIN

Copyright © 2011 by the University of Texas Press
All rights reserved
Printed in the United States of America
First edition, 2011

Requests for permission to reproduce material from this work should be sent to:
Permissions
University of Texas Press
P.O. Box 7819
Austin, TX 78713-7819
www.utexas.edu/utpress/about/bpermission.html

⊗ The paper used in this book meets the minimum requirements of
ANSI/NISO Z39.48-1992 (R1997) (Permanence of Paper).

LIBRARY OF CONGRESS CATALOGING-IN-PUBLICATION DATA

Cadet, Jean-Robert, 1955–
    My stone of hope : from Haitian slave child to abolitionist / Jean-Robert Cadet,
with Jim Luken.
        p.   cm.
    ISBN 978-0-292-72853-0 (cloth : alk. paper) — ISBN 978-0-292-72929-2 (pbk. :
alk. paper)
    1. Cadet, Jean-Robert, 1955– 2. Haitian Americans—Biography. 3. Children—
Haiti—Social conditions. 4. Haiti—Social conditions. 5. Cincinnati (Ohio)—
Biography. I. Luken, Jim. II. Title.
    E184.H27C335 2011
    977.1'043092—dc23
    [B]
    ISBN 978-0-292-73884-3 (e-book)

                                                                              2011022404

*For Katrina Marie Schrode,
who, at three years old, tamed me
like the Little Prince tamed the fox.
"You want to play a little game
with me?" she often asked.
As we played Candy Land and
shared laughter, I became unique to her
and she became unique to me.*

. . . we will be able to hew,
out of a mountain of despair,
a stone of hope.

—MARTIN LUTHER KING JR.,
in his "I Have a Dream" speech, Washington, DC, August 28, 1963

FOREWORD

"An earthquake has hit Port-au-Prince," I said into the phone. "I've heard. I'm going to try to get there as soon as possible," Jean-Robert Cadet, my husband, replied.

"Please be careful. I love you."

Jean would leave the next morning for Haiti, the country of his birth. I knew I could no more keep him from going there than, years earlier, I could have forced him to admit he was from there.

Growth is normal; it is expected. But its pace is not always predictable; our only role is to create an environment that encourages it. And so we live a good deal of our lives in hope until the seed sprouts, surprised by joy when the flower blooms. I think of my last trip to Haiti. It is this kind of joy that caught in my throat when I reached over to kiss our eighteen-year-old son good-bye when he dropped me off at the airport. His rough cheek beneath my lips, his muscled frame against my arms reminded me of his manhood and his own imminent departure plans. I was leaving to meet his father in Port-au-Prince on the 14th of July, our twentieth wedding anniversary. We had thought what a peculiar coincidence it was for two French teachers to be marrying on the bicentennial of the French Revolution.

Liberté, égalité, fraternité. France planted the seeds of its democracy with these words. Slaves toiling in sugarcane plantations revolted against France and created an independent Haiti, taking these same words for their new nation. But my husband did not grow up in liberty, equality, and brotherhood; his childhood in Haiti was spent in slavery, suppression, and isolation. He was a *restavek*.

"If you are within the sound of my voice and you have a child staying with you, please treat this child with dignity. Please remember that all children need love, that all children are God's children." I could not keep back my tears as I sat beside my husband in a radio studio last summer, listening to his voice broadcast over the airwaves of Port-au-Prince.

And now, despite this earthquake, I believe in Haiti's growth and expect it. It will flourish when all its children live in the sunlight of freedom and drink the waters of love.

Cynthia Nassano Cadet

ACKNOWLEDGMENTS

Various drafts of *My Stone of Hope* went through the hands of many friends, including my wife's. These wonderful people, whom I love dearly, gave me feedback and checked for spelling errors.

They are Kris Yohe, Linda Morris, Max Rabinowitz, Nicole Titus, Deborah R. Lydon, Jim Luken, Barbara Mustard, and David Mustard, who helped me focus on the theme of acculturation and put countless hours into improving the manuscript. I thank all of you for your contributions.

Most names of individuals and organizations have been changed.

My sole affiliation is now with the Jean R. Cadet Restavek Organization (http://www.JeanRCadet.org/).

MY STONE OF HOPE

PROLOGUE

O N JANUARY 12, 2010, I happened to be in Florida visiting my only childhood friend from Haiti, Carl Vilfort. We were driving to a shopping mall when we heard news of the massive earthquake that had struck Haiti hours earlier. Our friendship grounded both of us as we came to grips with those awful realities.

I had lived with Carl's family in Port-au-Prince for a year in the late sixties as a *restavek*, a domestic child slave. (In my first book, *Restavec*, I gave him the name Olivier.) We were about the same age and quickly became best friends, even though Carl was forbidden to play with me or even to have a normal conversation with me. In the presence of the adults, I had to address him as Monsieur Carl. Our clandestine friendship was a microcosmic example of the class system that still pervades Haitian society. He and I would meet secretly to swim or play together whenever we could. It may be difficult for the reader to grasp, but my friendship with Carl stands out in my memory as the one and only "moment" of loving contact in my entire childhood. When I was sent to the United States at age sixteen, I expected never to see him again.

Reunited as adults, our conversations often focused on the complex sociopolitical situation (including that of the *restaveks*) in our native country.

Back at Carl's home in Florida, we hurried to seek information about the earthquake on TV and the Internet. The reports were understandably vague, and the early death counts seemed relatively low. I recalled an earthquake I had experienced while living in California in the '80s. I didn't know what was happening. I thought I was experiencing vertigo. Then a few books fell off a shelf, but there was no damage. It was a *mild* earthquake. Carl and I were hoping for the best in this case too. But, as the night wore on, and knowing our native country intimately, we began to sense that the situation there had to be much worse than what we were hearing. When things go wrong in Haiti (and for centuries many things have gone horribly wrong), Haitian people often respond with a dismissive shrug. "Well . . . Haiti is Haiti," they say as if that should explain everything that fate seems to reserve, especially for the first black republic in the Western Hemisphere.

For my part, there were more than two hundred boys and girls in Port-au-Prince who were now living under the sponsorship of a large and growing organization that—at the time—bore my name. (Now the Jean R. Cadet Restavek Organization will carry forth my mission.) I was especially worried about two preadolescent girls, Magalie and Rachelle, who had been in *restavek* situations. They were in the process of being adopted by two American families.

A number of these children were part of a subclass in Haitian society known as *restaveks*, the word I used for the title of my first book. My foundation had been sending all two hundred of these children to various schools, paying for tuition, books, and uniforms. Additionally, we had become increasingly vocal in advocating that the government put an end to this cruel practice.

I myself had been a *restavek*. In Creole, the word refers to any child who "stays with" people who are not his or her immediate family. The word, as well as the concept of "staying with" others, might seem benign to outsiders, but, in fact, those Haitian children are unpaid domestic workers, often treated as slaves by the families they "stay with," just as I had been. They perform the most menial household chores: carrying water, scrubbing floors, cleaning chamber pots, and walking the owner-families' children to and from school. By the time of the earthquake, the faces of many of these children, whom I had come to know personally, had fixed themselves in my consciousness. At this point in my life's journey, at age 54, helping individual children in *restavek* situations (and eventually putting an end to this nationwide system of abuse) had become my passion. For the most part, *My Stone of Hope* details the strange, and for me, amazing story of how I came to realize my life's purpose.

Carl and I stayed up late into the night, dealing—sometimes in tears—with the worsening news about the earthquake. Both of us resolved to make our way to Port-au-Prince as quickly as possible. Weeks earlier, I had booked one of my semiregular flights from Miami to Haiti for January 14th. The staff of my foundation and I had planned to use our time in Haiti to begin writing and filming public service announcements to aid in an aggressive campaign against child slavery.

I assumed I could easily move my reservation forward one day. So I called the airline, only to learn that all commercial flights to Haiti had been cancelled (it would be three weeks until they resumed semiregular service). I called my wife, Cindy, in Cincinnati, to tell her that I would be trying to get to Port-au-Prince in any way possible. She already knew that nothing would keep me from getting there. She gave me her love and told me to be careful. Carl drove me to the airport, and we promised to meet up as soon as possible in our native country.

My best option was to fly to Puerto Plata in the Dominican Republic (DR), where I arrived on January 13, at 3:00 p.m. (Both Haiti and the DR are located on an island known, in colonial times, as Hispaniola.) From this remote airport I took a nine-hour bus ride to Santo Domingo, the Dominican capital, where I hoped to secure transport of some kind to the earthquake zone.

At one point during the long ride, I found myself listening intently to a Dominican radio station's call-in show blasting from the bus's speaker system. All the talk was about the previous day's earthquake in neighboring Haiti. I had taken four semesters of Spanish in college and could understand much of the conversation. Many of the callers were sharing their opinion about the "reasons" for the earthquake. These comments bore a remarkable similarity to the absurd statements I would later hear coming from some fundamentalist "talking heads" in the US. Some callers brought up the poverty of Haiti, which is so much more severe than in the DR. Some brought up the hurricanes that had devastated Haiti only a year ago. All this chatter was heading toward the same conclusion: that Haiti was a cursed nation. This may be true, but the curse has a human face, and an evil human history. I will never be convinced that God or nature has it in for Haiti.

A number of the callers were saying that my homeland's traumatic history had happened as the result of an *acuerdo con el Diablo* (a deal with the Devil), which some slaves, in order to gain their freedom, were supposed to have signed 230 years ago. One man even called Haiti "el campo del Diablo" (the land of the Devil). I was boiling mad, and for a long time I found it all but impossible to catch some much-needed sleep.

When at last we arrived in Santo Domingo, I found a hotel where I was able to connect my laptop to the front-desk computer and access my e-mail. Among my messages was a request from the BBC for an interview about the earthquake. Several months earlier, a BBC reporter had interviewed me about *restaveks* in Port-au-Prince and I had told him that I planned on being in Haiti once again in mid-January. Fortunately for me, I took a few moments to send a short reply saying that I was in the DR and would be trying to find transportation to the Haitian capital. Almost immediately, I received the following response: "Here's the cell phone number of a Haitian man in Santo Domingo, a fixer-translator who has worked with us. Give him a call." Fixers are bilingual locals used by news agencies to make connections for their reporters and camera crews, for whom they then translate. I placed a call to the fixer. He told me to meet a guy named Mike at a particular location in the Boca Chica. He said there was a group of reporters that would be leaving soon for Haiti. And, yes, they had room for one more person. This was incredible good luck. I realized that I could have easily been stuck in Santo Domingo for days.

I took a cab to the meeting place and met with the reporters near two big SUVs they had rented. Everyone was bristling with eagerness to cover so huge a natural disaster. But there was a glitch. Mike, the main reporter, told me there was no room after all. Instead of panicking, I assessed my situation. Finally, I got Mike off to the side. I was desperate to get to Haiti. This was no time for reticence.

"Look," I said, "you're a reporter, right? Well, I speak fluent Creole and I might be able to help you get some very special stories."

"But I've already paid the fixer."

"Does the fixer have international connections?" I explained that I was an advocate against child slavery in Haiti, that I had written a book, and that I was "known" in Haiti, as well as in the US and Europe. Mike remained hesitant. Finally I said, "You have an iPhone. Google me . . . Jean-Robert Cadet, C-A-D-E-T."

He promptly did this, and I watched as he scrolled down the list of "hits." His eyes widened a bit.

"Okay," he said. "You're in." I breathed a huge sigh of relief.

It was 3:00 a.m. when we left Santo Domingo for what would be a seven-hour drive to Port-au-Prince. At sunrise I began to notice several medical mobile units and trucks of emergency food rushing toward Haiti, courtesy of the Dominican people. This goodwill quickly washed away the bitter residue left in my mind by the radio call-in-show.

It was mid-morning when we arrived at the outskirts of Port-au-Prince. I began to see the effects of the earthquake in outlying towns. Many homes had collapsed into big piles of rubble, and I found myself wondering how many people were buried inside each of them. The city reminded me of an exaggerated war zone, although I had never seen one firsthand. Bodies littered the roadside, as if they had been shot by snipers in broad daylight. Many people were carrying off personal belongings that they no doubt had collected from their own ruined homes—or someone else's. I was struck by the weird stillness, the absence of the usual horn-honking din that had been the heartbeat of this huge, boisterous, city. People were shouting and moaning, "Jesus, help me . . . Jesus . . . Jesus!"

The entrances to many streets were blocked with the remains of fallen buildings and homes. We saw women and children sitting in small clots in the middle of the sidewalks, many of them still weeping, although this was the second morning since that unmerciful earthquake. More than once I saw a man, himself clearly wounded, carrying a severely injured woman on his back. "Is it his wife, his sister, his mother?" I wondered. And where was he going?

Over the years, there have been many stupid zombie movies made about Haiti. I had never encountered a zombie. But here at last, I concluded, were the walking dead. Hundreds of them. And these were only the people we could see as our SUV crawled toward the airport. I knew there had to be thousands and thousands of others like them, confused, dazed, homeless, desperate, walking around half-dead, much like Hollywood zombies, except that they were real, and—for the moment, at least—alive.

Finally, at the airport, we pulled in front of a big building that was identified by a large sign, in English, as the "International Media Headquarters." Reporters and television crews from all over the world seemed to have been transported almost magically to the earthquake zone, all of them ready to record and transmit the story of Haiti's latest misery into the homes of the secure and comfortable. Military cargo planes—mostly from the US and Canada—were roaring down the runway, coming and going, while Black Hawk helicopters flew reconnaissance over the city, as they would for weeks to come. Search and rescue teams from various countries were erecting their tents in the tall grass alongside the tarmac. I could see that some team members were exercising their body-sniffing dogs and returning them to their cages. The scene was one of organized chaos.

Later that day I accompanied my new friend Mike, the reporter who had transported me from the DR, on a short trip to Petionville, the wealthy suburb on the mountainside overlooking Port-au-Prince. I was keeping my promise to help him out. Mike wanted to locate the mayor of Port-au-Prince and have me translate his hoped-for interview. We found the mayor's house. It was severely damaged. In the front yard was a tent. We were told that the mayor had gone to visit a nearby hospital, so we went there to find him. On the hospital grounds we noted hundreds of small pup tents that had mushroomed into every available space. People were using these tents as waiting rooms, but in many of them, the injured had already died. In the heat of the day the stench was all but unbearable. It permeated our skin and clothes. We found the mayor, a tall and robust man, coming out of the hospital with his right arm in a sling. Mike and I approached him. "I am in a hurry," he said in perfect English, heading toward the gate. "We need tents. We need water. We need medical supplies. We need . . . ," he rattled as he hopped into a large SUV. Mike took a few notes and we headed for our car.

On the way down the hill we passed near the famous Hotel Montana, where the rich would stay when they came to Haiti. Now it resembled much of the rest of Port-au-Prince, a collapsed wreck that, in minutes, had become a tomb for hundreds of people.

By early afternoon we returned to the airport. Whenever I was hungry, I would visit a large tent alongside the tarmac occupied by American soldiers and ask for a box of MRE (meals ready to eat) and a bottle of water. "Help yourself," a soldier would say and point to a box on the floor. I could have asked the Canadian troops, who were a lot closer to the media headquarters, but since I had served with the 82nd at Fort Bragg, I felt a special connection to that unit, as if I belonged with these troops. That night (and several more to follow) I slept deeply on the tile floor of the main airport terminal, using a flattened cardboard box as my mattress, and my backpack for a pillow. No one needed to remind me that my sleep situation was infinitely better than that of most of the people in Port-au-Prince.

The next few days—indeed, that entire first month after the earthquake—are a chaotic jumble in my memory, a rolling, ongoing nightmare. It has been said that the best way to remember a dream (or a nightmare) is to *feel* your way back into it, which I will attempt to do here. Days and dates are fuzzy, but the primary recollections are set in stone, and the *feelings* about those memories still reverberate in my mind and in my heart. I have no doubt, they always will.

Thankfully, even before I left Miami, I had been in e-mail contact with the staff from Cincinnati. I was relieved to learn that they were safe in my foundation's compound in Port-au-Prince. I promised to join them later.

During those first few days in Haiti, I decided to accompany Mike, as guide and translator, on many of his attempts to report various stories for the English language branch of Al Jazeera, the famous Arab news network. For three days I had access to information, Internet, and e-mail at the media center. Often, I found myself rubbing shoulders with famous newspeople and major television anchors, like Diane Sawyer (my favorite). Mike, of course, had the four-wheel-drive SUV and a driver to get us to places that I would never have seen on my own. For me, this was a way of seeing the effects of the earthquake through a special lens, the eyes of an experienced reporter. As we traveled about, I sometimes played the role of a reporter, questioning dozens of my fellow Haitians regarding their experiences of the *evenman* (the "event," as most Haitians referred to the earthquake). Some said that it sounded like a thousand bulldozers rushing down the street. Others called it "goudou goudou," because the ground had made deep muffled sounds.

One thing no one who was there will forget from the aftermath of the "event" is the smell of rotting flesh. All over the city were thousands of bodies still entombed under the concrete and structural steel that had crushed them, along with bodies littering many of the streets, singularly or piled into mounds. Some were carefully wrapped up in bedsheets. Some were rolled in cardboard and tied up with ropes. Some were stuffed into burlap sacks or garbage bags. Many were so swollen in the sun that they seemed ready to pop, their skin having turned ghostly white after being stretched to its limits.

We inched past a large street-side grocery store that had collapsed. A man with a handkerchief around his face stood on the sidewalk leafing through an American passport. Another man wearing a surgical mask dragged himself out of a small hole in the debris holding a fistful of cash. Apparently he had picked the pockets of the dead. Later, driving past a pile of rubble that once had been a police station, we saw dead uniformed officers, buried up to their chests like the busts of statues. Another policeman was upside down, buried to his knees, the soles of his spit-shined shoes facing the sky.

Knowing how Haitians love to honor their dead with expensive funerals and ornate aboveground tombs, it seemed surreal that so many people's remains were—in a sense—trivialized, almost to the point of desecration, by the brutal realities surrounding those first days and weeks. As most will remember, due to the incredibly difficult (and dangerous) circumstances, thousands of good people had to be buried in mass graves. It couldn't be helped. All of Port-au-Prince went through a living hell, and the living coped as best they could.

Most of the world saw some of this horror on TV news shows, and many viewers, grief-stricken and torn, responded with incredible generosity. Perhaps I don't need to mention that, whatever grizzly bits and pieces television audiences may have endured, nothing can compare with the ongoing, numbing trauma of being there, of living through those seemingly endless days after the most devastating earthquake in human memory. I can say one thing without a doubt: You would *not* have wanted to be there.

O n Sunday, five days after the earthquake, I engaged a motorcycle "taxi" to take me to my foundation's offices on Route Frère, some five miles north of the airport. We had, a year before, rented space in the large walled-in compound owned by the Church of the Nazarene, one of the many fundamentalist megachurches that had sprung up in Haiti over recent years. The compound, located a significant distance from the epicenter of the *evenman*, had survived with little damage to its buildings.

I was overjoyed to find the foundation's Haitian staff alive. We were relieved to have come through our various ordeals, and to have found our way to this relatively secure situation where, almost immediately, we could begin planning our postearthquake work.

Considering the enormity of the chaos, we were not really sure of what exactly we should be doing. With so much need, with so devastated an infrastructure, with supply systems severely disrupted, and with many communications systems limping along, what could a small organization do? My impulse was to find Magalie and Rachelle. Hours after I had arrived at the compound, the couple who would be adopting Magalie informed me by e-mail that they had been receiving text messages from their daughter-to-be. Magalie was safe.

I drove to Rachelle's neighborhood. The entrance to most streets was blocked with debris. I parked on a main road and began to walk with a backpack. I had stuffed it with rice to give to Bertha, Rachelle's aunt, in case I found her. The stench of decomposed bodies was unbearable. Eventually, I located Rachelle's house. It was split in half, with the front section on its side. In the back room was a large wall hanging of the Last Supper. People had erected shacks near their destroyed homes to guard their personal belonging, buried in the rubble. I climbed on top of a pile of debris and yelled, "Rachelle, Rachelle. Bertha, Bertha." Finally I heard a voice. "Se Bertha, Map vini" (It's Bertha, I am coming). I saw her in a black dress, running toward me with Rachelle in tow.

I gave Bertha the rice and piggybacked Rachelle to the car. Back at the compound, I learned that the Haitian government and the US State Department had approved all adoptions that were initiated before the earthquake. In a matter of weeks, Rachelle and Magalie would join their American families in the states.

As a foundation, our course of action was determined, to a certain extent, by the arrival, providentially, the day before the earthquake, of a huge shipment (more than a ton) of rice, mixed with freeze-dried vegetables. We began to feed about two hundred people, roughly forty families, who had crowded inside the walls of the Nazarene compound. This turned out to be no small task. As I walked around their tents looking to see if they had children in servitude, I would encounter families who were diligently sifting through the rice and discarding those hard, scary little vegetable pieces. I explained that they could cook it just like rice, and the vegetables would puff up and taste wonderful mixed with their beloved rice. But they would not deviate from their cultural traditions, or habit, regarding food. They wanted their rice and beans. It was as if I were coaxing small children to try Chinese food for the first time, and it was a battle I finally gave up trying to win.

I continued walking, especially early in the morning, amongst the improvised tents and keeping a watchful eye for children in domestic slavery. Knowing my culture so well, I knew that during times of crisis, the plight of *restaveks* would only worsen. These children would be lucky to eat twice a day, as some families often saw them as extra mouths to be fed. Within days I was able to identify eight girls living with families in the compound. They were dressed more shabbily than the rest of the children, and they were constantly hauling water to their families' living space, or carrying plastic bags, often full of human waste, away from the tents to some outside area where they could dump it. I did my best to work with the families of these children. I told them the story of my own childhood and gave them extra food and blankets, explaining always that the children staying with them were sent by God and should be loved and fed like their own children. Before long, these eight girls were calling me "Pappy Jean-Robert" with the biggest smiles on their faces.

I noticed one little girl watching "her family" eating spaghetti. She was standing beside a mat with a plump toddler in her arms.

The child would cry when she sat him down. I asked her name. "Manouchka," she said. She was nine years old. Later, away from the family, she related her story. It was much like my own story. Her mother was dead. She had been "given" to her "family." They had not sent her to school. Now, like many city people after the earthquake, they were planning a move to the countryside of Lagonave, where they would have little need of her services. She said they were contacting other families in the area to see if they wanted a *restavek*. No doubt Manouchka would find herself in yet another bad situation. It was an old Haitian story. In disastrous situations (e.g., hurricanes), many *restaveks* are simply abandoned.

At one point Manouchka looked me right in the eyes. "Please take me, she said. "You can have me. They don't want me anymore." Hers weren't the limpid eyes of dog, begging for a treat from the table. Here was a child, begging for her life. With my heart breaking, the best that I could do was to see that her family received more food and supplies. In the hopes of showing them Manouchka's potential "value," I arranged that she would be the one to come and pick up these various goods.

When my foundation's supply of rice ran out, we went into high gear to obtain more food. It became clear that a lot of hoarding was going on by merchants and suppliers in the capital city. The foundation's contributors had made certain that we had plenty of money. At a time when very few organizations were getting food out to people, we did. In such desperate circumstances, we paid the inflated prices. Why not?

We began distributing tens of thousands of dollars' worth of food to Haitian groups that claimed to be working with children. Although we were very small compared to many organizations that had come to Haiti, we were agile in adapting to "market conditions." There is little doubt that we made a significant impact in terms of feeding our contact groups during this perilous time.

Two weeks after the earthquake, I tried finding my way to a "partner organization" called Foyer Ovide Xavier, or FOX, which, for many years, had been housing runaway *restavek* children and reuniting them with their birth families. I knew most of the girls by name in that prisonlike home.

Two years earlier, I had accompanied twelve-year-old Marika for a joyful reunion with her birth family in Benet, a mountain village in the south. A social worker had come along to secure the signature of the parent who would be receiving her. The road was treacherous. It had taken us nine hours to get there in a large SUV. When we arrived, Marika, who had been a slave for two years, ran into the house.

"Manman" (Mother), she screamed.

"Marika, is that you?" her mother asked, as if she couldn't believe her eyes. "Oh, Jesus, I didn't think I would ever see you again. Last year your uncle went to Port-au-Prince. He was told that you ran away. How did you get here?"

"A man named Jean-Robert brought me home," said Marika.

Before long the family, with three other children, appeared on the front porch. They greeted me warmly. In a matter of minutes the entire village had gathered in the yard. They had come to see who brought back Marika.

"Thank you, Jesus. Thank you, Mr. Jean-Robert for bringing home my child," said the mother, with tears of joy streaming down her face. Because dusk had begun to settle, I didn't want to prolong my stay. I asked Marika permission to show the crowd her scars. She nodded and I asked her to stand on a chair and face the house. She complied. "How many of you have a child living with strangers in Port-au-Prince?" I asked. Five women raised their hands. Everyone looked perplexed. I pulled up the tail of Marika's blouse. "Oh, Jesus, that's not right," a woman said. Every face expressed shock, looking at the whip marks that crisscrossed Marika's back.

"Jesus, Jesus," screamed Marika's mother, who quickly held her daughter in a tight embrace. "Look at what they did to my child," she said, moaning as if she were having labor pains.

"That's not right. That's not right," said her father.

"If you have children living with strangers in Port-au-Prince, go get them before it's too late," I said. Some women nodded. The crowd began to leave, shaking their heads. "How could they do this to Marika?" some asked.

"It's time to go. We have a long drive ahead of us," said the social worker. She handed Marika's father a document on a clipboard.

"Write your name here to show that we've delivered Marika to you."
She handed him a pen. The father printed his name awkwardly on the
signature line like a child who had just learned to write the alphabet.

The FOX girls' home was in downtown Port-au-Prince. I walked
into an area of town where I remembered the building had been
located. The neighborhood looked so different from the way it had
been before the earthquake. As soon as I saw the big steel gate, still
standing, I recognized a large image of Mickey Mouse painted on it
in bold colors. I had found it. But beyond the gate, I could see that
the three-story building, including the residence floors for the girls,
had collapsed into a huge pile of rubble. My heart sank.

At the top of the pile, two men were working with picks, obviously looking for bodies. I climbed carefully up to join them. At
first I tried to help, but my bare hands were all but useless on the
rough concrete and cinder block debris. I got down on my hands
and knees, peering into the area where the men were pulling away
concrete. I noticed something in the shadows that looked like the
arm of a white mannequin sticking up.

"Is that a body?" I asked. One of the men looked closely.

"Yes," he said without emotion, "it is." They began clearing away
the debris near the arm. After a few minutes we could make out some
hair on the back of the head. Then one of the men put his pick gently behind the head, turning it in our direction. The girl's face was
white with dust, but even so, I recognized her. I didn't remember
her name, but I knew her.

That had to be one of the worst moments of my life. I broke down,
crying uncontrollably. "I know her, I know her," I kept saying. One
of the men did his best to comfort me. After more work, we were
able to remove the girl's body from the clutches of the concrete. With
that, we saw another body, but could not recover it. "We would have
to pull her out in pieces," the man said. I left before the men carried
the dead child down from the pile. I couldn't take it. Later I learned
that at least four more girls were down there in the rubble.

A week later, a staff member and I visited the other facility: FOX
Boys, in the town of Medor, which was east of the city. I knew that
this area had been undamaged for the most part and that the girls
who had survived the tragedy in Port-au-Prince had been moved out

there. By this time, I had gotten more or less accustomed to some of the postearthquake realities in Haiti. Not all of these realities had to do with death and destruction, but they were almost as unsettling.

Partly, this had to do with the fact of "Haiti being Haiti," as mentioned earlier. Long before the earthquake, it had become almost a cliché to mention that Haiti was "the poorest country in the Western Hemisphere." Being so known, my birth country had gained a certain notoriety for attracting a huge number of nongovernmental organizations (NGOs) to help with Haiti's ongoing social and developmental problems. Unfortunately more than a few of these NGOs had become semiparasitic, feeding off various forms of aid money that poured (or sometimes trickled) into the country from foreign governments as well as private donors. Whenever I saw one of those huge SUVs driven by many of the NGOs, I would become almost sickened. "Why do they need such fancy gas-hogs?" I would ask myself, knowing, of course, that the question was rhetorical.

After the earthquake, this situation became even more pronounced. Haitians, at all levels of society, were aware that mountains of money would be coming to aid the victims of the *evenman*. No doubt there would be even more of these wasteful NGOs. Of course I am aware that there are many NGOs that are doing incredible work for the people of Haiti. The same can be said for many small groups and individuals, hundreds of whom were arriving every day, people who genuinely wanted to help.

When we arrived at the FOX Boys facility, I saw a teacher I had known from past visits standing near the entry door. I inquired how many kids were now living at the group home. He told me that, with the addition of the girls from downtown, there were about 120. That seemed like a large number.

Just then, six of those FOX girls came running up to me. I had visited with them in November, before the earthquake. They hugged me and touched me and, for the longest time, wouldn't let go. Considering what had happened at their living facility, I was happy to shower them with affection. But as our little reunion was taking place, I noticed a young boy in the recreation area leaning against a wall and weeping uncontrollably. I pulled myself away from the girls and walked over to him.

"Ki jan ou rele?" (What do you call yourself?), I asked, putting my hand on his shoulder.

"Jean-Woody," he said.

"And why are you crying, Jean-Woody?" There was another burst of tears.

"I want to go home," he sobbed.

"Where is your home?"

"Chuotte." (This is a town in the country, several hours from Port au Prince.)

"Who brought you here?"

"My papa."

"Your papa?" I asked. "Then you are not a *restavek*?"

"No, sir," he said.

"Then why are you here?"

The boy explained that a few days earlier, a man had come to his house in Chuotte and told his parents to bring him here. The man assured the family that the boy would be well treated and returned to them when he was eighteen years old. This was a new wrinkle in the *restavek* system. The FOX organization, which had in the past been housing and returning runaway *restaveks* to their birth parents, was now *collecting* children from their families and passing them off as displaced victims of the earthquake. The obvious reason: to get money from a major NGO. Like many charities in Haiti, it appeared that FOX had become part of a numbers game, one in which both the NGO and its grassroots partner benefited financially. It is a simple scam: the more children you are "helping," the more money you get. The longer you keep the children, the steadier the income. I found it incredible that the enabling NGO benefactor had failed to interview any of these kids and thus determine their actual status.

Several other children came to talk to me, with very similar stories. They kept asking me to call their parents. Every story ended with the same moral: "I don't want to be here until I'm eighteen. I want to go home." Three children from the Brice family, along with their cousin, had been brought to the compound. They begged me to call their father, and later that evening I did. He told me that representatives of FOX had promised that the children would be fed, schooled, and cared for. I was very direct with him.

"They are your children," I said. "You can't give them up like this. They will grow up hating you. They won't get any love in that camp."

He responded that he was afraid to go back there again to pick them up. To his way of thinking, the people who ran FOX represented the government, and he was afraid of them. All in all that day, I spoke with nearly two dozen very unhappy children at the facility. Their lives were in turmoil, not because the earthquake had destroyed their homes or killed their parents, but because some greedy people with power had decided what was best for them. This is an old story. In Haiti, and elsewhere.

Our foundation had always had good relations with Madeline Ganoud, the Haitian woman who ran FOX. I was shocked, as if I had walked into a sinkhole. "Madeline has been our partner," I said to myself. "I can't believe she is doing something like this."

I located our staff person and recounted the situation. He didn't seem too bothered by it. He said something about these being crazy times, and that Madame Ganoud was probably doing the best she could. He added that we needed to be cautious, because her husband worked for the government.

I told him that I wanted to go into her office right then and there and confront the woman. I wanted to ask her why she had brought all these children in from the countryside, kids who were neither runaways nor *restaveks*, kids whom her agents had coerced away from their parents. I saw this as another Haitian tragedy in the making.

Later, I contacted two major news organizations and related the story to them. They showed no interest.

On many mornings, accompanied by a few of the foundation's Haitian employees we called "child advocates," I visited tent camps. The advocates were so desensitized, they couldn't recognize a child in domestic slavery even if she served them a glass of water. In every one of these makeshift communities, I was easily able to identify *restavek* children and to establish that the earthquake didn't seem to have changed anything in the way they were being abused. Often, it had made things worse. The kids were slaving away, often for groups of neighbors, not just the family they were staying with.

On many occasions, I saw them being beaten with wooden spoons, or shoes, sometimes even whips.

I recalled when I was a child during another disaster, one of Haiti's worst hurricanes of that era. The government radio station was warning people not to send their children out of doors to fetch water, because people were being sliced in half by flying tin roofs that had been dislodged from so many makeshift houses. Guess who was sent out for water? Right. Me . . . and every other *restavek* kid I knew, boy or girl. Not much has changed.

Mid-February came. I had been in Port-au-Prince for a solid month. The first day after I returned to Cincinnati was my birthday, and Cindy tried to celebrate with me, as much as I would let her, but I really wasn't in the mood. Birthdays have always been difficult for me. As a child, not only was the date of my birth unknown, but celebrating a *restavek*'s birthday was unthinkable for the owner-family. In fact, the date of my birthday (February 15) is a fiction. I determined the time frame of my real birthday when I was an adult, but never the actual date. Cindy was sweet, and didn't push the birthday on me too hard. Cindy was teaching school at the time, but we managed some caring and comfortable times together, punctuated by various engagements related to Haiti, of course.

During my second week at home, I flew to Columbia University in New York for a major symposium on Haiti's *restavek* problem. The panel of speakers included a representative of UNICEF, one of the higher-ups from the Haitian consulate, and myself. There were two hundred people in attendance, including a man who was in charge of producing a proposed segment for the *60 Minutes* television show on CBS. He did not bring a cameraman, and I think he may have been there to make certain I would be returning to Port-au-Prince by the first week of March, when his crew was scheduled to film a segment with me.

Back in Cincinnati from New York, I conducted several major fundraisers for my foundation. One of them was a gala, including dinner and music at the University of Cincinnati. It had been arranged months earlier by one of the foundation's board members. I wasn't feeling very "gala," so in my twenty-minute speech following the buffet, I mentioned the earthquake only briefly. As the center-piece for my speech, I projected a photo from my laptop of a shab-bily dressed little girl walking another girl, in her pristine uniform, to school. "In a nutshell," I said, "what we are trying to do is to see to it that the other little girl can go to school as well."

There were several other fundraisers at local schools. Loveland Middle School raised $18,000. I was blown away by such generosity. Maybe, I thought, that was why the village was called "Loveland." Basically, my brief time at home helped cauterize some of the pain that was in my heart, stemming from what must have been the most traumatic month of my adult life.

In late February I returned to Haiti, and almost immediately I found myself involved in the *60 Minutes* project. These things tend to be more complicated than one would expect. I had been through tapings for CNN and *Nightline* on ABC in years past, but for me (and certainly for the children in *restavek*) this was a pretty big deal. In my mind, bringing attention to the *restavek* issue, on a show with the credentials of *60 Minutes*, would result in nothing but good for the children.

Carl, my childhood friend, came to visit me. I wanted him to see some *restavek* children in action (i.e., at work). At the first camp, we observed the "routine" of a psychosocial program director, hired by UNICEF to aid in the healing process for traumatized children. This guy was a genuine hoot, very animated and clownish, using a battery-operated megaphone as he worked his young crowd, rallying the children's spirits and regaling them with funny little stories. He was loud, very loud, jumping up and down all over the gathering space, telling one slapstick joke after another. Carl and I could see that the kids were really into it. His job was to come there every day as a sign of continuity for the children, and a boisterous hint that a normal, happy life might one day return for them. He reminded me of an energetic Haitian version of Barney, the beloved purple dinosaur of children's television. Carl, a gifted photographer, took pictures of the performance and the kids, including several *restaveks* who were returning with buckets of water.

Afterward, we treated the man to lunch at a little restaurant. I suggested that he use the megaphone to draw more children to his performance. I told him to roam through the tent camps urging parents to send their children to his event—*all* the children, including the ones who were doing chores. I cautioned him about using the "R" word. Over the last twenty years, the word *restavek* has become taboo, almost like the "N" word in the US. I suggested he tell them to send "ti moun ki rete ave ou" (the child who lives with you). After lunch, we accompanied this wonderful man to another camp for a second performance. I don't know how he summoned the energy, but he was doing this show three times a day. He followed our suggestion for using the megaphone to drum up business. Afterward he told us that more kids had joined in than usual. Thanks to Carl and our crazy friend, that day proved to be the most relaxing, positive time I had had in two months.

At the end of the month, I once again returned to Cincinnati. This was a few days before the Sunday evening *60 Minutes* piece was to be broadcast. I was exhausted and ready to simply hang out at home.

One day in early April, I received an e-mail from US Lieutenant General Ken Keen, who was the point person for the Army's Southern Command unit, which had been headquartered in Port-au-Prince since the earthquake. He wrote that he had been impressed by the *60 Minutes* piece and wanted to meet with me. In the televised interview, it had been mentioned that, many years earlier, I had been an enlisted member of an Army Ranger unit at Fort Lewis, Washington. It seems that General Keen had served in that same unit. Both of us found this an interesting coincidence. He invited me to visit his office in Port-au-Prince. Through the general's aide-de-camp (whose patriotic-sounding name was Major Betsy Ross), I quickly made arrangements to meet with the general. I sensed that this could be a very important meeting.

I made my third trip—this one very brief—to the earthquake zone. I located the Southern Command Headquarters on the US embassy's grounds in Port-au-Prince, a huge complex of massive army tents. As usual, I was wearing slacks and a T-shirt. I went to the main gate and asked to see General Keen.

"Who?" The guard, an enlisted man, asked.

"General Ken Keen," I responded.

The guard gathered his composure and then turned and called to several other enlisted men who were standing behind him.

"This guy wants to see General Keen," he announced, a wry smile coming over his face. I guess I couldn't blame him. Here I was, a smallish brown man with a Haitian accent, asking to see the commander of all US forces in Haiti.

"And why do you want to see the general?" he asked.

"The general wants to see me," I said. "He asked to meet with me." The man looked perplexed, so I added, "If you contact his aide-de-camp, she will vouch for me. My name is Jean-Robert Cadet. My last name is spelled 'C-A-D-E-T,' but pronounced 'Ca-day.'"

"And what is the name of this aide, Mr. Ca-day?" He over-emphasized the pronunciation.

"Betsy Ross. I believe she is a major."

Once again, that smile came over his face. "He says the general's aide is named Betsy Ross." Everyone within earshot sniggered at this.

"That's her name," I said. "Look it up in your directory. She made the arrangements for my meeting with General Keen."

After several additional exchanges, they contacted Major Ross. Within minutes she was there at the gate to escort me in.

"It's good to see you, Mr. Cadet," she said. "The general will see you now."

As the two of us walked off, I didn't turn around, but I pictured all the personnel at the guard station scratching or shaking their heads. I relished that image.

The major led me to another huge tent, at the end of which, sitting at a large table, was the general. We greeted one another and sat down with Major Ross to a long and circuitous conversation. He asked about my time at Fort Lewis.

"I learned a lot about leadership in that Ranger unit, sir," I said.

"I'm sure you did," he responded, "but how did you ever wind up in the army in the first place?"

So I told him about wandering into a recruiting station when I was just out of high school and admiring the posters hanging all over the walls. I told him I had asked the recruiter if I might be permitted to change the oil in a tank. The general smiled.

Then Major Ross brought up the situation of the *restavek* children. The two of them seemed pretty well informed about the problem. Ross told me of a recent meeting they had had with Haiti's president, René Préval. When they brought up the *restavek* issue, Préval had responded by telling them that even in the US, adopted children were not treated as biological children. Everyone in the room was stunned by this misconception. Someone from the US Department of State had gently corrected him.

"We tried to be respectful in informing the president that his understanding was not, in fact, the reality, and that adopted children in the US are usually well loved," said Major Ross.

I explained to them how, in Haiti, many parents turn their children over to strangers in the belief or hope, first of all, that they will be treated with care, and secondly that they will receive what the birth family is unable to afford: a basic education, which in Haiti promises a way out of systemic poverty.

"Unfortunately," I added, "that rarely happens."

"This is no different than colonial slavery," General Keen observed, shaking his head. "How can this practice be brought to an end?"

I told him that two vital components would probably be necessary: the decentralization of Port-au-Prince and mandatory public education. Then the general asked the million-dollar question:

"What do you think we can do for these children out of this office?" I was ready to respond.

"General, I've been knocking on hundreds of doors over the past twelve years, hoping that one of them might help open up the *restavek* problem and move it toward genuine resolution."

"What kind of doors?" he asked. I conducted a shortened litany.

"Well, I've spoken before the UN in Geneva four times. Three times I've addressed the International Labor Organization. I've testified before Congress. I've even been on the *Oprah Winfrey Show*."

"Wow, you've been around," the general said, and we all laughed.

"And General," I added, in total seriousness, "You are one of those doors. I made a special trip to Haiti in order to open it." Lt. General Ken Keen nodded his head.

Before we said our good-byes, I pulled out a copy of my book, *Restavec*, and inscribed it to him. Later, in my notebook, I wrote down—as carefully as I could remember them—the words I had written there:

Please help convince Washington to push Haiti's government to make education a mandated gift to all Haitian children; otherwise economic growth will not be possible and democracy will never take root.

· · · · ·

When I first started writing *My Stone of Hope*, using a snippet of MLK's "I Have a Dream" speech as its title, I had a straightforward reason for writing it, and a simple theme in mind.

In 1998, my first book, *Restavec*, had been a modest publishing success. I was a high school teacher when that book came out, and I felt more or less satisfied that I had done something that had certain relevance, even importance. I had written a book that, in recounting the typical life of a Haitian slave child (me), had, far beyond my expectations, helped place the issue of child slavery in public view. I was proud of this accomplishment, and felt that I had done enough. What else *could* I do? I was helping to raise a family. My deepest hope was that—with my story as a catalyst—some talented individual might be motivated to champion the cause of child slavery in my native country, and also perhaps in other places around the world, where this horrible practice perpetuates itself. In the years that followed, various writers detailed the horrors of worldwide modern slavery, authors like my good friends Ben Skinner (*A Crime So Monstrous*, Free Press, 2008) and Keven Bales (*Ending Slavery*, University of California Press, 2007). We should be grateful to them.

But no anti-slavery knight riding a white horse emerged on the horizon. Well over 300,000 Haitian children, according to UNICEF, are still living in a daily, loveless hell. By a kind of default, I became the leading spokesperson in the effort to bring an end to this horrible, dehumanizing institution.

The theme of *My Stone of Hope*, in that first writing, had to do with how the cards in US society are stacked against an outsider. There I was, a nonnative black man trying to make his way in the "land of the brave and the free." Early on, the book simply recounted my problems in acculturating, in being accepted. Even as the first draft came into existence, I more or less believed that all my issues were outside myself. My problems had often been caused by others. In a conversation about why good people sometimes do very bad things, a friend of mine made a universal statement that I disagreed with. "Let's face it, Jean," he said. "Everyone has *kinks*." Without a moment's hesitation, I responded, "Not me. I don't violate the innocence of children and hurt others on purpose. I live by the rules."

If the reader has waded this far through my unusual life, spent early on as a *restavek*, she can't help but know that my life here in the US was anything but an easy one. And the reader can't help but have seen a few of my "kinks." Pulling oneself up by one's own bootstraps can be a Herculean task.

Then, as the final drafts of this book were being tweaked and edited, came the unthinkable *evenman*. Haiti's earthquake shook everything, including the foundations of my being. Before the *evenman*, I thought I had become who I was supposed to be. I thought I had hewn my own little stone of hope out of that mountain of despair, and made a life (yes, a "me"). The earthquake, with its ongoing psychological aftershocks, was a sobering reminder to me and much of the world of the incredible fragility of just about everything, including, in my case, the image I had of myself.

These few remaining paragraphs will, I hope, bring down the curtain on all of that, and will do so in a way that is, if not healing, at least generative.

But other aspects of my situation were not as encouraging. The foundation that I had started in 2002, and later turned over to others whom I trusted to manage, was no longer living up to its mission. I was shocked and devastated beyond belief to discover that the foundation's legal papers had been amended without my permission. My name, and the names of two other officers, had been replaced with the names of those who had come to "help." The situation was so bleak that, on the advice of lawyer friends, I had little choice but to withdraw my affiliation and my name from this well-funded organization and start over from scratch.

The plight of children in *restavek* servitude is my passion. I know there are thousands of Marikas and Manouchkas whose precious childhoods are at this moment being spent in unending labor and isolation. For child slavery to end, the new generation must be sensitized with a curriculum on human rights, and Haitian artists must be mobilized to create images and music for social change. My life's mission would go forward, God willing.

In the midst of all this, I had the honor of being the commencement speaker for the graduating class at Northern Kentucky University, a thriving young school across the Ohio River from Cincinnati. The ceremony took place in an indoor stadium on a beautiful spring day. Just before I was to give my speech, I was awarded an honorary doctorate by the university president and was given a beautifully framed diploma. Nine thousand people were in attendance to listen to a capsulation of my life and my life's mission. As I received a standing ovation, I was moved to tears.

After the ceremony, I found Cindy and handed her the framed document. She looked at me, her own face stained with tears, and smiled at me with eyes that I could see were filled with pride and love. We joined Dr. Votruba, the president of the university, for a delicious lunch. Said Dr. Votruba, "In my fourteen-year tenure, this is the first time a commencement speaker has received a standing ovation."

Within days of the "divorce" from the old foundation, I made up my mind to create RESTAVEK NO MORE, INC., d/b/a Jean R. Cadet Restavek Organization. As this book goes to publication, this organization will have become official, a legal entity, with its own articles of incorporation. Its mission: to advocate for the demise of child slavery. Those who join with me in this new endeavor will be fighting the same odds. Bureaucracy, history, and the traditions of Haitian slavery will continue to be aligned against us. We will be fighting an uphill battle, against all odds.

And so we pursue the struggle. Dr. King tells us that "the arc of history bends slowly, but it bends toward justice."

In the hopes of accelerating that bending process, I hand each of you, my dear readers, this *Stone of Hope*.

CHAPTER 1

O NE WINTER'S DAY in 1971, almost two years after arriving in the United States from Haiti, I found myself walking into a strange situation in the lunchroom of my new American high school. Immediately, and as usual, I began searching for a hard-to-find seat at one of the few integrated tables. Every day, I faced the same search. At this point, I still did not know enough about American history and culture to understand why most black and white students sat at separate tables on opposite sides of the cafeteria. But I had figured out my own situation. In my mind, I was neither black nor white. I was Haitian.

Nonetheless, I carefully avoided a table occupied every day by a handful of Haitian immigrant students, who usually spoke to each other in French, Haiti's official language at the time. That was the last place I would sit.

Because of my own background and history, I could fluently speak only Creole, the language of the Haitian masses. If I had mixed with these kids, I was certain my identity would be found out. In Haiti, I had been a *restavek*, a slave child, the lowest of the low in a class-based society. I was afraid of how these other Haitian students, who obviously came from the middle and upper classes, might react to me.

I continued to drift among the tables with my tray, all the while knowing that something had intruded upon the usual chaotic ambience of the lunchroom. A speech was coming over the PA system.

Even to my ears, still new to the language, this was a very powerful speech. Until that day, I had never heard anything but school announcements coming over those loudspeakers, announcements that were pretty much ignored by the lunch crowd.

I could feel myself being drawn into the eloquent ebb and flow of this moving speech. The orator's cadences, his melodious voice, and his passionate delivery mesmerized me, like some exotic melody that I was hearing for the first time.

To my recollection, I had only heard one other speech in my entire life. That one had been delivered by "Papa Doc" Duvalier, Haiti's infamous former dictator. I was perhaps seven or eight years old at the time. I remember some of his words, "Liberté, Egalité, and Fraternité." I didn't know what they meant, but I sensed they were important words, because he repeated them several times. I remember that the people gathered around the little radio, listening to their "President-for-Life," were jovial as Duvalier solemnly repeated these words.

The most striking thing about the situation in the cafeteria this day was the lack of joviality, the general hush, the absence of the normal teenage din. Why? And who was doing the speaking? It was obvious, even to me, that this was a powerful African American voice. My English had improved to the point where I could make out most of the words I was hearing, and much of their stirring syntax. It was almost as if this man were singing a powerful song, directed only to me. I fell into a kind of trance.

Finally, I noticed someone getting up from one of the tables that were exclusive to us "misfit" students, black and white. I took the seat without being acknowledged by my table mates. There was nothing new in that. Every day we would eat our meals in total silence. I refocused my attention on the incredible voice coming over the PA.

It was so baffling to me. *Why*, I pondered, *on this ordinary school day, was this kind of speech being played for the students of Spring Valley High School in Rockland County, New York?* As one who had been trained not to question his betters, I knew I couldn't bring myself to ask any of the students around me about this strange occurrence.

But I did notice that I wasn't the only one caught up in the speech. Most of the lunchroom crowd seemed genuinely captivated by this man's powerful oratory. At one point near the end, the man repeated the refrain, "I have a dream," over and over.

To this day, I remember asking myself: "Why is he speaking about a dream he's having *now?* He should be saying, 'I *had* a dream last night.'" In Haiti, I recalled, people often told each other about dreams they had had the night before. Then sometimes, using a book called *Tchala*, they interpreted the symbols of their dreams into lottery numbers, which might yield their one chance for a better life. But the speaker wasn't talking about numbers or money. I could tell that he was pleading for justice, freedom, and equality for Negroes, but I didn't understand why. I didn't get it. America was still so new to me.

As the man finished his speech, I observed the black and white American students at my table exchanging strange embarrassed glances between bites of hamburgers and fries. But no one said a word.

The only person I dared ask about the "dream" speech was Mr. Rabinowitz, my tenth-grade history teacher who, a year earlier, had helped me sign on to the welfare system after he discovered that, for want of a home, I had been sleeping in an all-night Laundromat. He was one of several compassionate teachers at the school who took me under their wings.

After I finished my lunch that day, I scrambled over to Mr. Rabinowitz's room, where he sat me down and explained, in very simple English, that the speaker was Martin Luther King Jr., a civil rights activist, who in this speech was appealing for racial equality during the March on Washington eight years earlier, in 1963.

"February is now Black History Month in the US," he said. "Reverend King was a great black leader, but he was assassinated. He's dead. The school administration thought that it was important for the student body to hear this famous speech." I caught on to what he was telling me, more or less. But I spent the next few days puzzling over the notion of a "Black History Month." I knew what "history" was. And I knew what "black" was. But I couldn't put the two notions together. English was my favorite subject, and I liked the color blue. I found myself hoping that March or April might prove to be "Blue English Month."

In spite of such crazy issues with the language, my overall cultural awareness was growing. I had been attending Spring Valley High long enough to have memorized the Pledge of Allegiance, but not long enough to have learned that "liberty and justice for all" was not to be taken too literally by anyone whose skin color was similar to mine. I believed blacks and whites were the same here in America, even if they sat on different sides of a big room.

In those days, whenever I watched news segments of civil rights protest marches on TV, I thought that black Americans were acting silly with their big Afros, their clenched fists, and their incessant demands for equality. My thinking often went something like this: *Why are they making trouble? I'll never wear an Afro. Don't they know that white people are good to them? They can get jobs, welfare, food stamps, and free education for their children. Why aren't they happy? Many of them even drive Cadillacs. What is their problem?*

One thing is certain. My understanding of the way things worked, or didn't work, between the races of my adopted country spiked dramatically the day I listened to Reverend King speaking of his famous "dream."

That very same afternoon, my eleventh grade history teacher began our class by passing around a cigar box with names of black historical figures inside. He assigned each student the task of creating an oral presentation about the person he or she had picked. I drew the name "Dred Scott." I had never heard of him. As we marched off to the school library that day to begin our research, I felt excited and eager to learn about this man with an ominous-sounding name.

I learned that Dred Scott had been born a slave in Virginia in 1799, on a plantation owned by a man named Peter Blow. Blow sold him to a Dr. John Emerson, who took Scott with him in 1830 when he moved his family to St. Louis, Missouri, a free state, where Scott remained the property of Emerson's wife after the doctor died.

Dred Scott sued for his freedom in 1846, on the grounds that Mrs. Emerson had beaten and mistreated him. He also argued that, by virtue of having resided for a time in the free territories of Illinois, Wisconsin, and Missouri, he should have been given his freedom. Scott lost the suit. Mrs. Irene Emerson won the right to keep her "property."

As I moved through this little research project, I often found myself wondering if Dred Scott had endured the same cruelties to which I had been subjected as a child slave on the impoverished island nation of Haiti. I wondered if his masters had passed him around to friends as mine had, with everyone living more easily off my labor. I wondered if he had ever gone to bed hoping never to awaken, to sleep forever. I wondered if slavery had stolen every moment of his childhood, as it had mine. I wondered if, like me, he had been taken away from his family as a toddler, never to lay eyes on them for the next thirty years. I struggled to interweave the history of slavery in the United States with my own background, because child slavery was then, and is *to this moment*, being practiced in all areas of Haiti.

I read Justice Roger B. Taney's ruling, often referred to as the Dred Scott decision. "Blacks," he wrote, "are so inferior they have no rights that a white man is bound to respect." I was shocked that a highly educated white person could be so ignorant and so malicious. Throughout my boyhood in Haiti, I had always heard that white people were generous, extremely intelligent, sincere, and almost saintly. Since many of my teachers, like Mr. Rabinowitz, were so kind to me, I speculated that this type of prejudice existed only a very long time ago in the US. Surely, nowadays, all whites had truly internalized the values of the Pledge of Allegiance, which they recited daily at school, and elsewhere, with their right hands over their hearts. I thought that when a person spoke with his hand over his heart, it meant: "This is my word of honor. I cannot go back on it."

Each day during Black History Month, I listened to my classmates present the stories of Malcolm X, Booker T. Washington, Frederick Douglass, Harriet Tubman, and others. When my turn came to speak, I read verbatim what I had learned about Dred Scott. As I read my essay, I noticed the teacher nodding in agreement and smiling. For one of the first times in my life, I felt proud of my achievement. Even then, I could sense the irony of that moment: *Unknown to anyone in the room (except me), a modern-day slave was relating the pain-filled saga of a famous historical slave.*

At this point, perhaps I should lay out for the reader a brief account of my childhood, as I have detailed it in my previous book, *Restavec*. For twelve years, as a child, I had been the *restavek* of a woman named Florence Cadet, a dark-complexioned prostitute and an amateur *mambo*, or *vodou* (voodoo) priestess. *Restavek* is the word for child slave in Haitian Creole. Literally, it means "one who stays with someone." The fact is, I was *owned* by Florence.

Florence was a tall, beautiful woman with an hourglass figure. She did not purchase me from a slave market like those Haitian slaves brought from Africa by French colonists. Instead, as a four-year-old, I had been given away by my biological father, who was white and somewhat wealthy. My mother, his housekeeper at the time of my conception, was a black, very poor, and illiterate peasant. Thus I was too low-born and too dark to be worthy of my father's name or to be raised as his son.

I was never told what name my mother had given me when I was born, but Florence called me Bobby. When she barked "Bob," my stomach would churn. That meant I had failed to perform a chore to her satisfaction. In a rage, she would sometimes whip me ferociously, saying, "I have to get that bad blood out of you." I guess she was referring to my mother's blood.

As a boy, I would occasionally overhear a *granmoun* (a particular adult) say to a friend, "I need a *timoun* [child] to help me in the house." Then, a few days later, a preadolescent would appear on the person's doorstep, brought to them from the countryside, just as I had been.

Like me, these children would be the first to rise and the last to sleep, often on the kitchen floor or under a table. We would sweep the yard, haul trash, light the charcoal, empty and wash chamber pots, fetch water, wash dishes, scrub laundry, clean the house, and make the beds. We would walk the family's children to and from school. As much as possible, we stayed out of sight, but always within the sound of the voice of an adult. A *rigwaz* (cowhide whip) was on hand to beat us if we refused to work or caused the adults any real or imagined displeasure. Some adults disciplined their own children with the *rigwaz*, but never as viciously as they wailed on their *restaveks*.

When newly acquired *restavek* children were sent on errands and got lost, the police took them to radio stations to be described on the air. "We have a *ti-fi* [little girl] named Dieula, between nine and twelve years old. She wears a pink, adult-sized dress. She's barefoot and has dark skin. She has a basket of charcoal and green plantains in her hand. We also have a *ti-gason* [little boy] named Luc, between ten and twelve years old. He's barefoot. He wears khaki shorts and a blue shirt. If these *ti-mouns* [children] belong to you, please come get them," the radio announced. Everyone knew a shabby-looking *restavek* when they saw one. In this situation, *ti-fi* and *ti-gason* were code words for *restaveks*.

Sometimes *restavek* boys ran away from their families and became street urchins. When this happened, the adults would simply get new children from the countryside. They thought that once a *restavek* had tasted freedom in the streets, he or she could never again be trusted.

The cinder block house where I lived with Florence had two bedrooms, a large living and dining area, a bathroom with shower, and a kitchen that featured a three-burner coal stove and a table. Water was only available outside the home, so I washed dishes at a faucet, which hung over a cement basin in the yard. Two metal drums served as water storage for the home.

The yard sported a large shade tree, a small mango tree, a few clotheslines, and a rock-pile on which to whiten hand-washed laundry in the sun.

In Florence's bedroom was a framed picture of the Sacred Heart of Jesus above her bed. Pope John XXIII was on the left wall, facing the Virgin Mary on the opposite wall. At the foot of her bed was a mahogany cabinet that opened to become a *vodou* shrine, which included supernatural pictures, a white bowl, some hand-dipped candles, and several bottles of rum and cola to be used as offerings for the *lwas* (voodoo spirit gods). On a vanity table with a large round mirror were two wigs, a Bible, a jewelry box, a makeup kit, and a large bottle of perfume.

For twelve years, I slept under the kitchen table on rags that served as my bedding. Between five and five thirty a.m., I took my bedding outside, and then I scrubbed my teeth with a wet finger dipped in ashes from the charcoal stove. I was not allowed to use the toothpaste.

As a growing child I became totally accustomed to the role of being a *restavek*. I had absolutely no memory of family love and care. In a very real sense, I believed that I was less than a person, unworthy even of human kindness. Every day it was made clear to me that my only purpose in life was to perform household chores for the one who "kept" me. Over a period of time, I came to believe there was something missing from inside me, something that would make me worthy of being cared about by someone, anyone. I imagined a hollow place inside my chest where my heart should be, a void.

My first chore of the morning was to light the charcoal and heat a pot of water. Then I filled a white basin and matching bucket from the water storage and carried them into the bathroom. Afterward I poured the hot water into the bucket and put ice cubes from the refrigerator into the basin. Florence washed her face in the basin and her *derriere* in the bucket. She believed that since white people came from a cold climate, washing her face in chilled water would lighten her complexion. As a young child, I often wondered why Florence wanted to lighten her face but not the rest of her body. I had heard her say, "Peyi frèt se peyi blan; peyi cho se peyi nèg" (cold countries are white people's countries; hot countries are Negroes' countries). (*Nèg*, which means black, is the word Haitians use to refer to themselves.)

I was never permitted to question Florence, nor to laugh in her presence. I only spoke when spoken to. Because all the *restaveks* I knew were treated the same way, I believed my situation was normal. I thought we all had "bad blood."

The ritual for Sundays was almost always the same. After Florence bathed, I fastened her bra, zipped up the back of her dress, handed her a wig, and fetched her shoes. As she left for Catholic Mass, I flushed the toilet with water from the bucket and washed the chamber pot with water from the basin. I was not permitted to use the matching bucket and basin for my bath. I bathed outside, standing on the rock-pile, and used the floor-washing bucket to rinse my body.

The moment Florence returned from church, she opened the *vodou* shrine and prayed there. Often I could hear her asking the *lwas* to improve her financial situation. When the cook-laundress arrived, she made breakfast and juice. After Florence ate, I cleared the table and scraped the leftovers from her china into my aluminum plate. I was never permitted to eat at the table.

Florence often called me into the bedroom to help her undress. After she took off her girdle and wig, I unzipped the back of her dress and unhooked her bra. If the polish on her toenails was chipped, I gave her a pedicure. Then I blew on her nails with my mouth, to dry the polish. In all the years I spent with her, never do I remember her thanking me.

At one point when I was six or seven, Florence purchased a *matinet*, a whip with a wooden handle and four leather strips, to punish me. As I got older, she replaced this with the infamous *rigwaz*. It was almost three feet long, stiff and twisted like a drill bit, narrow at the tip and rough like concrete to the touch. Each strike felt like a burn and often scarred like a burn.

When the faucet ran dry, as it did regularly, my duties included fetching water from elsewhere to keep the metal drums full. I satisfied my own bathroom needs in the bushes and wiped with rocks or leaves. I was afraid to use the bathroom when Florence was home because she'd get upset that I had wasted water and used her toilet paper.

Every month, one of my responsibilities was to wash Florence's feminine napkins, twelve pieces of white cotton cloth. She would hand them to me in a white canvas bag, along with a small bag of detergent, and say: "Wash these. If you lose one of them, I'll cut off your ears." I was not allowed to take the rags outside to dry until all stains were obliterated. She was fearful that if an enemy got possession of a rag with her menstrual blood in it, it could be used as a *wanga* (a tool of black magic) to kill her. For many years I lived in ongoing, very real fear of having my ears severed.

The first time I washed Florence's sanitary napkins, I was perhaps seven years old. They had been soaking in a covered bucket in the bathroom. When I took off the lid, a smell like rotten meat hit me in the face. Not understanding the sight of all this blood, I was convinced that Florence would soon die. Oddly, that thought plagued me with anxiety for several weeks. Not that I cared anything for this woman, but I worried about where I would go if she were dead. I had no one else. To the entire world, except to Florence, I was worthless. I didn't exist.

The following month, when Florence asked me to wash the rags again, I determined that she must be having bouts of bloody diarrhea. It would be years before I figured out the mystery of the bloody rags.

In the evenings, after the cook-laundress left, I prepared Florence's bath with stove-warmed water in the bucket and three trays of ice cubes in the basin. I flushed the toilet with water from the basin. If she had a "client" that night, I reserved the water in the bucket to wash his car while the man "dallied." The coin I'd often get for washing the car went right to Florence. I sensed that that bit of money should be mine. Each time she took the coin from me, I felt the ground disappear under my feet.

Florence's favorite clients drove cars that bore license plates bearing the word *OFFICIEL*, meaning the clients were important government officials. She often served them food that the cook had prepared earlier in the day, and they would give Florence a brown envelope with money so new I thought the men had printed the bills themselves.

One evening, one of these preferred clients arrived and sat down in the dining area waiting for Florence to bring his food. I stood behind the kitchen door and watched her at the stove, ladling goat's head soup into a bowl for him. Then she reached under her skirt, pulled out a menstrual rag, and dabbed it on the meat while mumbling to herself. She then held the bowl with both hands and bowed three times. I was shocked and confused.

"Bobby!" she yelled.

"Plait-il" (If it pleases you), I replied.

"Go put this on the table," she said, handing me the bowl. I was petrified, wondering why Florence wanted to poison this well-liked client. I carried the soup inside, placed it out of his reach, and hoped he would not eat it. "Bring it closer," he said. My hands shook as I moved the bowl toward him. I left the room quickly to avoid watching him die. As Florence went to join him with her bowl of soup, she said to me, "Now go wash the car. When you're done, stand beside it with the rag."

"Oui," I responded. Standing on a stepstool to wipe the windshield, I wondered why I should wash the car of a man who would soon be dead. After I washed the tires, I waited nervously near the driver's door, holding the rag. When I saw the man coming out with Florence in tow, I was deathly afraid, thinking Florence had put his soul in a bottle and transformed him into a zombie. Because I had often heard housekeepers say that people should never look zombies in the eye, I lowered my head, stepping back. "*Ti-gason*, take this," he said, reaching in his pocket. I closed my eyes and held out my hand. He handed me a fifty-cent piece and drove off. "Give me what he gave you," demanded Florence, holding out her hand. I reluctantly placed the coin in her palm.

It was only much later that I learned why Florence dabbed her menstrual rag on food she served her favorite clients. One day I overheard two housekeepers chatting, and one said to the other, "To keep a good man from going after other women, you must cast a charm on him with fresh menstrual blood." I figured that Florence's charm didn't work, because the men in her life never stayed around long.

One afternoon, Madame Beauchamp, a neighbor, came and asked Florence to loan me to sweep her yard before she and her husband came out to sit under the almond tree. I knew she wanted to have a *restavek* of her own because she had asked Florence, "Where did you find your *ti-gason*?" Florence had replied, "He came from Grand Hatte. He was a gift to me from his father, who had him with a domestic." Florence often chastised me with the words, "San sal, pitit chen. Mwen pa ras ou" (Dirty blooded, son of a dog. I am not of your race). These words made me feel inferior to everyone, except other *restaveks*.

"Go sweep Madame Beauchamp's yard," said Florence.

"Oui," I replied and left with the broom, which was twice my size. I didn't know my own age. Florence never bothered to tell me.

As I swept the yard, Monsieur Beauchamp, a mulatto, came out of his house and shouted to neighbors, "They've just announced on the radio that President Kennedy has been assassinated in the US." Most people went about their business as though the news had no significance. I felt sad, because I believed that President Kennedy was a generous man. It was during his administration that secondhand clothes began arriving in Haiti from the US. Before that day, I had mostly heard the word "Kennedy" used to describe secondhand clothing that was sold at the market. Housekeepers often said behind each other's back, "Look at her! She walks as though her dress is new. I bet it's a Kennedy." Now that I realized Kennedy had been a person, I wondered what he looked like and why people had been insulting him. I was certain that the *Tonton Macoutes* (secret police) would have decapitated anyone who referred to "Papa Doc" Duvalier as secondhand clothing.

One morning, a few months after the news of Kennedy's assassination, Florence said to me, "A *blan* [white person] named Philippe Sebastian is coming to visit today. This man is your papa, but when you see him, don't call him papa. Say, 'Bonjour, monsieur,' and then disappear. If the neighbors ask you who he is, tell them that you don't know. Philippe is such a good man. We have to protect his reputation. This is what happens when men of good character have children with dogs." I felt ashamed of myself, yet I was very anxious to see the man (the white man!) who was my father.

Before noon, a black car pulled into the driveway and a handsome man with light brown hair emerged from it. As I tried to make eye contact with him, he waved at me and then walked quickly to the front door before I had a chance to say, "Bonjour, monsieur." It was the first time I had ever seen a white person. Flooded with strange feelings and ideas, I tried to put it all together. *How could this almost godlike man be my father? And why had he never shown the slightest interest in me?*

Since I had never heard anyone refer to a black as "a man of good character," I thought only white people possessed good qualities. As Florence ushered him into the house, I went into the backyard thinking my father had given me to Florence because I had dog blood in my body. For that reason I couldn't imagine this man as my father. In my mind he was much more important than the men whose licence plates said OFFICIEL. Shortly thereafter, I heard his car leaving the yard. I felt happy to learn that I actually had a father, and I wished to say his name and feel his smooth brown hair, but I was never allowed to question Florence about this "apparition" whom she said was my father. It would be years before I would see him again.

As soon as Florence left the house after Philippe's visit, I went into her room and peered into the mirror to see if I bore any resemblance to this man who was supposed to be my father. I couldn't see even a remote similarity. But after that day, I began to pay more attention to the three pictures on the wall: the Sacred Heart, the Pope, and the Virgin Mary. All three were white. I thought maybe my father's reputation had to be protected because he was related to these white saints. I found myself wishing the Virgin Mary were my mother. I hated the idea of having bad blood in my body. Sometimes I imitated Florence, praying to the Virgin Mary. "Saint Virgin Mary, please improve my situation. Make Florence forget to beat me when I wet my bed. Make her care about me," I said, staring at the lily-white icon.

If I completed my chores in time, Florence would sometimes allow me to attend class at Ecole du Canada, a literacy center for boys in abject poverty. Khaki shorts and a yellow shirt were standard, but not mandatory, especially for *restaveks*. I wanted so much to have a uniform, thinking it would make me feel and look like a regular child.

Since I could not be admitted without a proper name, Florence registered me under the name Cadet. "I am lending you my family's name. Don't do anything that would tarnish it or I'll cut off your ears and call you Bob Joseph," she threatened. Joseph was a commonplace name, which everyone thought was worthless.

The center was a three-room, tin-roofed cinder block building with no electricity or indoor plumbing. In the backyard was an outhouse, and students often brought pieces of rags with which to wipe themselves. When I was at the center, I could be more expressive and felt almost good about myself, as if my heart might somehow grow back to fill the void in my chest. After school, walking back to Florence's house, I could feel myself becoming numb again, almost dead, a zombie child.

My teacher at the school, Madame Antoine, a mulatto in her late twenties, had brown hair. She often dressed in a blue skirt and white blouse. Behind her back, we called her Madame Zje Chat (Mrs. Cat Eyes). She assigned seats in accordance with skin tone. The darker a student's skin, the farther back his seat. Sitting in the first row, I tried not to feel superior to my classmates. I suspected that they didn't know I was a *restavek*.

The first time Madame Antoine took attendance, she called out, "Jean-Robert Cadet" several times. When I didn't answer, she then went on to the next name. Florence had picked the name "Jean-Robert" and provided it to the school without telling me. After going through the roster, Madame Antoine inquired, "Is there anyone whose name I didn't call?" I raised my hand.

"What is your name?"

"Bobby," I said.

"Bobby who?"

"Bobby Cadet."

"If you don't even know your name, Jean-Robert, go sit in the last row." My feeling of superiority was short-lived.

Whenever Madame Antoine walked into the classroom, we rose with arms crossed over our chests. She led us in the Lord's Prayer and one Hail Mary in French before she motioned for us to sit. Then she wrote at the very top of the board: "L'homme propose et Dieu dispose" (Man proposes and God disposes). She never told us what it meant. No one spoke in class until called upon by Madame Antoine. Occasionally, she wrote a short poem in French on the blackboard and pointed a stick at each word for the class to repeat after her. No one understood the words because everyone spoke Creole. Permission to use the small outhouse in the yard was sought by raising two fingers in a V. Her stern expression and angry demeanor caused us to feel fearful whenever she called upon us. No one dared ask her a question as she paced the room, *rigwaz* in hand, looking over our shoulders. She whacked those who arrived late, gave wrong answers, or demonstrated poor penmanship. She clearly displayed less brutality with us lighter-skinned students, who, she apparently assumed, were more intelligent than our darker peers.

One afternoon, as Madame Antoine wrote the alphabet in calligraphy on the blackboard for everyone to copy on his slate, Andre, the tallest boy in class, took a ball out of his pocket and held it high for his friends to see. It was white with red stitches snaking across its surface. Although Haitian factories had been making major league baseballs for many years, most children had never seen one. This was my first time seeing such a ball. Before Madame Antoine could turn around, Andre hid it in his lap. When recess was signaled, the students rushed out to the yard, begging Andre to show them the ball. Everyone was anxious to play soccer with it instead of using the usual rag ball, an old stocking stuffed with pieces of rags. Andre handed the ball to Paul, who quickly realized how heavy and hard it was after tapping it to his forehead.

"We can't play with this; it's too hard. What kind of ball is this?"

He slammed it on the ground. "It doesn't even bounce," he added and gave the ball back to Andre.

"That's the kind of ball *ti-blans* [white children] play with in New York," said Andre. None of us could imagine what kind of game could be played with an object so small and hard.

"Can I touch the ball?" I asked. The boy handed it to me, and I turned it round and round as if it were magical. I couldn't take my eyes off the ball.

"I'll trade you the ball for your cup of milk," Andre said. The center often gave a cup of powdered milk to each student during recess. As hungry as I was, I agreed without a moment's hesitation. Then Andre pulled a fistful of waxed red threads out of his pocket. The strings were uneven. Most were one to two feet long and some others, much longer.

"Where did you get the ball and the strings?" I asked.

"My dad gave them to me," replied Andre. "It's the same thread they use at the factory to stitch the balls." I helped him untangle and tie the pieces of thread end to end, so they could be used to fly a kite, sometimes in aerial combat.

"What games do *ti-blans* in New York play with the balls?" I asked Andre.

"Nobody knows. My dad counts the balls and drives them to the airport in a truck to be flown to New York."

"Wow! I wish I could fly to New York to see what game they play with these crazy balls." It was the first time I had dreamed of leaving Haiti. The notion that I might someday actually travel to New York went way beyond such dreaming.

Whenever Florence left the house, I tossed my new ball in the air and caught it, again and again. "Maybe they throw it at something," I thought, but couldn't imagine what that might be. But I found many things to do with my prized possession. I especially loved rolling the ball around and around in a tin bucket to make a sound like a drum-roll. Then I would bounce it in the bucket to produce the beat of a drum. "That's it! Maybe they make music with it," I said to myself. Sometimes I would spin it on the tile floor like a top, watching the red stitches make the whole ball look pink. Whenever I wasn't play-ing with the ball, I kept it with my clothes in a cardboard box. One day I was curious to know why the ball was so hard, and so I cut the stitches just a little to see what was inside. I felt driven to understand the true purpose of the strange ball.

The schoolyard was the only place where I could express myself freely. I joined other boys playing soccer with rag balls, hollowed out grapefruits, or anything that could be kicked with bare feet.

Florence often hired cook-laundresses, none of whom stayed in her employ for more than a few months or years. Sometimes I would ask them various questions that were always filling my head. The maids were the only people I was allowed to address, but they seldom had the answers I sought.

"Why don't I pee the same amount of water as I drink?" I'd ask.

"Oh-ho, what kind of question is this, little boy? Leave me alone," the woman might say. I would persist. "If I don't drink any water, will I stop peeing in my rag bed at night?"

"You crazy, boy? You gotta drink water or you die." I had become desperate to stop urinating in my bed, because Florence would sometimes smack me while holding on to my testicles. This was one of her methods for solving my bedwetting problem.

I preferred school to home, where punishment was linked to Florence's unpredictable moods. At school, punishment was always related to a specific transgression. Madame Antoine sometimes praised my work, either verbally or with a nod. I always tried my best and seldom transgressed.

Every evening, before the regular electricity blackouts, I would listen to neighborhood children reciting their French lessons out loud to memorize them. I wanted so much to recite my own lessons, but my voice was not to be heard in Florence's house. After their third or fourth recitation, I would repeat the same lessons in my head as if they had been assigned to me by Madame Antoine. "Christophe Colomb est né à Gênes en Italie en 1451" (Christopher Columbus was born in Genoa Italy in 1451). "Il aima la mer" (He liked the sea). "Il découvrit Hispaniola en 1492" (He discovered Haiti in 1492).

CHAPTER 2

WHEN I WAS between ten and twelve years old, Denis, Florence's son, who had been living on his own, moved into "our" house with his wife, Lise. Under this new arrangement, Florence's clients stopped coming to see her. Since there were now four people in the house, counting me, I seldom had time to attend Ecole du Canada, the literacy center. I had more shoes to polish, more dishes to wash, three chamber pots to empty and clean, more water to fetch, more baths to prepare, and worst of all, more adults to fear. In the following years, two children would be born to the couple.

One day, not long after the move-in, Denis came home with a strange and heavy wooden box and put it in the living room. I took a good look at it when I cleared the table after dinner. It had three knobs and sported an oval-shaped window that seemed to be shaded from the inside. I thought it was a new kind of radio. In a way, it was.

That evening Denis turned on the radiolike box, and the family sat down to stare at it. The language coming out of it sounded strange to me, and I ran to the back of the house to look through the window. I was surprised to see *blans* in their own living room inside the box. When a funny red-headed woman began to cry with her mouth wide open, I muffled my laugh, pressing my hand over my mouth to keep from being heard. I was hooked. I fetched a cinder block and stood on it to have a better view of the glossy images in the box. "How did those people get in there?" I asked myself.

At eleven o'clock, the glossy images gave way to a rain of rice, and when Denis turned a button, the rice gathered into a bright dot and vanished. I performed my last chores and made my bed under the kitchen table. I could not sleep, wondering what was inside the box. The next morning before I set the table for breakfast, I peeked into a small hole behind the box. There was nothing to see. The machine remained a mystery to me because I was not permitted to ask even the most basic of questions.

But soon, the word "televisyon" became part of my vocabulary, and I heard the adults call the show with the funny red-haired woman *I Love Lucy*. I could even make out what seemed to be those words on the screen. I thought it was the funny woman's name and wondered why her parents didn't call her "Love I. Lucy." Sometimes an episode of *Tarzan* would come on after Lucy. Tarzan was a handsome *blan* in a loincloth who swung from thick vines in a jungle somewhere. At various times, he carried a monkey on his shoulder as though it were his son, and he often risked his own life to save African men from lions and crocodiles, leaving me with the impression that, in addition to their being of good character and intelligent, *blans* were extremely kind and brave. "What a lucky monkey," I thought, as Tarzan smiled and played with the animal. I almost wished I could trade places with it. When I was sent on errands, I practiced the sounds that Tarzan always made. "A-uh-a-u-aaa."

Around this time, our neighbor, Monsieur Beauchamp, acquired a fourteen-year-old-boy named René as his *restavek*. I was glad because I hated to be borrowed by his wife to sweep and wash her dishes. René and I quickly became fast friends. When his grown-ups and mine were not home, René would tie a long rope on a tree branch, and we'd take turns swinging from it like Tarzan. Being older, René became my street-smart mentor.

Running errands at the crowded market, I saw René with a straw bag, buying rice. Each time a *restavek* girl walked by him, he called her "La Pou Sa" (Here for That) and laughed. The girls would get upset and curse René's mother.

"What is the 'sa' in 'la pou sa'?" I asked René.

"It's what men and women do in bed. We're better than *restavek* girls because men do *that* to them, but not to us boys," he said, grinning. I felt like telling him that a nephew of Florence, who had come to visit, had done *that* to me while I slept under the kitchen table, but I was too ashamed to bring it up, afraid my friend might jokingly start calling me the terrible name. As a display of camaraderie, I joined René in calling *restavek* girls "La Pou Sa."

"You have marbles?" asked René one day as we walked together toward the market.

"No, I don't have any."

"Why don't you make commissions for yourself on what you buy?"

"How do you make these commissions?"

"What did you come to buy?"

"Goat meat and charcoal," I said.

"Buy the meat for five cents [one US penny] less than the amount you were given. It's a small amount. They will not miss it. Do the same when buying charcoal. Pick up small lumps of charcoals on the ground to make up the difference. These are the only two items you can cheat them on. Then you'll have money to buy marbles and candy. But never keep the coins you've stolen in your pocket. They'll make noise. Hide them under a rock in the backyard."

On the way back home we each purchased a marble. Within a few weeks, I had accumulated twenty marbles. Whenever René and I went to fetch water, we played a round of marbles in back alleys with some of the street boys.

René was a wise counselor, and I often followed his clever suggestions, even if sometimes they bordered on the unsavory. The new "marketing" system meant I could now eat a third small meal some days.

We often watched white tourists buying souvenirs from street vendors in front of a nearby hotel. I'd look at the *blans*, thinking they were saintlike because they resembled the images in Florence's bedroom. Haitians assumed, almost by instinct, that *blans* possessed incredible wealth and could never run out of money. For that reason vendors raised their prices when selling to whites. Often we talked about our favorite fantasy, which was to be taken *lòt bò dlo* (across the sea) by some generous *blans*.

"Many people say that, across the sea, where the *blans* live, there's money in the streets, and their homes are like paradise," René said.

"I wish they could adopt us. We would go to school in uniforms and have plenty to eat and never run out of money," I said.

"Me, too, I wish the same thing," replied René.

One afternoon we saw a group of *blans* giving coins to street boys who whined in English: "*Blans, blans*, give me five cents." We had no idea what the phrase meant, but suspected they had learned it from tourist guides. So we decided to imitate the boys. To our surprise, a tall, blue-eyed *blan* with a big grin on his face gave us each a nickel, twenty-five cents in Haitian currency. It was the most money I had ever had at one time. We were bursting with happiness. René and I purchased bread and lemonade from a sidewalk vendor. Since the *blans* had eyes like the Sacred Heart, the Virgin Mary, and the Pope, René and I were convinced they were saints and could perform miracles.

"I wonder if they poop like regular people," I said.

"Maybe they do, but their poop is probably white and doesn't stink," my friend mused. We both laughed at that idea.

"Do you believe the pope poops?" I asked.

"I don't believe so. After God is the pope, then the *blans*," said René. "*Blans* are better than us *nègs*," he added, chewing on his bread.

"Yea, even their president was good. He was better than ours. They called him Kennedy," I said. René laughed.

"Don't be an imbecile. Kennedy is not a person. Kennedys are secondhand clothes," said René.

"They call the clothes Kennedy because President Kennedy was sending them to the markets," I said.

René laughed again. "What *nèg* told you that lie? I am telling you Kennedy is not a person," he insisted.

"It's not a lie. It's the truth, white people's word. Before you came to live with Monsieur Beauchamp, I heard him say, 'They've assassinated President Kennedy.'"

"No president would let his name be dirtied like that," René swore.

"I bet you a marble Kennedy is a person," I insisted, and we sealed the bet with our pinkies.

"Excuse me, ma'am," I said to the lemonade vendor. "Is Kennedy a person or a secondhand dress from across the sea?" She looked at us head to foot with disgust and sucked air between her teeth, making a long chirping sound.

"Hurry up with the bottles," she snapped.

I thought of asking well-dressed pedestrians, whom I knew were educated, if Kennedy was a person, but I worried they would scold me because I was a *restavek*. When we returned the empty bottles, the vendor said, "Kennedy pa moun" (Kennedy is not a person).

"Pay up," said René, laughing.

"I'll let you watch *Tarzan* with me behind the house tonight," I said.

"If you don't pay up, you'll have to call me Tarzan. I'll call you *Ti-makak* [little monkey]."

"No, I am Tarzan and you're the *makak*," I insisted. I paid him the marble, knowing I would be getting my marble back when I found someone to verify my story. My friend may have been a thief, but with me, he was always fair.

When René's owners went out at night, he and I would stand on the cinder block watching *Tarzan* and *I Love Lucy*.

One morning, as I walked outside to sweep the yard, I saw Monsieur Beauchamp in his backyard, *rigwaz* in hand, whipping René, who was kneeling on two rough stones. His muffled screams caused my stomach to churn. Afterward, he drove René to what I believed was the police station to get a second beating. I had often heard owners threatening their *restavek* boys with a police beating. Florence's maid told me that René had stolen money to buy food. Later that day, I saw my best friend, my only friend, sitting on the rock pile in Monsieur Beauchamp's yard. His face was disfigured, almost unrecognizable. He had been severely beaten by the police. I was afraid to go talk to him. That was the last time I would ever see him. If one day René's parents had come to visit him, they would have been told matter-of-factly: René ran away. I didn't know where he went. And there was no one I could ask.

Several days later, a girl who looked to be about nine years old was brought in from the countryside to replace René. This is the way the child slavery system works in Haiti. There's no government interference or regulation, and so it runs informally—and efficiently.

Watching *Tarzan* and *I Love Lucy* was never the same without René, who had been more than a big brother to me. Whenever I went to market I continued to skim my penny from the top of large purchases, each time whispering a little "Thank you" to René. Often when I fetched water, I begged tourists for money, always wishing one of them might take me to their home across the sea. Now that I had begun stealing from my owners, I was aware that what had happened to René could be my fate also.

One night, after the television was turned off, Florence and Lise went to their rooms. I sat on a step stool in the kitchen waiting for Denis, Florence's son, to come home. I was not allowed to make my bedding until all the adults went to bed. I slept sitting on a step stool leaning against the wall. In the morning when I went outside to sweep the yard, I noticed Denis's car was missing. Later that day, I overheard the cook mention that Monsieur Denis had left for New York. His wife, Lise, and the children had gone to live with Lise's mother in another part of town.

With that, two of Florence's former clients came back, but not regularly. I returned to the literacy center in the afternoon and was placed back in the level II class, because I had been absent for such a long time.

For financial reasons, no doubt, Florence moved into a small apartment in Bourdon, another suburb of Port-au-Prince. There, the faucet often ran dry. So the cook would send me to fetch water at a home where her aunt, Mrs. Theodore, worked as a housekeeper. Mrs. Theodore was in her sixties. She told me to be careful not to come when a black car was parked in the driveway. It was a two-story, modern house with a colonial exterior and a long cobblestone driveway that circled the front yard. In the backyard was a small, windowless bungalow where Mrs. Theodore slept. The faucet was beside the swimming pool near a lovely rose garden.

Over a period of months, from Monday to Saturday during the noon hour, I would often see a long black Mercedes with red velvet curtains in its side windows sitting in the driveway of that house where Mrs. Theodore worked. This pattern of visits became the shadowy gossip of the neighborhood. The car was chauffeured by a muscular man in a trim khaki uniform. A patch on his right upper sleeve bore the image of a guinea fowl. As I watched from a distance, the silver frames of his sunglasses flashed and glistened in the noon sun. He often took up a position behind the gate and waited there patiently.

The "client" was a tall man, always dressed in a dark suit. His hair was gray, and his stomach hung over his belt. His license plate bore the familiar word *officiel*. It was clear to me that this guy was much more "official" than any of Florence's government clients.

The woman of the house was a mulatto, tall and incredibly beautiful, in her mid-twenties, I guessed. Her hair was reddish-brown, curly, and shoulder-length. She had caramel eyes and full, red lips. I never missed an opportunity to go there to fetch water. Many of those times, I would see the beautiful woman sitting out on the balcony. In my memory, she is always playing the same song on her phonograph.

The song began with a sudden explosion of wind instruments and a loud bang, followed by a Spanish melody from a lone trumpet. Then the singer, Charles Aznavour, sang in French:

Your eyes are lifeless; you lie pitifully bruised and pale. Your body is half-nude and covered with a white sheet. Your glittering clothes, stained with blood, are thrown in the dust.

The chase continues while you give up your soul. Too bad for the vanquished—he deserves his fate. The victor's name is cheered much more than the pain that pierced his body . . . Alone and abandoned, you see death coming.

As I grew toward adolescence, I became more and more accustomed to hearing French spoken on the radio and by upper-class people on the street. After hearing this song a few times, those words took shape in my mind. I could understand these French phrases as if they were being sung in Creole. I remember them, somberly, to this day.

On the morning of January 1, Haiti's Fourth of July, Florence left to spend the day with a friend, a true *mambo* who often came to visit our apartment. On her visits, the two of them stayed in her room with the door closed. Before Florence left, she "loaned" me to one of the neighbors to fetch water. I took Florence's bucket and left for the house where Mrs. Theodore worked. The morning air on January 1 always smelled of pumpkin soup, the traditional meal of Independence Day. The soup had a special significance, because in the years before the overthrow of the French in 1804, the slaves had been forbidden to prepare it for themselves. For my efforts the neighbor gave me her soup pot to lick. After eating, I washed the dishes and went to fetch water for her little reservoir.

In honor of the holiday, our street, a major artery, was decorated with red and blue paper garlands that bore pictures of President "Papa Doc" along with his personal logo, the guinea fowl. The words *à vie* (for life) were printed below each picture. Large posters of the same picture were plastered on walls, light posts, and trees. "Papa Doc," in reading glasses, had a neutral expression, and his dark complexion contrasted with a patch of white hair. The guinea fowl, in profile and facing "Papa Doc," was charcoal gray with small white dots from its neck to its drooping tail feathers. According to street lore, the dictator had chosen the bird because of its keen eyesight and acute sense of hearing. Apparently, it could detect danger from afar and then would quickly disappear into the underbrush.

At a designated time that morning, the national anthem could be heard playing loudly on every radio, all but drowning out the street noise. Then the president began to address our Creole-speaking nation in French. People like me, walking on the sidewalks, stopped in front of stores to listen to "Papa Doc's" words, we poor folks trying desperately to understand them as best we could.

Many of "Papa Doc's" words stayed in my mind, though I could not understand all of them. He began in his familiar whining, nasal voice.

> Liberty, equality, fraternity. Haitians, my brothers, today we celebrate our independence day. . . . We broke the chain of slavery to seize our own sovereignty. . . . Liberty, equality, fraternity. Haitians, my brothers, we are proud of our freedom for which our ancestors paid in blood and in gold francs.

After the speech, the radios played a song called "Duvalier! Duvalier! Duvalier!" as if Duvalier were a god. I believed he would never die.

Upon reaching the mulatto woman's yard, I saw that she was standing on the balcony, almost as if she had been waiting for me to come. When I got to the faucet, I looked up and our eyes met.

"Bonjour, Madame," I said bashfully.

"Bonjour, petit bonhomme" (Good morning, little gentleman), she responded and smiled. "Here, catch this." It was the first time anyone had ever spoken to me in French. I held the bucket out toward her, and she dropped two caramels and a coin into it. "That's your New Year's gift," she added in Creole. At that moment, I was happier than I could ever remember being.

"Merci," I said, using the French pronunciation, and put the gift in my pocket. She went back inside. I unwrapped one of the caramels and chewed it slowly, savoring the texture as much as the taste. I had never eaten such a treat before. I stood there for a long, euphoric moment. The woman had put her favorite song on the phonograph once more, and I could hear her singing along with it. Although there was no way I could have understood the concept, I knew I was in love, for she was the only person who had ever called me a little gentleman. For that brief interlude, I was no longer society's outcast. I was no longer a *restavek*.

On the way back to Florence's house with the water, I saw a crowd lining up on both sides of the street. Suddenly a parade of motorcycles with deafening sirens thundered through the corridor of people. They were followed by jeeps mounted with machine guns occupied by heavily armed men in green fatigues and dark glasses. A black Mercedes with a Haitian flag mounted on each fender appeared. It had black velvet curtains on the sides and rear windows. The crowd screamed, "Papa Doc, throw me a New Year's gift." A few dozen motorcycles, cars, and jeeps sped by after Duvalier's car had passed. The crowd thinned down, only to regroup later when "Papa Doc's" entourage returned, heading back to the National Palace.

That night, I framed the mulatto woman's smiling face in my imagination, like one of the pictures on Florence's wall. The woman's kind words echoed again and again inside my head. I imagined myself sitting on her lap and kissing her, as I had seen *blans* kiss on TV. During my entire boyhood, I had never had such feelings for any person.

I returned there often to fetch water, even when it was not needed, each time hoping to catch a glimpse of her. I would turn the faucet on low in order to fill the bucket ever so slowly. On those occasions when she was out on the balcony, I couldn't bring myself to look up and say hello.

Six months went by. Then, late on a very hot July afternoon, I found myself making yet another trip to fetch water from my benefactor's yard. The air was heavy with the smell of melting asphalt from the road, and the sidewalk felt fry-pan hot, even to my calloused feet. Approaching the driveway, I heard several loud "pops!" coming from the house. "Fireworks," I thought. Then I saw four soldiers in dark sunglasses, some with pistols still drawn, climbing into a green jeep on the driveway. The patches on their fatigues bore the infamous guinea fowl of the dictator's inner circle. In no apparent hurry, the jeep pulled out of the yard. With that I heard the housekeeper, Mrs. Theodore, screaming, "Oh, God! Oh, Jesus, Mary, Joseph!"

I ran into the kitchen and saw the mulatto woman lying on the checkered ceramic tile floor. She was covered in blood. Her arms and legs were awkwardly bent. Her head was one big gaping wound. A large piece of her skull with a lock of hair attached to it lay beside her shoulder, and fragments of bone were scattered about. The walls and refrigerator were spattered with blood.

Most unforgettable for me, the beautiful woman's favorite song was playing upstairs in her room and reverberating through the house. Mrs. Theodore continued weeping and screaming as she knelt near the body.

In complete shock, I took off running with the empty bucket. When I reached Florence's house, I found her in her rocking chair on the porch. She was fanning herself with a fan that bore the Sacred Heart's image. Out of breath and drenched in sweat, I wanted to blurt out what I had just seen, but I was programmed not to speak until she questioned me.

"Where's the water?" she asked.

"The faucet was dry," I stuttered, still unable to tell my grim story.

"You didn't think to go to another house for water," she barked. So I turned away and slowly walked back to the dead woman's yard. Mrs. Theodore was sitting on the front steps crying. We said nothing.

Angry, confused, disoriented, and trembling, I filled my bucket. Then I carried it back to the only place I knew as home, focusing my total attention on keeping every drop of water in the bucket. I see now that this was my way of staying sane, and of dealing with the horror that had just enveloped me.

That night and for many nights thereafter, I lay awake for hours, seeing my beloved lady friend lying in that pool of blood. I never spoke to Florence about it, but a few days after the killing, a neighbor came to chat with Florence. I was washing dishes in the cement basin outside the kitchen.

"Did you hear about the murders? Two different houses in broad daylight," the neighbor said in a loud whisper. My heart thudded. I knew she was talking about the mulatto woman. But I had no idea that any others had died.

"I heard the story of Gustave Flambert's attempted coup d'état," Florence said.

"Yes, and Papa Doc shot him in the head at Fort Dimanche," the woman responded.

Florence needed no prodding. "It's terrible," she whispered. "And they said the *Tonton Macoutes* went to Flambert's house and killed his wife and all his children."

"You mean you didn't hear about his mistress?" the woman continued. "She lives right up this road from here. The *Macoutes* killed her too! It's criminal. No one is safe. People are leaving the country every week by the hundreds." I could see the neighbor glancing left and right, to make sure no one but me was listening.

My knees felt weak. The mulatto woman's song played in my head, and tears welled up in my eyes. I felt powerless, but I wanted to do something. I imagined myself sneaking up on Papa Doc's limousine and letting the air out of all his tires.

"My dear, everyone in this country is living in fear," Florence said softly, scratching her throat. "Most of the intellectuals have already left. I am glad my son is living in New York," she added. Florence dropped her voice further, looking in every direction. "Last year, three of my friends were arrested. No one knows where they are. No one dares ask." She shot a sidelong glance at me.

"I have to leave this country," she said, knowing I would hear.

I spent the next weeks wondering what would become of me if Florence did leave Haiti. I imagined myself in a landfill collecting pieces of red strings to sell to kite flyers.

Not long after the killings, Lise left for America to join her husband Denis. She left their two children in the care of her mother. It became clear that Florence would be joining them when her travel papers were in order. Desperate for money, she sold the television and bought her own *Tchala*, to help her pick good lottery numbers. I was deeply upset, because I could no longer watch my favorite programs.

Not surprisingly, the man Florence had charmed with her menstrual rag began returning once a week to consult the *lwas* in Florence's head, and to meet some other needs. I often wondered why her *lwas* never gave Florence a winning lottery number. Each week, while the man was at the apartment, I was sent to fetch water from a nearby ravine to wash his car.

As I walked across one of the neighbor's yards to reach the ravine, I saw a young girl with vacant eyes in a dress made from a burlap sack. Painfully thin and dark complected, she often sat on a rock in the yard scrubbing laundry. I could not imagine being in her place, washing bedsheets, pants, and dresses, seemingly from sunrise to sunset. The two of us would exchange a glance but never a greeting, because René had told me that *restavek* girls were my inferior—La Pou Sa. I didn't know her real name, but she answered to "Little Girl" when called by her owner, a heavyset woman who always seemed to be angry at something.

As I approached the *restavek* girl's yard one afternoon, I heard a piercing scream that traveled to the pit of my stomach. I rushed in and saw a few women gathered around the girl, who was pinned to the ground, a tiny person under all the weight of her owner. The woman was holding a hot chili pepper in her right hand. "Spread your legs, little whore. I am not of your race, you hear?" shouted the woman as the girl continued to scream and kick. The neighbors, mostly women, laughed as the girl was punished in the most despicable way imaginable. At that moment, I wanted to be like Tarzan swinging from a vine and landing amongst the women to rescue the girl. I wasn't sure what was being done to her, but I knew she was in excruciating pain. Adults often dehumanized us *restaveks* with words like "Imbecile!" or "I am not of your race!" No doubt, long ago, the French had berated their slaves with that phrase. One thing was certain; I actually believed that we *restaveks* belonged to an inferior black race, and the other Haitians to a superior black race.

When the girl was released, she ran to the ravine and sat in a stream, still screaming. I filled my bucket and left her there, unable to imagine the pain she was in. From then on, I stopped using the taunt "La Pou Sa" when I encountered *restavek* girls. I could see that, in some ways, they had it worse than we boys.

On the last day of the Mardi Gras carnival, I went to fetch drinking water and saw the same girl in the same burlap dress with an empty bucket in her hand. I followed her into a yard with a running faucet on the edge of a cement basin. Four men were playing dominoes, smoking cigarettes, and drinking cola in the shade of an almond tree. I felt like speaking with the girl as we stood facing each other, but I didn't know what to say. Her eyes were focused on the bucket being filled, and mine on the scars, fresh and old, on her arms and legs.

"Let me help you," I offered after her bucket was filled. Together we lifted the bucket, and she moved her head under it.

"Mèsi" (Thanks), she said and left the yard. To the domino players, she and I were invisible.

I placed my bucket under the faucet and listened to the domino players' conversation. "*Blans* are a great deal more intelligent than *nègs*," began one, as he looked at the ice in his glass. "They invented a machine that makes little cubes of ice." He sucked in the last drop of liquid from his glass and chewed on a piece of ice.

"That's nothing," interrupted his partner, dangling an unlit cigarette from the corner of his lips. "What about the airplane, which is twenty times bigger than a bus and capable of flying around the world with hundreds of people in its belly? Now, that's something special."

"Eh, are you forgetting the television and films? Sometimes, when you're watching a movie, you believe it's real," a third man said. He had a number of clothespins attached to his ears as penalty for having lost a few games.

"When I saw *Samson and Delilah*, I wished I had the power of Samson. With that kind of power, everybody would respect me."

"When God was creating people, He made the *blans* with His hands and the *nègs* with His feet," said the third man's partner, who had clothespins attached to both of his ears. He slammed his last domino hard on the table and removed a few clothespins from his left ear. "Now, respect this," he added and grinned.

As I lifted the bucket of water to my head, Florence's words came back to me, "When it comes to intelligence, my son Denis is *blan*." Another familiar line came to mind. "The truth is white people's word." Several times I heard her say to vendors, "Don't worry. When it comes to paying my debts, I am *blan*."

The following day, while fetching water from the ravine to wash a customer's car, I gathered two lumps of mud the size of small human heads. Then I sat down on a rock and carefully tried to shape a face on one lump with my hands. Then on the other, as best as I was able, I used my bare feet. I picked up the crude, foot-made face in my left hand. Then I took the hand-made version in my right hand. I probably looked something like Rodin's famous statue, as I pondered my creations for a long moment. It was so obvious. *The domino players must have been right about how God created people*, I thought. The face I made with my feet was grotesque and looked stupid, nothing like a face. The one I shaped with my hands was much better, almost human. My thinking about this went even further. I concluded that God must have used white clay when He made *blans*, and mud when He made us *nègs*. "God only gave the ability to invent great things to *blans* because He made them with His hands," I told myself. I assumed that many black people had broad noses because God had not been able to make them straight with His toes. As bizarre as all this must sound, I believed it in the deepest part of my soul. That internalized belief would stay with me for a very long time.

CHAPTER 3

I COULDN'T FIGURE it out. Florence had been in a jovial mood for weeks, although she had lost money playing the lottery. She had even purchased new fabric and hired a dressmaker. Florence wouldn't think of wearing Kennedys. "Why does she seem so happy?" I'd ask myself. Then one day, I overheard her talking to her *mambo* friend.

"The American Embassy has finally granted me and the children our visas so we can join Denis and Lise in America." Boom! It was as if an anvil had fallen from a window, just missing me. She and the *vodou* priestess were in the bedroom asking Erzulie, Florence's favorite *lwa*, to remove all obstacles that would prevent her from leaving Haiti.

Fifteen years old now, I began dealing with a great deal of new anxiety. Since it was the habit of many people to release their *restaveks* into the streets before going across the sea, I wondered if Florence would do the same to me. If so, I knew of only two options for me: I would become either a shoe shiner or a vendor of kite strings. But where would I live?

On the day of Florence's scheduled departure, I awoke with my stomach churning. It didn't stop churning that day, or for weeks afterward. *What will become of me? What am I going to do?* Life in this woman's house was unpleasant, but after eleven years I was used to it. It provided food—usually—and it had its routines. This was the only life I had ever known.

Early that afternoon, a relative of Florence's arrived with Florence's two grandchildren to take the three of them to the airport. I helped carry her luggage to the car, shaking, tears welling up in my eyes. As they drove off, out the window, Florence waved me goodbye. I sobbed uncontrollably watching the car disappear in traffic. She hadn't spoken a word about my future.

But later that day, to my complete surprise, I learned from a neighbor that Florence had made arrangements to send me to live with her own mother in Petite Rivière, a farming village north of Port-au-Prince. I felt a huge sense of relief, because I had been there with Florence, years earlier, visiting her mother, "Grannie," who had been kind to me, at least kinder than her daughter had ever been.

Now, under instructions from the neighbor, I left for the bus station with all my belongings in a cardboard box. Florence had given the woman my bus fare and a little extra, so I bought a lemon for the trip. Someone had told me that sucking on it would help me avoid car sickness.

After the six-hour ride over rough and dusty roads, the bus pulled into a large marketplace in Petite Rivière. Using the directions I had been given, I found my way to Grannie's house, a two-room bungalow with indigo blue doors. Grannie was bedridden and alone, dying of old age. She had not been told I was coming. She didn't even remember who I was. I felt totally abandoned and worried about my survival in so strange a place.

Soon, Chelaine, Grannie's niece, arrived to care for Grannie. I was relieved that she remembered me from the previous visit and seemed almost delighted to see me. It had been a long time.

"Did Aunt Florence go across the sea?"

"Yes, she did," I replied.

"Did she send money with you?"

"Non," I answered. The delight left her face as if a shade had been drawn.

After Chelaine cared for Grannie, she invited me to her house for a meal. She lived with a companion, a man named Antoine. He was tall, in his forties, and made his living as a tailor. After Chelaine served him cornmeal with beans at a small table beside the bed, she and I ate behind the kitchen hut. After dinner, I returned to Grannie's for the night.

Upon arriving, just after dark, I learned that Simon, Chelaine's younger brother, also lived in the house. I could feel my new situation was turning toward disaster. Simon was in his late twenties and had come to stay with Florence in Port-au-Prince four or five years previous. I hated him more than anyone I had ever known.

During that long-ago visit, he had grabbed me as I slept under the kitchen table and sexually molested me. I could tell no one at the time. As a *restavek*, my duty was to be as useful and silent as a table or a chair. Who would have believed me? The incident stays lodged in my memory to this day, even the feeling that I had somehow done something wrong. After all these years, I still feel ashamed.

That night, as I lay on a mat in a corner of the second room, Simon came near me again, but this time I was prepared. The moment he touched me, I began screaming and kicking. Had he continued, even the neighbors would have heard the commotion. Simon gave up and went back to his bed, laughing at me. He never tried again.

I relied on Chelaine for food, and every few days she would ask, "Will your father send money to care for you?" I knew that if I said no, she would eventually stop feeding me. So, I always answered, "Yes, I'm sure he will." Aware that this awkward situation couldn't go on for very long, I did what I could to buy some time until I figured out how to return to Port-au-Prince to join the street boys.

"Does your papa know you're here?" she'd asked.

"Yes, he knows where I am. He'll be sending you money soon. I'm sure of it." Chelaine, who had lived in the countryside all her life, could have no idea what happened to children when they were handed over to strangers in Port-au-Prince.

"Write a letter to your father, and I'll give it to the bus driver," she suggested.

"Oui," I responded. A letter? I had never written a letter, and I had no idea where, in Port-au-Prince, my father lived. Since my father was a *blan*, Chelaine must have assumed that he had been supporting me. Who knows? Maybe he had. That wasn't something Florence would have shared with me.

to be accepted at a school. "I am going swimming in the Artibonite Canal to celebrate," I added. It was a good distance from the house.

"Be sure and take a calabash shell with you," she said. Townspeople often carried water back from the canal using the shells of these large pumpkinlike plants.

"And I won't spill a drop," I promised, as I rushed out of the house.

On Monday morning, I went to school and saw Maitre Jean-Charles standing at the gate with a *rigwaz* in his hand. When class began, he escorted me to the second classroom. My teacher was Maitre Roger, and he, too, had a *rigwaz*. All these whips made me nervous just looking at them. An older student from Maitre Jean-Charles's class walked in and handed me a notebook and three booklets, math, history, and grammar. "These are from Maitre Jean-Charles," he said. And a smile spread across my face.

Maitre Jean-Charles kept an eye at the gate from his classroom window. A student who arrived late would receive twenty lashes on the palms of his hands.

I loved school, but one day I arrived late. Terrified to be found out by Maitre Jean-Charles, I crawled through an opening in the cactus fence, which pricked me several times on my back. I stood behind the door of my classroom, waiting for Maitre Roger to start writing on the board. As he did, I sneaked into my seat, heart pounding. Moments later, before the teacher turned around, a boy from Maitre Jean-Charles's classroom came in with a smile on his face and said, "Jean-Robert Cadet, Maitre Jean-Charles wants to see you." I could feel myself beginning to sweat. The teacher shot a glance at me and grinned wickedly. I was in trouble.

Stepping outside the classroom, I stared at the gate, my only escape route. I thought of going home to avoid the whipping that awaited me, but I knew Maitre Jean-Charles would never take me back. My stomach boiled with fear. I took a deep breath and walked to the threshold of Maitre Jean-Charles's classroom. He came toward me with the *rigwaz* and I held out my hands, palm up, first one, then the other. Teeth clenched, I counted out the twenty lashes. After the last stroke, I dropped to my knees, crying quietly. "Now go back to class, wild pig," he said. I returned to my classroom and sat with my palms up in my lap. Blood trickled out where the tip of the whip had made cuts on my wrists. My classmates bit their lips to contain their amusement.

At home, Antoine and Chelaine were getting impatient with me about the money that my father was supposed to send. Chelaine suggested that I give a message to Louis.

"Who's Louis?"

"He buys coffee for *Blan* Philippe to export and goes to Port-au-Prince every two weeks," said Chelaine.

"Where does he live?" I asked anxiously. She gave me directions to the house and I ran all the way there. Out of breath, I opened the gate and walked in.

A woman in a new dress and sandals came out of the kitchen hut. She looked at me inquisitively and said, "You are the child of the deceased Henrilia Brutus. You look just like *Blan* Philippe. Louis has told me all about your mother," she said. *I don't look like my father*, I thought. *He's a blan.* In my mind Philippe was barely real, more like a character in a movie. Shortly thereafter, Louis arrived. He was in his forties, of medium build. He, too, was excited to see me.

"Did you come with Madame Cadet?" asked Louis.

"No, she went across the sea," I said. In Louis's mind, Florence had been treating me like her child because my father was an important *blan*.

"Will she send for you?" Louis inquired.

"I don't know," I replied. "How did you know me?" I asked.

"I worked for *Blan* Philippe at the coffee factory. Now I buy the coffee beans that he exports."

"Can I live with you, Monsieur Louis?"

"Of course. You're welcome to."

"Thank you. I'll come back after school," I said and returned to Chelaine's, happy to have found a new place to stay.

"Did you find Louis?" Chelaine asked.

"Yes, I found him and he invited me to live with him." She looked surprised.

"Antoine wants his money," she cried. I collected my belongings and ran to Louis's house. Before sunset Chelaine came into the yard of my new home.

"Onè," she shouted, announcing her presence.

"Respè," replied Maude, Louis's wife. This is the traditional Haitian greeting in the countryside.

"I've come to get Bobby," said Chelaine.

"He wants to live here," said Maude. Louis entered the yard.

"Bobby was sent to live with me, and I want him back," demanded Chelaine.

"Bobby lives here now," said Louis. Almost politely, he asked Chelaine to leave his yard. It was strange watching people argue over me. For a few fleeting moments, I felt almost important, as if I had value. But I understood the reason. Whoever I lived with expected a substantial repayment.

One Sunday morning, Louis took me with him on a long walk to watch the local cockfights, which in Haiti are something like Sunday afternoon football for the men. Crowded into the small arena, I watched them bet on their favorite rooster, screaming and shouting as the animals tried to spur one another to death. At one point, Louis placed a bet on a strange-looking red rooster, which sent its opponent scurrying off half blind. Louis was happy for the rest of the day.

We walked back home along the banks of the River Estère. At one point we came upon a place where the old pilings of a footbridge stood. The bridge had collapsed long ago. Louis pointed across the river toward the mountains in the northern distance. "That road over there goes to Grand Hatte, where your father's factory was. It's been closed for a long time," he said. I tried, without much success, to imagine such a place. Louis told me that I had been born there in Grand Hatte. I felt an urge to see the place of my birth, but it didn't occur to me to ask if I still had relatives there. The notion of having relatives was foreign to me. Other than Philippe, the man who was supposed to be my father, I had never met a single relative.

The river crossing was a strange sight. On our side were men in suits and hats and women in colorful patterned dresses returning from church services in Petite Rivière. They were heading back to their homes in Grand Hatte, a five-kilometer walk, Louis had explained, with a river running through the middle of it.

Before crossing the river, the women removed their shoes and pulled their dresses up between their legs. The men took off their shoes, socks, and pants, covering their genitals with their hats as they walked across the waist-deep water. A shirtless man in cutoff pants gave a woman a piggyback ride to the other side. This was part of the life in rural Haiti. A hard life. Even on Sunday. To this day, I remember wishing that the bridge were still there to make things just a little easier for the poor people from the town of my birth.

For a few weeks, Louis treated me as if I were his own son. He even allowed me to learn to ride his bicycle. But suddenly, after he returned from a trip to Port-au-Prince, I knew I was no longer special in his eyes. It was clear to me what had happened. Louis had discovered that my father didn't care about me. Nonetheless, Maude, his wife, continued treating me well. On Saturdays, Louis insisted that I work in his fields, planting rice or harvesting potatoes. I felt it was a matter of time before he'd ask me to leave, and I knew that I could not return to Chelaine's.

Late one night, I awoke to the cries of Louis's wife and carefully pulled the curtain aside to see what was going on. The lamp in their room was lit. I saw Louis straddling Maude and slapping her viciously. I imagined myself as Tarzan and jumped on Louis's back to rescue Maude. "Leave her alone," I screamed. Louis dragged me back into the room and slapped me several times in the rear. The next morning Maude told me that Louis was beating her because she could not bear him a child. When Louis was home, she stayed as close to me as possible, as a protection for us both, I assumed.

More and more, I wanted to leave for Port-au-Prince. I felt ready to take my chances there. But how? I had no money for transportation.

Louis had mentioned that my father lived in the suburban town of Pont Morin. That piece of information gave me an idea, and so I began planning my trip back to the city. One night in July, I packed my box of belongings, including a lemon I had picked. Before daylight, while everyone was still in bed, I grabbed the cardboard box and ran to the market, where I knew the bus that had brought me to Petite Rivière would be waiting to leave for the return trip to Port-au-Prince.

Breathlessly, I told the driver I was being sent on an errand. I would get money in the city and pay him on my trip back home. As far as he knew, I lived there in Petite Rivière. His bus was the only way back. "Okay, get on board," he said.

When I reached Port-au-Prince, I thought of visiting a landfill to search for strings like the ones used to stitch that ball I'd seen, but decided first to try to make contact with my father.

I made the long walk to Pont Morin. There, I asked different street vendors for directions. "I'm looking for a *blan*. His name is Phillipe," I would say. Finally, I found it, a big yellow house with a large yard. I was certain that this had to be the home of my wealthy father. The gate was open. A black Volkswagen and a white Plymouth were parked in the driveway. I stood across the street, clutching my box of belongings and observing the yard. My heart pounded with nervousness as I imagined standing before him. "If only I could speak French," I thought, "he might allow me to live with him." But the only French I knew were my memorized recitations from school. Finally, I saw my father coming out of the house and heading for the Volkswagen. I crossed the street and went into the yard.

"Bonjour, Monsieur," I said. My two secure words of French.

"What are you doing here?" he asked in Creole. Clearly, he was angry.

"I want to live with you," I answered, trembling.

"You can't live with me. That's impossible. Damn! Now what am I going to do with you?" I said nothing.

"Get into the car," he snapped. I put my box in the backseat and climbed into the passenger side next to him. From the corner of my eye I looked at his smooth, light brown hair, again longing to touch it for a moment.

He drove a few miles to another neighborhood and pulled into the driveway of a two-story, colonial-style house with a detached kitchen.

"Wait in the car!" he said and walked toward a plump, brown-complexioned woman on the porch. After speaking with her for a few moments, he waved me to come forward. "You're staying here with Madame Laroche until I send you to Florence in New York," he said in Creole. He then gave Madame Laroche a few dollars, kissed her good-bye, and drove off.

I could not believe what my father had just said. New York! *Lòt bò dlo* (Across the sea)! I recalled my old wish to go to New York in order to see what game children played with the heavy white ball laced with red strings. I recalled hearing any number of housekeepers gossiping about how the streets of New York were full of money. I smiled an inner smile, bigger than any I had ever smiled on my face. I imagined walking the streets of a strange land with a rickety wheelbarrow and filling it, coin by coin, with money I found on the ground.

"What's your name?" Madame Laroche asked in Creole, clearly annoyed at the situation.

"They call me Bobby," I said.

"Bobby who?" she asked.

"Bobby Cadet," I said, feeling ashamed that I didn't have my father's last name.

"I am not running a guesthouse, and don't behave like a *pitit kay* [a child of the house]. Put down your box, get the broom beside the kitchen, and sweep the porch," she said. Clearly, Philippe had not told her that I was his son. If I had my father's last name she would not have put me to work. Now it felt as though I had a new owner and a new set of rules to follow.

Later that afternoon, two young people, a boy and a girl, wearing school uniforms arrived with their books and kissed Madame Laroche on the cheek.

"Bonsoir, Maman," they said.

"Bonsoir, cheris," replied Madame Laroche, smiling proudly at her children.

"Who's this boy?" asked Madame Laroche's son, Jerome, who looked to be sixteen or seventeen. The girl, Marie-Claire, was older than he.

"They call him Bobby. I am keeping him as a favor to a friend, *Blan* Philippe Sebastian, until he sends him to New York," said Madame Laroche.

On a cool mid-December night, I sat alone beside the gate watching the street. The Laroche family was in the living room listening to Christmas songs on the radio and decorating an artificial tree. Suddenly, as if called by instinct, I walked in the direction of my father's neighborhood. When I arrived at the street, I stood for a long while, staring at his house. Perhaps because it was Christmas, I wandered into the yard, hoping for some kind of contact with the only "family" I had. The housekeeper, who had apparently seen me talking to Philippe the day I showed up from Petite Rivière, let me come into the house.

After a while, I wandered into the dining room and spied a bottle of rum, a bowl of brown sugar, and cups on a tray. I ate spoonfuls of sugar, and downed most of the rum. I couldn't stop myself. I wanted to enjoy something from my father's house before sneaking away. Rum proved not to be the best choice. I heard a car pull into the yard. I panicked. My head began to spin. A white woman in her twenties walked in. "Who is this boy in my uncle's house?" she yelled. The maid rushed in.

"He's Monsieur Philippe's son."

"What is he doing here? He's drunk. Where does he live?" she asked. In my nervousness and fear, I vomited on the floor. The woman's driver volunteered to take me home. "Where do you live?" he asked. As best I could, I gave him directions to the house where I was staying. When he pulled into the yard, Madame Laroche came out onto the porch. The driver told her about the "scene" at *blan* Philippe's home. I stumbled into the house with my head pounding.

After the driver roared off, Madame Laroche pulled me by my ear into the shower, which was ordinarily off-limits to me. As I stood there helplessly, she turned on the faucet full blast, soaking my clothes with cold water. "Your father is such a good man. How dare you go to his house and embarrass him and his family like that? Philippe is such a saint," she repeated. Then she dragged me from the shower and forced me to my knees. I was shivering and covered with goose bumps in my wet clothing. The woman rushed upstairs and returned with a thick leather belt. For a moment, I was relieved it was not a *rigwaz*. I expected a dozen stinging lashes, a "normal" whipping. When the first stroke landed on my back, sending water splashing onto the walls, I reeled in shock. It sounded like the pop of a balloon, but it felt like I had received a severe burn. The wet clothes had tenderized my skin and made it doubly sensitive to pain. As she beat me, Jerome and Marie Claire stood in the doorway, laughing. I silently implored the two children with my eyes to stop their mother, but they laughed even harder as I screamed with each vicious stroke.

Then I heard a voice from outside the house. "When you're done skinning him, send me his hide to make a drum," shouted a man, apparently walking by on the street.

After that night, I became deathly afraid of Madame Laroche, and I would shake in terror when she called my name. I wanted to run away, but I remained there at her house only because my father had said he was sending me to New York.

Each time Madame Laroche assigned me a chore, she'd say, "You'd better do it well, or I'll wet you down again." When she sent me to the store, I'd run both ways, for fear of another beating.

One morning in mid-January, Madame Laroche told me to bathe and put on my clean shorts, shirt, and canvas shoes. "Stay on the porch. Your father will be picking you up," she said. I filled the wash bucket and bathed behind the kitchen, where I also dressed. A short time later, my father arrived in his black Volkswagen and handed Madame Laroche some money. I heard him say, "Please buy a suit and a suitcase for the boy." I felt ashamed that he didn't refer to me by name.

As we drove, I looked at him again from the corner of my eye. I still could not believe this stern white man was my true father. He parked in front of a travel agency, and I followed him inside.

Philippe signaled me to sit on a chair while he approached the clerk, a mulatto woman. I sat watching him speak in a low tone in French with the clerk. "Come here," he said to me in Creole, and I followed him into a small room in the back. As I entered the room, I saw a man standing behind a camera on a tripod. "He needs to have a picture for his passport," my father said. The man took my picture. It was the very first time I had ever had my picture taken.

Then my father drove me to another building and parked. I followed him inside. Again, he approached the counter.

"This boy needs to be vaccinated for a trip to New York," he said. The clerk began to write on a sheet of paper.

"What is your name?" the clerk asked me in French.

"My name is Jean-Robert Cadet." I wished with all my heart that my father would say, "No, his last name is the same as mine. He is Jean-Robert Sebastian.

"Mother's name?" he asked.

"Florence Cadet," replied my father.

"Father's name?" he asked. I turned my head and looked up at my father. He stared at the clerk.

"*Inconnu* [unknown]," he replied. At that moment, I wanted to disappear off the face of the earth. But I didn't. Then, the man sent me to a room for the vaccination while my father waited outside.

As we drove back to Madame Laroche's in silence, my heart still longed for contact with this man, my "unknown" father. He stopped at the gate without saying a word. I got out of the car, and he drove off.

A week later, Madame Laroche went shopping and returned in a taxi with several bags. I was standing on the porch. "Come get the bags," she barked at me. As the driver handed me a small brown suitcase, I felt my heart smiling. In my imagination I was jumping around, dancing and shouting all kinds of crazy things, "I am going to the white people's country." "I'm going across the sea." I couldn't believe it was actually happening.

"Put down the suitcase and get the bags," Madame Laroche yelled, jarring me from my mental celebration.

"Oui," I replied. I carried the two large paper bags inside and placed them on a table. Madame Laroche came in and pulled out a shoebox from a bag and handed it to me along with a pair of black socks. Written on the box were the words "STEP OVER" in English. It was the store's name. I didn't know what the words meant, but I will never forget them. "Go wash your feet and try these on," she said. Again, my heart smiled. I washed my feet in the wash bucket outside and put on the shoes. Madame Laroche came outside.

"They fit?"

"They're a little too big," I said, without a hint of complaint.

"You'll grow into them."

Later that afternoon, a tailor came and took my measurement. Before he left, Madame Laroche handed him a gray fabric with which to make my traveling suit.

Several days later, the tailor returned with my suit on a hanger and handed it to Madame Laroche. She paid him and put the suit in her bedroom.

At noon on February 15, 1969, Madame Laroche handed me a plate of rice and beans with a tiny piece of goat meat on top. Although no one in the house would have known it, this was the day my father had selected as my birth date when he applied for a passport. I fetched my spoon and cup from the dish basket on a rock pile in the sun. "Come see me when you're done eating," she said. After I washed my plate, I went to see Madame Laroche in the dining room. She and her children were having dinner. She handed me a pair of white underwear from the empty chair beside her. "Go take a good bath and put these on, and then come see me again," she said.

"Oui." I was shaking with excitement. She had never told me to take a "good" bath. Clearly, I was not supposed to take any of Haiti's dirt to America. I took off my ragged *restavek* clothes and placed them in a pile on the ground, knowing deep inside that I would never need to wear such a "uniform" again.

I filled the wash bucket with water from the drum and bathed behind the kitchen. I lathered up, scrubbed, and rinsed my body. One thing was certain: I had never been so clean. After I dried myself and put on the new underwear, I went back inside to see Madame Laroche.

"Go get dressed in Jerome's room and then pack your suitcase. Philippe will pick you up at two o'clock," she said.

"Oui." Since I had always dressed myself behind the house, now I was even more convinced that I had to be almost perfect in order to travel to the country of the white people. I went upstairs into Jerome's room. My suit, tie, shirt, and socks were on his bed. After I put on the shirt, Jerome tied my tie around his own neck, took it off, and then slipped it over my head. He adjusted it carefully under my collar.

After packing my suitcase, I went to the porch and faced Madame Laroche in her rocking chair. She looked at me head to foot.

"Amazing," she said, "You resemble a real person." Then she told me to sit down.

"Merci," I replied, thinking what she said was a compliment. It was my first time sitting so close to her. Soon, my father came to take me to the airport. He approached Madame Laroche and kissed her on both cheeks.

"Thank you for everything," he said.

"You're welcome," she replied.

"Go get in the car," said my father. Stiffly, I carried my suitcase to the car.

"Don't you forget us, you hear," said Madame Laroche.

"I will never forget you," I replied. And, for many reasons, I meant it.

On the long trip to the airport, I watched my father from the corner of my eye. Perhaps I sensed that these were the last moments I would have with him. As on our previous trips, neither of us said a word. He pulled the car into a lot in front of a huge two-story building. "Dr. Francois Duvalier International Airport" was written in large letters on the wall. *So Papa Doc was a real doctor,* I thought, *and this is his very own airport.* I removed my suitcase from the back seat and followed my father, who had a brown envelope in his hand.

All the other passengers were well dressed, as if they had come to a wedding reception or a funeral. I was so grateful for my new clothes, so happy not to stand out. My father approached a counter and handed some documents to the clerk, a young woman. A blue sign on the wall read: PAN AMERICAN.

"Is he traveling alone?" asked the clerk in French. I understood the question.

"Yes, he is. Someone will pick him up in New York." And I was relieved to understand Philippe's response.

The clerk returned the documents to my father, who handed them to me. I looked up at him, wanting to shake his hand, but thought I was too inferior to touch him, even now, at this strange moment in our father-son relationship.

A group of passengers were lining up to walk toward the plane. "Well, what are you waiting for? Go, get on the airplane," said my father in Creole, motioning me away with his hand. Even in this moment, he had managed to make me feel worthless. I followed the other travelers to the tarmac and up a stairway that piggybacked an orange pick-up truck. I did not turn to look back on my papa—or my homeland.

Stepping inside the plane, I couldn't believe my eyes. The interior was light blue and very clean. I recalled the domino player's remark that intelligent *blans* had invented the airplane. A flight attendant gave me a window seat, and I began to examine my travel documents.

Staring at my passport photo, I wondered how I had gotten the scar on the right side of my mouth. The information on my birth certificate was handwritten in red ink.

Name: Jean-Robert Cadet. Mother's name: Florence Cadet. Father's name: unknown. Date of birth: February 15, 1955. Place of birth: General Hospital, Port-au-Prince, Haiti. I knew that everything in the document was false. Florence had been my "owner," not my mother. My father was known, not unknown. The name "Cadet" was an alias, not my own. I opened my passport once more. Nationality: Haitian. At least that was correct. *When I arrive in the United States, what will I be?* I asked myself.

During the flight, I recalled having seen Florence washing her face with ice water so many times. I wondered if her skin had become lighter since she began living in a cold climate. *It won't be long before I see for myself,* I thought, feeling a smile form at the corners of my mouth. I looked down at the vast ocean under the plane. It was still like a dream. I was flying *lòt bò dlo* (across the sea).

CHAPTER 4

THE PLANE LANDED in New York. It was winter, 1969. I believed that I was more or less sixteen years old, a kid from a backward country who had been magically transported in the belly of a shiny aluminum bird to a totally different world. Everything about it would be new, except for me, and the very limited set of life experiences that I carried with me. In Haiti, I had walked out alone onto the tarmac and climbed a stairway to the plane. At this airport, I stepped out of that plane into a long, cold tube. Was this a birthing canal? Or was I walking a kind of plank? I moved along the tube like an alien, just arrived from another planet. I followed the throng of passengers toward an enormous room, illuminated by more electric lights than I had ever seen anywhere.

A sign on the wall said: "Welcome to John F. Kennedy International Airport." I didn't know what the word "welcome" meant, but I felt a warm sense of justification that proved, once and for all, that Kennedy was a real person, a president who owned an airport a thousand times bigger than Papa Doc's airport. I wished my old friend, René, were there to see it for himself. I was scared, but happy to be in the country of so kind a man as President Kennedy, who had sent all those secondhand clothes to Haiti before and after he was assassinated.

In the far end of the room were glass booths occupied by white men in blue uniforms. Written above the booths were words I didn't understand: "U.S CUSTOMS AND IMMIGRATION." I moved toward the booths with the other Haitians.

Behind the booths were people waving at the passengers. I spotted Florence and her son, Denis, in the crowd. They were as black as the day they had left Haiti. When they noticed me, they waved and I raised my hand bashfully. My heart pounded. Would they make my life happier now that I was in America?

After I went through customs, Florence greeted me with a smile, something I could not recall her ever having done before.

"Ki jan-ou ye?" (How are you?), she asked, in Creole of course.

"Mwen pa pli mal, non" (I am not too bad, no), I replied. It was so strange trying to find a comfort zone around this woman who had made my life so miserable for so long a time.

Walking out of the airport, I was amazed that the air felt colder than anything I had ever imagined. *So this is a cold country*, I thought, convinced that it would stay this way forever, just as the air in Haiti stayed always warm or hot. Immediately I noticed that the cold air had no smell. In Port-au-Prince the breeze often carried a variety of smells: fried food, rotted garbage, smoke, car exhaust, coffee, urine, dried fish, etc.

Following my grown-ups to the parking lot, I began searching the ground in the pools of lamplight for all the rumored money. I saw nothing, not a penny, but was amazed at the cars, hundreds of them sitting side by side, as if they were about to march in some immense parade. Each one stood between two white lines.

Getting into the backseat, I felt a huge, embarrassing tension. Denis had never driven me anywhere. The thing I most remember from my first car ride in America was the silence on the streets. In Haiti, drivers blasted their horns incessantly. All during the long ride, I listened, but heard only the occasional honk. I couldn't wait to get to the family's home so I could get out of their sight. I had never sat so close to these people who had kept me hidden behind doors and under tables.

It was late when we arrived at their two-story brick home in Spring Valley. Denis went to bed, leaving me in the kitchen with Florence. I put my suitcase beside the table and stood there looking in every corner for a step stool to sit on because in Haiti the furniture was off-limits to me.

Sensing I was ill at ease, Florence asked me to sit at the table. She set out a bowl of stew for me, and then pulled out a chair and sat across from me. I was so nervous. Although it was delicious, I could barely swallow the food. It was the first time Florence had ever shared a table with me.

"Don't be embarrassed. Eat," she said.

"Oui." I downed the stew quickly so I could get out of her sight and feel safe.

Looking around the kitchen, I wondered why the faucet had two handles. Selecting the handle on the right, I washed my bowl and drank some of the water. It tasted funny with a faint smell of Clorox, the bleach I had so often used on Florence's menstrual rags. "Maybe one handle is a spare," I thought. I felt like asking if the faucet ever ran dry. Then, I puzzled about the stove. *Where is the charcoal?* I wondered. I was still afraid to ask Florence any questions. Of course, I assumed I would continue to heat water for her on the stove to wash her derriere.

"Bobby, don't call anyone in this house 'Monsieur,' 'Madame,' or 'Mademoiselle' in the presence of guests," Florence warned.

"Oui," I answered. I thought of asking why, but I couldn't vocalize the word.

That night, for the first time in my life, I slept in a real bed. It was in a small room that had been the porch. As I drifted off to sleep in this new world, I couldn't help wondering how long I would be "staying with" this family of virtual strangers.

The next morning, I got up, went to the kitchen, found a small bucket, and filled it from the sink. Denis caught me as I headed outside to wash the car.

"We're in February, Bobby, winter season. It's too cold to wash the car," said Denis. I didn't understand what Denis meant by "winter season." I understood corn season, mango season, coffee season, avocado season, bean season, tobacco season, rain season, dry season, kite flying season, vacation season, and school season. I felt like asking Denis if America also had these seasons, but I was too afraid of him.

I emptied out the bucket and placed it in the closet. Soon, Lise came downstairs with Denis Jr., a toddler who was lighter than either of his two siblings. I thought maybe his light skin was the result of his having been born in this cold climate.

Because in Haiti my place had always been outside, I felt extremely uncomfortable being inside with the family. I wanted to use the bathroom but was afraid to ask. So I began following my old routine of peeing discreetly outside when no one was paying attention. But whenever I had to use the bathroom for bowel movements, my heart pounded with nervousness as I flushed. I believed I was wasting their water.

At some point several days later, Denis explained that I did not need to pee outside, and that I should flush even after urinating. I was astonished that saving water was no longer a concern. So many astonishments! And these wonders would be part of my life for a long time.

Off the hallway to my room was the door to Florence's room. I peeked in and saw a dresser beside her bed, but no mahogany cabinet, no *vodou* shrine. I couldn't imagine Florence without her *lwas*. The only familiar object was a framed picture of the Virgin Mary, different from the one she had had in Haiti.

That first morning, after Florence bathed, I waited beside her door in case she needed me to fasten her bra and zip up her dress. She told me that she didn't need my help anymore.

When it was time for my own shower, I went into the bathroom with an old towel and a bar of soap that Madame Laroche had given me for my own use. I stepped into the bathtub and turned on the right-hand faucet. The water was so cold, I turned it off quickly. I thought of asking permission to heat a pot of water on the stove, but I was still afraid of the adults. *How did they tolerate water so cold?* I hadn't noticed anyone heating up water for a bath. "If everyone can shower in water this cold, I can too," I said to myself. I clenched my teeth, contracted my muscles, and turned the water back on, but this time using the other handle. It was cold for a few seconds, and then suddenly, it became the hottest water I had ever felt, spraying against my face and chest. I jumped out of the tub, falling on my back and banging my head on the toilet. I had grabbed the shower curtain as I fell, and pulled it down on top of me.

"What's going on in there?" yelled Florence. My heart thudded. "Nothing," I said, and turned off the faucet. Steam was filling the bathroom. I imagined the hot water being piped from a dam with thousands of charcoal stoves underneath it. I tried to reinstall the shower curtain bar, but it would not stay on the wall. "They're going to kill me," I thought. My heart pounded. I sat on the edge of the tub, looking at the faucet handles. Written on one was the word "HOT" and on the other was "COLD." The meaning of these new words was now very clear to me. *FRÈT* and *CHO*. This was my first English lesson in America. I turned on the cold very gently, and then the hot. I played with the mixture until it felt perfect, then I climbed into the shower once more. How exotic it felt! After drying myself, I used the towel to soak up the water on the floor. I left the shower bar and curtain in the tub.

"What was that noise in the bathroom?" asked Lise. My heart sank.

"The curtain fell down," I said. Less annoyed than I had expected, she went to the bathroom and fixed it.

On Saturday morning, Florence put soap powder in a sandwich bag and asked Denis for a ride to the Laundromat. Then she ordered me to put my dirty clothes in a pillowcase. Denis drove two blocks down from our street and stopped in front of a brick building. I followed Florence inside with the clothes bag in my hand. A few black women with large afros sat on long benches, folding laundry. I wondered why they didn't braid their hair, or wear wigs like the women in Haiti. I wondered how long they had been living in the white people's country for them to be speaking English so fluently.

"This is where you'll do your laundry," Florence said. "Lise doesn't want it done in her washing machine. Put your clothes in a machine." She pointed to a white metal box with a round glass door.

"Oui," I said, and stuffed in my dirty clothes. She handed me the bag of soap.

"Pour it in and close the door," she said, handing me two quarters. I recalled placing in her hand the coins I had earned washing her clients' cars in Haiti. Now it was as if she were giving them back to me.

"Here, put these in the slot," she said, standing beside me. After I put in the coins, I watched in amazement as water shot out of holes inside the washing machine, as the clothes spun, and the box hummed. "'This is like magic," I thought.

"This place never closes," said Florence as she sat on an empty bench that was bolted to the floor. I looked at her and waited for instructions to sit.

"Sit," she said.

"Oui," I said, and sat two feet from her with my knees together, heart pounding, hands crossed in my lap, staring at the machines. I was still uncomfortable being so close to her. I wanted to investigate everything in the room but was afraid to move. I looked at a box that was shaped like an armoire with "Coca-Cola" written on it. A much smaller box was white with metal rods sticking out of it. On its surface was the picture of a yellow and red box with the word "Fab" written in blue. It was the same brand I had used to scrub our clothes in Haiti. I visualized the black women in the Laundromat sitting topless along a riverbank, scrubbing away on the big rocks. The thought made me smile.

After the machine stopped humming, Florence ordered me to remove the clothes and place them in another round box with a glass door. This time she placed one coin in my hand and I put it in the slot. I returned to the bench and watched again in awe as the clothes spun inside the box. When the clothes stopped spinning, the machine made a buzzing sound. "Take your clothes out of the machine, put them on the table, and start folding them," ordered Florence.

"Oui," I said. Once again I was amazed that the clothes were not only dry, but hot. *How did this happen?* I wondered. By the time I finished folding them, Denis had come back to pick us up.

The following Saturday Florence gave me seventy-five cents, and I walked down the street to wash my clothes in the Laundromat. This time, I investigated everything in the room freely, pushing buttons and pulling metal rods of each machine. "The domino players must have been right about the *blans* being inventors of everything. God really did create white people with his hands," I thought.

One day, Alix, a relative of Lise, came to visit. He had known me in Haiti as a *restavek*.

"You have to send Bobby to school. It's against the law in this country not to send a minor to school," he said.

Florence grimaced and sighed. "Could you take him for me?"

Alix drove me to Kakiat Junior High. The school was like a palace, absolutely beautiful. At the office Alix handed my passport to a white woman and said something in English. Alix translated my birth certificate to her. She asked which school I had attended in Haiti, and I wrote Ecole du Canada on a sheet of paper.

After Alix left, two boys escorted me to a classroom. I had never seen white teenagers in Haiti. There were lots of girls in the hallway. "They look just like the Virgin Mary," I said to myself.

Before long, a strange buzzing sound came out of a wall speaker, and all the students began to leave the room. A boy showed me to another classroom, and I wondered why we were moving. "Is something wrong with the other teacher?" I wondered. After that, I followed the schedule and sat silently in each class, listening to a language that sounded like people speaking nonsense with their mouths full of stones. But I knew what they were saying—especially the teacher—was important. Hearing real people speak English was completely new to me.

When I went into the "BOYS" room, I was amazed to see boys urinating into rectangular white basins attached to the wall. "White students are the luckiest in the world to have a large bathroom with a separate place to urinate," I thought. As a white boy left a bathroom stall, I went in and saw that he had not flushed after himself. "Oh-oh, his poop is the same color as mine and smells just as bad," I thought. Then I thought of my *restavek* friend René. He had been wrong about Kennedy, and about this, too. *Blans'* poop was not white, and it definitely was not odorless.

For the first time in my life, I didn't feel guilty when I used the toilet and, especially, the free toilet paper. Before I left the bathroom, I pushed the silver handle atop each urinal and watched the water come down like curtains washing away the urine.

I hated to go home after school because I would often find Florence angry. She had to wash dishes and clean the bathroom—chores she had not been accustomed to doing in Haiti. Although I was no longer being whipped, Lise and Denis often looked at me with disgust.

Several months later, in early spring, the gym teacher took us outside. The trees were coming back to life with new leaves. When I had seen them leafless during the winter months, I assumed they were dead forever. Trees in Haiti lost leaves over time, but they always stayed green. That day, the morning sun felt good on my face. I realized, happily, that it would not stay cold forever in this land across the sea.

I watched two boys carrying a bunch of wooden sticks that, to me, resembled chicken legs. Another boy had a canvas bag filled with leather gloves that looked like oversized hands with banana fingers. When a fourth boy carried a bucket of balls stitched with red thread, my mind began racing with excitement. I couldn't believe my eyes. I would at last see the game that white children played with the leather balls, like the one that had been my first toy in Haiti.

On the grassy field, I watched the coach position four white canvas cushions to form a large square and heard him refer to them as bases. Then I watched in wonderment as the boys who wore the gloves walked into a big field outside the square. Then one boy stood in the middle of the square and threw a ball to a boy who was holding a stick. The boy with the stick hit the ball with it and ran toward one of the bases. A boy wearing a glove chased the ball down as he ran.

"I knew it! I had always imagined that the ball had to be thrown at something. That's why it's so heavy," I thought. As I continued watching, I imagined whoever caught the ball before it hit the ground would be the winner. Then I changed my mind. Maybe whoever hit the ball the farthest would be the winner. It was a crazy game, very complicated. "Maybe whoever accumulates the most balls wins," I said to myself.

As I tried on a baseball glove, a boy tossed a ball at me, and I jumped back to avoid being hit.

"Why didn't you catch the ball?" asked the boy. I shrugged and smiled. When it was my turn to hit the ball, I held the big stick on my shoulder. A few boys laughed. The coach frowned and moved me into the proper position. A boy threw the ball at me, and I swung at it. The bat flew out of my hands and nearly hit the pitcher. Everyone laughed. I was embarrassed, but also happy that my wish had come true. At last I knew that the mysterious ball with the red stitches was a "baseball."

The coach sighed and shook his head. I picked up the bat and tried again. I swung at the second pitch, and the stick once again flew out of my hands. The coach scratched his head and mumbled to himself. He had a stern expression on his face, and I felt badly that I had made a white person mad. He stood behind me, placed the stick in my hand, and held my grip in place. He then bent me slightly forward like a mannequin.

I hit the ball on my third swing, sending it rolling onto the grass. I stood still and watched two boys running to pick it up.

"Run!" yelled the coach. "Run! Run, damn it, run!" I was happy that I hit the ball. I hadn't figured out that I was supposed to run somewhere. I walked off the field and went back inside. The coach never included me in anything again. He was the only teacher at the school I didn't like.

At the end of the school year, I attended remedial summer school classes. In September, I transferred to Spring Valley High School. I was placed in the tenth grade. A teacher introduced me to a Haitian boy named Nicholas, who had come to Spring Valley High the year before. I was glad he spoke to me in Creole rather than French. I wanted to keep my social status a secret, if possible. Since we were in different grades, I rarely saw him at school.

During lunch, Mr. Rabinowitz, my history teacher, fetched me from the cafeteria with a smile on his face and escorted me to his office for tutoring. English was now making sense to me, although I could not understand many of the words I heard.

He placed a chair beside his desk and motioned me to sit.

"L'État, c'est moi" (I am the state), he said in French and asked, "Who said that?"

"I don't know," I replied shamefully, in English.

"Louis XIV. Who was Louis XIV?" he asked.

"I don't know," I said.

"Louis XIV was king of France, the Sun King. Like Papa Doc Duvalier, Louis XIV was the law and the state in France." Then he spoke to me about "Papa Doc" and the *Tonton Macoute*. I was surprised that he knew something of their crimes against the Haitian people, and of many of the bad things that were so much a part of Haiti's history.

As for me, I had only learned good things about America. In my old mind, there had been an American president called Kennedy who loved poor Haitians so much that he sent them used clothes. There was also a big white man named Tarzan who often saved Africans from lions and crocodiles. In my new mind, I learned that Tarzan wasn't a real person, and that the used clothes came from the US, but Kennedy himself hadn't sent them.

I always sensed that Mr. Rabinowitz was challenging me to learn more and more. Sometimes my heart pounded, and I thought he might throw me out of his class if I didn't know the answers to his questions.

Often when Mr. Rabinowitz escorted me to his office, he put his arm around my shoulders and said, "Let's go, Wise Guy." Since *restaveks* were sometimes given new names by their grown-ups, I assumed teachers in America could also call their students by different names. "Wise Guy" sounded good to me. I wanted to keep it for myself, but I didn't know how. After a few weeks in the classroom of this wonderful teacher, I no longer felt empty. School became my refuge, even more than it had been in Haiti. Although there was no corporal punishment at school, I worried each time I was called to the counselor's office, as if I were once again being summoned to be whipped.

"I wrote to your school in Haiti asking for your academic records, but I have not received them," the counselor said one time. "Is this the correct address?"

"Yes, Ecole du Canada, 2nd City, Saint Martin, Port-au-Prince, Haiti."

"I also wrote to the Department of Education in Haiti, asking for your records, but nothing came," said the counselor. I left her office, heart pounding, and worrying that I'd be thrown out of school.

One night in November, I waited for everyone to go to bed before sitting at the kitchen table to do my homework. The children came downstairs unexpectedly, playing and running around me at the table.

"Hey, stop it. Go back upstairs. You're shaking the table," I said firmly. Suddenly, Lise appeared from nowhere with anger in her eyes and a stern expression on her face. Denis was right behind her.

"How dare you? Who do you think you are, talking to my children in that tone? It's their house and their table. I want you out of my house right now," she screamed. I was petrified, yet I had always known that it was only a matter of time before I'd be forced to leave. Then Denis added, "And stop using the name Cadet, it's our name. Get yourself your own name."

Once again, I wished my father had recognized me with his own name. I could still hear him say, "Unknown!" to the clerk in the vaccination office. I went to my room. I reached under my bed and pulled out the suitcase from Haiti. I stuffed my clothes into it, along with my books, and walked out of the Cadets' house.

It was cold and dark. I looked left and then right. "Maybe I'll go sleep in the Laundromat," I whispered to myself. Florence had said it was never closed.

I walked down the street and stopped in front of Nicholas's house. Nicholas had just moved into the neighborhood. I could see him moving around in his room. I took a deep breath and went into the yard. I knocked softly on his window.

"Nicholas, open up. It's me, Bobby." He opened the window.

"What's the matter?" he asked.

"They threw me out," I said.

"What did you do?"

"I raised my voice at the children." He was surprised.

"They're not my parents. I was staying with them." I could see his mind at work. Click . . . click . . . click. He had figured it out. I was a *restavek*. He let me in through the window and put a blanket on the floor for me to sleep on.

"If someone knocks on my door, roll under the bed," he said, and turned off the light. I thought that, despite the nasty weather, being homeless in America could not be as bad as being homeless in Haiti.

In the morning, as Nicholas was getting ready for school, I asked if I could leave my suitcase under his bed.

"Go out through the window and knock on the front door. I'll pretend you came to pick me up. I'll share my breakfast with you," he said. This became my daily routine. Sometimes I brushed my teeth and showered in the school gym. After school each day, I sought shelter from the cold in the Laundromat. For hours I did my homework, sitting on the benches and listening to the whir of the machines.

I befriended Mike, an African American classmate, who lived a few blocks from Florence's street. One Friday afternoon, I went to his house and hung around until dinnertime. His single mother fixed the two of us a lovely dinner of pork chops and mashed potatoes.

"Thank you very much," I said after dinner.

"Any time," was her reply. I was dumbfounded to think that Mike's mother would be willing to feed me at any time.

The next morning, bright and early, I left Nicholas's room through the window and went looking for breakfast at Mike's house. I knocked at the door, and his mother yanked open the second floor window, looking at me as if I were an intruder.

"What are you doing here so early?" she asked with an angry tone. I was confused, thinking she had forgotten her promise to feed me.

"Is Mike awake?" I asked.

"Go home!" she barked.

It took me a while to figure out that in America, "any time" was another way of saying, "you're welcome."

During this period of homelessness, I was always hungry. One day I grabbed a partly eaten slice of pizza from a table in the school cafeteria and noticed a white girl looking at me with disgust. Each time she and her friends saw me in the hall, they pointed my way and pretended to vomit. A few days after this incident, Mr. Rabinowitz asked that I stay after class.

"What's wrong, Wise Guy?" he asked. "You don't seem like yourself."

I was hesitant to respond. "I don't have a home anymore. The people I had been living with kicked me out last week. I stay mostly in the Laundromat, and at night I sleep under the bed of a friend."

"You're kidding?" he said with a frown. He seemed genuinely shocked. "The Cadets are not your parents?"

"No, they're not my parents. I worked for them in Haiti. They don't want me anymore." I was too ashamed to tell him that I had been a *restavek*.

Several days later, Mr. Rabinowitz handed me an envelope and directions to an address in New City, New York. "Take this there," he said, pointing to the address. "They know you're coming." I assumed it was a place where I would be given some kind of job. When I arrived, I handed the envelope to a woman at a counter. She read the letter and escorted me into a room, where another woman was seated at a desk.

"You are eligible for food stamps, money, and medical care," she said.

"I don't understand. Please say that again." I thought I misunderstood what she had just said.

"You're eligible for full benefits, as long as you're unemployed," she said. I couldn't believe it. "This is the best country in the entire world," I whispered to myself as she typed out my information.

The woman sent me into another room, where a man took my picture. When the picture was developed, he handed me an ID card and sent me back to the woman's office. She handed me a small booklet of food stamps.

"Come back for your first check on the 15th," she said.

"Thank you," I said, looking into her eyes with deep gratitude. I simply could not believe that these strangers were helping me.

Nicholas's father, who had learned of my homelessness from Nicholas, introduced me to a Haitian man from whom I rented a room in his two-bedroom apartment.

After a few months on public assistance, I applied for a job at a gas station and was hired as an attendant. I worked four to midnight. After I received my first paycheck, I stopped collecting welfare and food stamps. I liked the work, and I wanted to become self-sufficient.

CHAPTER 5

IN EARLY JUNE 1972, a few weeks before I graduated from Spring
Valley High School, my English teacher, Mrs. Rosenberg, sent
me to fetch a movie projector and a film from the library. She had
named me "Media Technician," and I was grateful to her for giving me that title, although I didn't fully understand the meaning of
"Media." In preparation for our assignments, we had been watching
films of famous people giving speeches.

Returning from the library, I carefully loaded the film through
the projector's tracking channel and onto the take-up reel. The film
began with President Kennedy campaigning for the presidency of
the United States. As Kennedy shook people's hands, grinning as if
they were his friends, I wondered why I had never seen "Papa Doc"
doing this with Haitian citizens on television. I had seen many pictures of him, but never with a smile on his face.

President Kennedy stood at a podium speaking passionately about
his vision for the country. By this time, my English had improved
dramatically. I cherished each word the young president spoke. Part
of the speech contained a directive that had become famous to most
Americans, although I was hearing it for the first time. "Ask not what
your country can do for you; ask what you can do for your country."
These words imprinted themselves on my consciousness. It was my

understanding that Kennedy had more or less *ordered* Americans to be good citizens and to serve their country well.

Nine years after his death, I assumed the deceased president's "orders" were still being carried out by his citizenry, because, to me, everything seemed so wonderful in America. The streets were clean, education was mandatory, my teachers treated me like a regular person, laws were enforced, the electricity almost never went off, and the faucets ran all the time. Most important to me was my growing awareness that children of all classes were protected under the law. Feelings of deep well-being and pride-of-country engulfed me as the documentary film proceeded through various moments of Kennedy's life.

Now a senior in high school with a regular job, I had stopped collecting welfare. I found myself wondering at times what exactly I could do for America, the country that had provided me this opportunity for a new life of freedom and physical well-being. I remembered that "Papa Doc's" main concern seemed to have been to kill communists and anyone who spoke ill of him. I recalled seeing swollen cadavers of men lying on sidewalks with signs that said *kamoken* (communist) tied to their chests. I was still angry at "Papa Doc" because his stooges had killed the mulatto woman whom I had fallen in love with as a little boy. To me, there was no question that President Kennedy was a much better man than the "President-for-Life" in my country.

Now on the screen were blurred images of Kennedy and his wife in the back seat of a slow-moving convertible. They smiled and waved at the people lining the road. My classmates hushed. I didn't know why. The projector's rattling sounds filled the silent room. I had never seen this footage, but I sensed something terrible would soon happen to JFK. Suddenly, the images turned even blurrier, and Kennedy, in slow motion, collapsed in the back seat. His wife crawled onto the trunk of the limousine. My heart was thumping in my chest. Tears welled up in my eyes. The film ended. A collective gasp went up in the classroom. The teacher turned on the lights.

Getting up from my seat, stunned, I rewound the film and placed it gently in its round metal box, almost as if I were handling the remains of President Kennedy himself. As I rolled the projector back toward the library, I realized that the adolescent fantasies of being Tarzan, which I had been carrying inside me for so long, had been suddenly replaced by the desire to imitate a real human being, President Kennedy. JFK was now my best hero, and I wondered what I might do to please him, or to honor his memory.

Graduation day came and went. I was proud of my academic achievement and honored to shake the principal's hand as I received my diploma. But that was all overshadowed by the fact that, unlike my fellow graduates, I had no parents or relatives beaming with pride in me. Not a single person. There were no graduation parties to attend, not even a special meal in my honor.

A few days after graduation, I took a long walk and came upon a storefront that had captured my curiosity some time earlier. A sign on the window read: US Army Recruiting Station. I stood at the window and looked inside. I saw several posters of tanks and aircraft on the walls. Intrigued, I went inside to have a closer look.

"May I help you?" asked the man at the desk. He was in uniform, and his jacket was decorated with a cluster of tiny rectangular ribbons. I was curious, but I didn't really understand what he could help me with.

"Are tanks difficult to drive?" I finally asked. The man introduced himself as Sergeant Williamson and shook my hand.

"Have a seat, young man. What's your name?"

"My name is Jean-Robert." I used the French pronunciation.

"How do you spell your name? Write it down for me, will you?" He handed me a pen and a notebook.

"May I call you John?"

"Yes, sir," I said.

"Where're you from, John?"

"I am from Haiti."

"Tanks are easy to drive, John. And fun. A child can drive a tank." I formed an image of myself as a child playing with a tank, rather than a baseball in a tin bucket.

"What kind of work do you do?"

"I work in a gas station. Is it easy to change oil in tanks?"

"You've come to the right place, John," he said.

"You will teach me how?" I asked in disbelief. Since Florence had always told me that I would never be anything but a shoe shiner, I had been quite happy working in the gas station.

"We can do better than that, John. We'll teach you to drive it, load it, and fire it. Are you interested in doing something like that?"

"Yes, I am, sir," I said excitedly. "I'm very interested."

"Have you graduated from high school?"

"Yes, I did. Two weeks ago."

"Will you bring me your diploma tomorrow morning?"

"Yes, sir," I replied. He shook my hand.

"White people are so good," I said to myself as I exited the office.

Just before the door closed, Sgt. Williamson called out, "Bring your birth certificate, also." My heart thudded, and I immediately panicked. *I hate to show a document that has nothing in it but lies to a* blan, I thought.

"Yes, sir," I said glumly.

The next day, I returned to the recruitment office with the requested document along with my diploma. I handed them to him, hoping he would not understand the word "Inconnu," which appeared beside my father's name on the birth certificate.

"It's in French. Show me your date of birth," he said.

"February 15, 1955," I said, pointing at the date. He typed it on a form.

"What's your mother's name?" he asked.

"My mother is Florence Cadet," I said, hoping he'd skip my father's name.

"Father's name?" he asked.

"Philippe," I replied. He typed "Philippe Cadet."

Sergeant Williamson drove me to a large building in Manhattan, where I spent half a day taking written tests with young adults. Afterward, some people were sent home, and he congratulated those who remained in the room. "Get on your feet, raise your right hands, and repeat after me," he said. We repeated these important words, each one of us using our own name.

"I, Jean-Robert Cadet, do solemnly swear that I will support and defend the Constitution of the United States and the State of America against all enemies, foreign and domestic; that I will bear true faith and allegiance to the same; and that I will obey the orders of the president of the United States and the orders of the officers appointed over me, according to law and regulations. So help me God."

A huge feeling of pride washed over me at that moment. I, Jean-Robert Cadet, would be obeying orders from Richard Nixon, the president of the United States.

I was thrilled to be taken into the United States Army. I found myself imagining driving a tank. It was the first time I had ever dreamed of actually becoming something. Spring Valley's guidance counselor had never spoken to me about my future plans. Although on several occasions I had heard my classmates talking about the universities they planned to attend, I had no future plans. Sgt. Williamson gave me some papers that I signed without ever reading them, and a few days later, the other recruits and I were driven to a very large military facility in New Jersey. I had no idea exactly where we were going. I didn't really care. At the entrance was a large sign that said: "Fort Dix." When the driver stopped, a tall black soldier boarded the bus and yelled, "Get off the bus and line up in front of the building." I was surprised to see that his shoulder patch bore an eagle. Since the symbol of "Papa Doc" was the guinea fowl, I assumed the eagle was the logo of the president of the United States. *I hope I get to wear that eagle on my uniform*, I said to myself.

We lined up in front of the building, and the soldier paced back and forth, looking at us.

Where're you from?" he asked a recruit.

"New Jersey, sir!"

"Only hippies, pimps, and drug addicts live in New Jersey," shouted the soldier.

"How does he know that?" I asked the young man next to me.

The black soldier stepped in front of me.

"Who gave you permission to talk?"

"No one, sir," I responded timidly.

"Are you a faggot?"

"No, sir!" I knew what a faggot was and I knew I wasn't one.

"Then stop standing like one. Straighten up, soldier. I hate faggots," he said. I stood up as straight as a flagpole.

"From now on, you all belong to Uncle Sam, and for the next eight weeks I'll be your mama and your daddy," said the sergeant. I raised my hand.

"Who is Uncle Sam, sir?" I asked. Some recruits chuckled. I honestly had never heard of him.

"Are you a comedian?"

"No, sir," I said.

"Wipe that damn smile off your face," barked the sergeant.

I tried to wipe off whatever was on my face, but it wasn't a smile. The last thing I would do at this moment was smile.

As he marched us to our barracks, he kept repeating, "Left, left, left, left, your left, right, left . . . " I stepped with my left foot, dragging my right foot behind. We all looked disorganized, as if no one knew his left foot from his right. We would learn.

After he assigned each of us a bunk and lockers, he marched us in the same manner to another building, where a supply sergeant issued us boots, socks, uniforms, ponchos, underwear, helmets, and other gear that we stuffed into duffle bags, which were also issued.

Back in the barracks, the sergeant explained the purpose of each piece of gear. He put a helmet liner inside a helmet. "This is a steel helmet. In combat this could save your life," he said, holding it high for emphasis. Immediately, I assumed it was bulletproof. I couldn't wait to wear that helmet.

I wonder why they don't make our clothes out of the same kind of metal. That way our bodies would be protected too, I said to myself.

Most of the recruits in my unit hated Army life. But not I. It was as if the late President Kennedy had spoken to me personally, man to man, and said, "This is what you can do, Jean, for America."

What I *did* do was everything that I possibly could to be a good soldier. I often volunteered for extra duties in hopes of fulfilling Kennedy's wishes. I wanted to serve America beyond the call of duty. To put it simply, I loved America. America had given me so much: access to education and a quality of life I couldn't have dreamed of in Haiti.

For the first time in my life, my teeth were examined by a dentist who filled in two cavities. I even felt proud of my fillings. Around the same time, I also received my first-ever medical examination.

In spite of an impoverished childhood, the doctor told me I was in "tip-top shape."

During the first week of orientation, an officer in his mid-forties stepped to the podium and introduced himself as Captain Walker, Company Commander. He spoke about the importance of honor, truth, and the consequences that could occur if we went AWOL.

"Absence without leave is a serious offense, punishable under the military code of justice."

I was bewildered. *Why would someone go AWOL, when the army provides everything we need?* I wondered. And I wondered this many times thereafter, when this guy or that guy would disappear from the base.

"If you have a problem that your noncommissioned officer cannot solve, come speak to me about it instead of going over the wall. If you feel the problem is too personal to discuss with your noncommissioned officer, tell him that you want to speak to me," said the captain. Then he talked about the consequences of using illegal drugs. "You cannot be effective on the battlefield when you are high on drugs, and using them is punishable under the Military Code of Justice," he said.

"Who is he talking to?" I thought. I wondered why anyone would want to use illegal drugs in so nice an army.

Later that day, the recruits were asked to review their personnel files for accuracy. "If you have knowingly given false information to your recruiter, I encourage you to come forward and tell the truth . . . otherwise you will be prosecuted under the Military Code of Justice and discharged for lying," said a lieutenant. Once again, my heart banged like an old door on the walls of my chest, as I recalled giving the recruiter my fake birth certificate. *Oh, God, am I going to lose this too?* I thought. Not if I could help it. I requested permission to speak to Captain Walker.

"Private Cadet, requesting permission to speak with you, sir." The captain returned my salute.

"Stand at ease, Private! What's the problem?"

"Sir, I am sorry, but I gave the recruiter a fake birth certificate."

"Why the hell did you do that?" he asked.

"I've never had a real one, and I don't even know my age. The name

Cadet does not belong to me. The people who brought me to America from Haiti are not my parents. My father didn't recognize me as his son." I rattled off my life's sins as if I were in the confessional.

"Were you adopted by the Cadet family?"

"No, I was their . . ."

"Their what?"

"Their boy. I used to live with them," I said. I simply could not admit that I had been a child slave.

"Okay, soldier, take it easy. I'll take care of it. Not to worry," he said.

"Thank you, sir," I said with an almost loving sincerity. I snapped back to attention, and saluted the captain. As I walked out of the office, I let out a long sigh of relief. I trusted him. He was an officer in the United States Army. And he said he would take care of it. I would remain a soldier, ready to defend the country I loved.

Later that day, the other recruits and I took a series of written tests in a large room in order to determine what jobs we would be assigned after Basic Training. Some tests required that we arrange puzzle pieces to form pictures. With my English still limited, I felt I did fairly well on the test. And I was right.

We spent the second week marching with our M16s on our shoulders, singing lots of army chants. In the afternoons we learned to disassemble and assemble our rifles in a matter of minutes. At the firing range I imagined myself fighting in all the World War II movies I had seen, shooting at German soldiers. From the start I was a very good shot. I almost always hit the bull's-eye at fifty yards and felt good when the sergeant nodded at me approvingly. I was happy and content. Life was good. Even the food was good, so much better than what I had eaten most of my life. No more gas station jobs for me. In my mind, I could see myself staying in the army forever. Maybe until I became a general.

One day, after a session at the firing range, I was feeling very cocky as we recruits fell out for lunch. I put my bull's-eye target on display for everyone to see. Looking at my fellow recruits in their helmets, I remembered watching a western movie in which the cowboy hero knocked a bandit's hat off his head with one shot.

"I bet you five dollars that I can shoot the helmet off your head at fifty yards with one shot," I said to the recruit sitting next to me. I wasn't really serious, but I was certain that I could do it.

"Are you nuts?" he yelled.

"I always hit the bull's-eye at fifty yards. Don't worry, I'll aim high. Besides, the helmet is made of steel. The bullet cannot penetrate it," I assured him. He walked over to the sergeant.

"Sergeant, Cadet thinks my helmet is bulletproof. He wants to shoot it off my head." The sergeant came toward me with a stern expression on his face, snatched the helmet off my head, and threw it far out in the dirt. He then inserted the magazine clip into my M16 and shot at the helmet from about twenty yards. Another sergeant, laughing, retrieved it from the firing range. It had a hole in one side and another hole out the back. I was stunned.

"Private, how can you be so damn smart and so damn stupid at the same time?" he yelled.

"But you said the helmet was made of steel and would protect my head," I stuttered. No new helmet was issued. I wore my helmet with the holes that let daylight shine through from front and back. The soldiers began calling me Gomer Pyle. I didn't mind. I had no idea who Gomer Pyle was. That TV show had never made it to Haiti.

After my group met qualifications with our M16s, we went through another phase in our training. At an outdoor class, we sat facing a life-size picture of a Vietnamese soldier in a khaki uniform. "Know Your Enemy" was written above its head. When the instructor referred to the enemy soldier as a communist, images of those swollen cadavers lying in the streets of Port-au-Prince flashed in my mind. Now, my head was filled with questions: "Does America have any communists in it?" If yes, "Why don't we kill the ones here, rather than go to Vietnam? How can you tell a communist from a noncommunist? Are all Vietnamese communists?" It would be years before I had learned enough about politics and war to answer questions like these.

In early September 1972, after I had completed eight weeks of Basic Training, I was sent to Advanced Infantry Training at Fort Jackson, South Carolina. By that time, the long, deadly Vietnam War was nearing the end. But military exercises and training continued unabated, as if another war would soon begin, as it always does.

After the recruits had completed Advanced Infantry Training, the first sergeant called us to formation.

"If anyone wants to volunteer for Jump School, step forward," he said. Because I still wanted to serve America with all my heart, I stepped forward, as did a few other soldiers. The first sergeant took our names, and we soon received orders to report to Fort Benning, Georgia. One of my fellow recruits asked me, "Cadet, why would you be crazy enough to jump out of a perfectly good airplane?" But the thought didn't scare me. I had seen posters of soldiers jumping out of airplanes and vividly imagined myself doing it. "Why not?" I responded. "If my chute doesn't open, nobody would care but me."

At Fort Benning, parachute training lasted four weeks. When it came time for our first jump, we were trucked to an airstrip where a C-130 aircraft and a large truck loaded with parachutes were waiting for us. The plane's engines were roaring. The door under its tail resembled the entrance to a dark tunnel. My heart pounded as I walked forward, wearing my parachute like a seat cushion against my chest. Attached to the chute was a yellow cord with a metal hook.

We lined up facing our sergeant, the jump master. Sewn to his shirt were a parachutist's wings and a Combat Infantry Badge. "I'd like to earn those patches," I told myself.

"If anybody wants to change his mind, now is the time. This plane will land with no one on board but the pilot," he promised.

We marched single file into the plane. It had no seats. A steel cable ran from front to back like a clothesline. We sat on the floor with our backs to the walls. I had the misfortune of sitting close to the door. As the plane took off, a red light behind the pilot came on. When we reached the right altitude, the jump masters opened both side doors, and a cold wind burst into the plane, stronger than any hurricane I had lived through in Haiti.

The light turned yellow. "Stand up," shouted the jump master. Everyone rose. "Hook up," he yelled. We all snapped our hooks onto the cable and then checked one another's gear. All of a sudden, I wanted to change my mind, but it was too late. There was no turning back. My stomach churned. As fate would have it, I would be the first on my side to jump. "Stand in the door," barked the jump master. That meant me. I had no other choice. I stood on the door's edge, looking straight ahead. Before me was nothing but blue sky. The light turned green. "Go, Go, Go, Go," shouted the jump master. I stood still, paralyzed by fear.

The next sensation I felt was a hard kick on my rear, and I fell headlong out of the plane, screaming. But I was the only one who could hear my screams. The wind filled my mouth and pressed my tongue back in against my gums. A second later, the rip cord pulled the parachute open, jerking me violently heavenward. Then, feeling relief and a surge of hero's pride, I floated down like a falling kite. It was beautiful. I tried searching the clouds for angels, though I knew they weren't there. After a while I landed and rolled, as trained, in the tall brown grass of a large field.

The subsequent jumps were progressively less terrifying. No more screams. I found myself really enjoying the last of them. At the Jump School "graduation," my company commander pinned a silver wing to my chest. Jean-Robert Cadet, a former *restavek*, was a US Army paratrooper.

Soon afterward, I received orders to report to the 82nd Airborne Division, in Fort Bragg, North Carolina. I reported to the company clerk, a white corporal, who escorted me to the second floor of the barracks. The white soldiers, who were the majority, occupied the right side of the barracks. On the left were a few Puerto Ricans. The clerk assigned me a wall locker and a bunk at the back end of the left side, where African Americans were housed.

"Hey bro," a black soldier said to me.

"Good morning, everyone," I replied, and they looked at me oddly from head to foot. I was used to it. With my accent and my manner, I was always a little different.

The next morning we packed our gear and went out on an extended training exercise and returned to the barracks several nights later. After we had cleaned and turned in our weapons, I went to the latrine for a shower. When I got back to the barracks, I was shocked to see some of my bunkmates sitting on their bunks smoking marijuana. This was my first assignment where I had seen weed being smoked publicly. As crazy as it may sound, I admit to being shocked.

I recalled Captain Walker in Basic Training warning the recruits about the danger of using illegal drugs. *How can they serve their country well when they're violating the rules?* I thought. I decided it was my duty to set them straight.

"Excuse me, please," I said. "You should not do this. President Kennedy said, 'Ask not what your country can do for you; ask what you can do for your country.'" They looked at me as if I were the strangest human being they had ever seen. No doubt, I was.

"Man, get the hell out of my face," said one.

"Haven't you men read the quote on the wall beside the first sergeant's office?"

"What quote?"

"The quote that says: 'We have done so much with so little for so long, we can do almost anything with nothing.' That means we have to be very good soldiers," I said. They proceeded to curse me and my mother. One of them threatened to throw me out the window.

"I guess they don't like this country," I told myself. Undeterred in my stupid resolve, I went to see the staff sergeant, who had his own room on the first floor.

"Sergeant, the guys are smoking marijuana. They're not being good soldiers," I said. He, too, stared at me oddly, shaking his head in disbelief.

"I'll take care of it," he said. I waited for him to come in to talk to the guys, but he didn't come. On Monday morning before breakfast, I went to see the first sergeant.

"First sergeant, the guys smoked marijuana all weekend long. They will not be effective on the battlefield in case we go to war," I said. He, too, looked at me strangely.

"Where're you from, soldier?" he asked.

"I grew up in Haiti," I replied. He sighed and scratched his head.

"Okay, I'll talk to the troops," he said.

Later during formation, the first sergeant spoke to the troops. "Anyone caught smoking marijuana in the barracks will get an Article 15," he warned, and dismissed the troops. But that still didn't stop them. Both these sergeants were black. In fact, all the sergeants in my unit were black. So I assumed black soldiers didn't really care about their country or about being successful in wartime.

Soon, I found myself being ostracized and threatened with more violence. I began to fear for my safety. My locker was broken into and my clothes scattered on the floor when I was out of the barracks. In my mind, if important rules were being violated within the military, America would no longer be the perfect society that I thought it was. One day, during formation, an officer came and asked those with a General Aptitude Test score of 110 or above to step forward. So, I did.

"What's your score?" he asked.

"One hundred twenty-two, sir," I replied. He smiled and nodded. The next day I was sent to clerical school on the base. After a few weeks, I could type forty words a minute.

When the troops realized that I would be working in Battalion HQ with the officers, they stopped threatening to kill me. But they still would have nothing to do with me.

After I completed clerical school, I reported to HQ and was assigned a desk with a manual typewriter. I typed Article 15's, Court Martials, and Officer Evaluation Forms. I was stunned when I typed my first Court Martial. A soldier had stolen a jeep engine, taken it apart, and mailed it piece by piece to his father in Kansas. I could not understand why anyone would steal from the same army that gave him food, shelter, uniforms, and money. It just didn't make sense to me. *Why are these people so ungrateful and unpatriotic?* I would often ask myself. But I could never figure it out.

The Officer Evaluation Forms, however, were always full of words like, "pragmatic," "substantive," and "meticulous." I relied on a dictionary to learn what words like these meant. Because the officers in Battalion HQ were all white men, these laudatory adjectives applied to them, but probably did not apply to all the noncommissioned officers, who were black. I assumed the officers were nearly perfect human beings, like some of my teachers at Spring Valley High, who were also white. All this made a special kind of sense to me because, throughout my childhood, Haitians always spoke so highly of whites. "The domino players were absolutely right," I kept thinking. In my desire to fully understand why the officers were unlike regular soldiers, I approached a second lieutenant in the office.

"Sir, what is the difference between an officer and an enlisted man?" He thought for a moment.

"Their rank," he said, having no idea what I was getting at.

"How did you become an officer?"

"I graduated from West Point."

"What is West Point?" He looked at me oddly.

"It's a military academy," he replied, but I couldn't imagine what that might be.

"Did all the officers graduate from West Point?" I asked.

"No, but they're all college graduates," he replied.

"Thank you, sir," I said. Then I came up with a strange notion. I concluded that college graduates, who, I assumed, were all white, didn't commit crimes. It would be years before I realized the convoluted, racist nature of my own thinking. At that moment, I felt a desperate urge to be a college graduate and an officer.

At this point in my military career, I had not yet seen a black officer. Haitian people do not really understand racism unless they come to the United States for a long while. I seldom looked in a mirror, and even when I did, I couldn't see myself as black.

In November 1974, I was sent to Fort Lewis, in Seattle, Washington. I reported to the first sergeant, who saw in my personnel file that I had been a battalion clerk.

"Report to S-2 at HQ," he said. I didn't know what "S-2" meant. On a door at HQ I saw "S-2" and knocked. The "S" in S-2 meant security.

"Come in," said a voice. I walked in and saw an officer at his desk. Behind him was a large steel vault.

"Corporal Cadet reporting for duty, sir," I said, and saluted. He returned my salute and handed me a folder. On the wall was a poster of a battleship that read: "LOOSE LIPS SINK SHIPS." A strange figure in a long coat was hiding inside the ship. His hat partly covered his shadowy face. I wondered how he had gotten onto the navy's battleship.

"Log these before I lock them in the safe."

"Yes, sir," I said. In the folder were several documents about Russia that were numbered and stamped "SECRET" and "CONFIDENTIAL."

"Sir, how do loose lips sink ships?" I asked, pointing at the poster on the wall.

"The enemy is always seeking information about our ships. So we've got to be careful what we say," he warned.

In addition to logging the documents, I continued typing Officer Evaluation Forms. As usual, they were full of high praises using big words. By this time, I had acquired a fairly rich vocabulary.

One morning, after a few months of my working in S-2, a colonel came to inspect the office. I was alone. He showed me his ID and asked to see the log.

"I detect an accent. Where're you from?"

"I am from Haiti, sir," I replied.

"I assume you're a naturalized citizen," he said.

"No, sir," I replied. No one had ever asked me that before.

"Corporal, should I assume you don't even have a security clearance?"

"That's correct, sir." I wasn't sure why he asked me that.

"How long have you been working in this office?" he asked.

"About three months," I said. He picked up the phone and placed a call to my company commander. The colonel dismissed me in order to speak with the commander in private. Because I had pledged allegiance to the flag of the United States of America in high school, I did not understand the concern with my lack of security clearance. I was so secure in my respect for the United States Army that I had listed it as "beneficiary" on my life insurance policy. I remembered the clerk looking at me oddly when he read that form.

I reported to the first sergeant, feeling nervous. I found myself again thinking, *I hope they don't kick me out of the army.*

"Why the hell didn't you tell me you were not a US citizen?"

"I didn't think of it," I replied, wondering what all the fuss was about. "I told the recruiter I was Haitian," I added.

"We'll be working on your US citizenship, Corporal."

"Thank you, First Sergeant." I breathed another sigh of relief. The thought of becoming an American citizen had never occurred to me.

While I waited to see what would happen, I continued to do the same work, but in a different office.

One early evening, at the base's PX, I spied a corporal with a black beret on his head. The word "Ranger" was written on his shoulder patch, and on his chest was an airborne wing. So I approached him in my straightforward manner.

"How can I join the Rangers, Corporal?" I asked.

"You would need to speak to my first sergeant," he said.

The very next day, I visited the 75th Ranger Battalion and asked to speak to the first sergeant.

"I see you're jump qualified," he said, looking at the wing sewn on my shirt. "What's your GT [General Aptitude] score?" he asked.

"One hundred twenty-two," I said.

"That's good. We don't have potheads and dope addicts in this unit. This is an elite outfit. Who's your first sergeant?" he asked.

"First Sergeant Roberts," I said.

There and then, he phoned my first sergeant and spoke with him briefly. "Go turn in your gear and come back with your clothes," he said. Sometimes, that's the way it is in the army. Things can happen fast.

"Thank you, First Sergeant."

With that, my new home became Company C, 75th Ranger Battalion. In this unit we were constantly preparing for war in different environments and on various types of terrain. We trained especially hard at night, even when the weather was at its worst. I liked it when we camouflaged our faces down to our necks. I felt good being in "green face" since it made everyone the same color.

The following month, my platoon sergeant asked me to put on my dress khaki uniform.

"Where are we going?" I asked.

"You're about to become an American citizen," he said, and smiled broadly. I was shocked. I couldn't believe this was actually happening.

The sergeant parked in front of the Federal Building in downtown Seattle. I followed him inside. In an office on the first floor, a secretary escorted us into a room where a tall, gray-haired white man in a black robe sat at his desk. My heart pounded.

"You must be Corporal Cadet?" he asked, rising to greet me.

"Yes, sir," I replied. His robe reminded me of a picture I had seen of the Sacred Heart of Jesus.

"Raise your right hand and repeat after me," he said. I repeated his words, phrase by phrase, my pride, my intense joy, growing with each promise that I made. Being a soldier in need of a security clearance, I thought this oath was written especially for me.

"I, Jean-Robert Cadet, hereby declare, on oath, that I absolutely and entirely renounce and abjure all allegiance and fidelity to any foreign prince, potentate, state, or sovereignty of whom or which I have heretofore been a subject or citizen; that I will support and defend the Constitution and laws of the United States of America against all enemies, foreign and domestic . . . so help me God."

By the time I had finished taking the oath, I was misty-eyed, and feeling more proud of myself than I had ever been. In my mind the words "so help me God" made the oath a sacred promise. I also believed that it meant I could never commit a crime or do anything that would compromise the ideals of my newly adopted nation.

"Congratulations, you're now an American citizen," the judge said. He shook my hand and handed me a copy of the oath. I saw this as the most important day of my life. I couldn't stop smiling.

"How does it feel to be an American citizen?" asked the sergeant, driving back to our unit.

"It feels so good. I wish every enlisted man were given this oath," I said.

"What do you mean?"

"They would stop breaking the rules and become better soldiers, like the officers," I said.

"What rules?"

"They steal equipment from the army and do drugs. Some even rape our female soldiers."

"Taking that oath will not make someone a better soldier."

"I think it will, especially if they raise their right hands and say, 'So help me God.'" The sergeant shook his head, unconvinced.

In the days to come, I memorized the oath as if it were a poem assigned to me by my English teacher at Spring Valley High. My Certificate of Citizenship soon arrived in the mail. It was in gold calligraphy on beige paper and looked very valuable. To me it was priceless. I thought if I didn't keep the promises in the oath, the army would take back the certificate. *I can't believe I am an American, exactly like all other Americans,* I told myself. Actually this was my first time being an actual citizen of any country. In Haiti, I had been an undocumented slave child, without a legal status.

A few days later, I received my security clearance from the FBI, finally allowing me to handle top secret documents that I had been unofficially handling for three months.

In June 1975, my first sergeant called me into his office.

"Cadet, as you know, your three-year hitch is up. Do you want to reenlist, or go to college under the GI Bill?" I remembered talking to the lieutenant from West Point about what it takes to be an officer.

"How does the GI Bill work, Sergeant?"

"Simple. Because of your service, you receive a scholarship that covers your college education for four years," he replied. As much as I loved the army, I made my decision on the spot.

"I think I'll go to college," I said, remembering that with a bachelor's degree I could come back and continue my army career as an officer and a perfect gentleman.

"Good for you," said the first sergeant, "I wish you luck."

I had another notion that came into play at the moment I made my decision. *Maybe*, I thought, *my father might finally recognize me as his son if I become a college graduate.* At that particular moment, anything seemed possible.

CHAPTER 6

I T RAINED THE day I received my honorable discharge from the army. I felt a deep sadness about leaving the military, so the weather matched my mood. I packed my duffle bag and important papers and took a taxi to the Seattle International Airport. I wore my dress uniform proudly.

As crazy as it may seem, I had not picked a final destination for my flight. The only thing certain was that I had decided to take up a new challenge: higher education. As we approached the departure area the taxi driver asked, "Which airline?" He caught me by surprise. "Northwest," I said. It was the first sign I saw.

I paid the driver from a wad of bills I had in my pocket. The wad contained several thousand dollars, all the money I had saved while in the military. I walked to the Northwest Airlines ticket counter with my duffle bag and approached a clerk. "Excuse me, ma'am. I'd like to go to a warm state that has a college," I said. The woman looked puzzled.

"Where exactly would you like to go, sir?" she asked, clearly annoyed. I'm sure she thought I was clowning around.

"I would like to go to a place where it does not snow and where there is a college. I want to use my GI Bill to get a four-year college degree," I said. Her eyes got bigger as she realized I was serious.

"And you have no idea where you're going?" By now she was

thinking I might be mentally slow. I thought for a moment, and then repeated myself.

"Ma'am, if you have a flight going to a warm place that has a college, you can put me on it."

"Well, okay, sir. There's a flight leaving soon for Tampa, Florida. It's warm there. How does that sound to you, sir?" She continued to stare at me as if I were an imbecile.

"Do they have a college in Tampa?" I asked.

"Yes, I think several," she said.

"Then I will go to Tampa. Thank you very much." I reached in my pocket and pulled bills from the wad to pay for my one-way ticket. She stared at the money in my hand and then looked up, staring directly into my eyes. I didn't blink. "Thank you very much," I said again, without smiling.

When I arrived at the airport in Tampa, I looked in a telephone book under "Colleges" and saw Hillsborough Community College. Then I walked out of the terminal to the taxi waiting area.

"Take me to Hillsborough Community College."

"Which branch?" he asked.

"It doesn't matter." I was nervous, anxious to use my GI Bill as quickly as possible, afraid the offer might evaporate before I had found a place to study. We drove into a suburban area not far from the airport. As we approached the entrance sign for Hillsborough Community College, I noticed a motel along the highway called the Pink Flamingo.

"Let me out here," I said.

I rented a room at the motel, stored my bags, and then headed immediately for the campus. At the registration office, I filled out an application and made an appointment to see an academic advisor. Afterward, I went for a walk. Not far from the motel, I picked out a 1962 Dodge Dart at a used car dealership. I purchased it for $250 cash. Several weeks later I found an apartment on Kennedy Boulevard. It felt good to be living on a road named after JFK, my greatest hero.

The following Saturday morning, in my new used car, I took a little sightseeing drive. It didn't take long before I wound up in an all-black neighborhood where I spied a barbershop. I went in for a haircut and found myself listening to several customers' conversations with the barbers. Not surprisingly, the topics were racism and boxing. Sonny Liston was compared to Joe Lewis, Joe Frazier to Jack Johnson, and Sugar Ray Leonard to "The Greatest," Muhammad Ali. The men were especially animated when they spoke of Ali.

"The white men wanted to destroy his career," said a voice.

"Tha's right. And Jack Johnson too," said another.

"Shit, they wanted to kill him for messin' with them white women," said the barber.

"They sho' did! White folks even rooted for that Nazi fighter against Joe Lewis," said an old, toothless man. I couldn't quite believe what I was hearing. *Are they speaking about the same white people who had treated me so kindly since the day I registered in an American high school?* I asked myself. It didn't occur to me to consider how little time I had spent among African Americans since I came to the states.

"They're evil, I tell you. White folks just plain evil," claimed another gray-haired man. My mind flashed back once again to the four domino players in Haiti speaking so admiringly about the *blans.* In this mental debate, I couldn't help siding with the Haitian men's opinion.

The more I listened, the more irritated I became. I told myself, *From now on I will only go to white barbershops.* A month later, I would learn that trying to get a haircut at a white barbershop in the South would come with its own set of problems.

When registration opened up at Hillsborough Community College, I returned for my appointment with the advisor.

"What are you interested in?" he asked.

"I don't know. I want to use my GI Bill to become a college graduate." He looked at me oddly.

"What would you like to become? A teacher, a nurse, an accountant . . . ?" he asked. I thought I was going to college. I hadn't even considered that there would be options. Feeling pressed for a response, I replied, "I think I would like to be a teacher." Partly I said this because of Mr. Rabinowitz, my favorite high school teacher.

"We have an excellent pre-teaching program," the man said, "and your credits will be transferable to the University of South Florida." All this was new to me.

"Why would I transfer to the University of South Florida?"

"We're only a two-year college."

"But I want four years of education."

"Like I've said, your credits will all be transferable to a four-year college." The advisor handed me a class list, and I registered for four classes. Several weeks later my GI Bill check came in the mail. It was for two hundred dollars per month.

At the end of my very first class, on a Friday morning, my professor of Western Civilization, Mr. Collins, a Caucasian in his thirties, announced that he would be at the Sunset Club at nine o'clock that night. He said we could meet him there. The Sunset club was not far from campus. I had often driven past it.

That evening I reviewed the chapter that Mr. Collins had covered in class and wrote down some questions on a sheet of loose-leaf paper. I thought that the nighttime event would be an informal study session. When I arrived at the bar, my professor looked at me oddly.

"Why did you bring your book?" he shouted through the noise.

"Just in case you wanted to discuss the lesson," I said. He smiled and shook his head. Because I had never seen army officers fraternize with enlisted personnel, I assumed college professors didn't socialize with students either. I looked around the table at my fellow students. Weird looks everywhere. Not that I wasn't used to such looks. I excused myself, went outside, and put the book in my car.

When I returned to the bar, an attractive young woman I recognized from school was perched in the seat I had vacated. She invited me to sit beside her. She had blue eyes set in an almost porcelain face. She wore a black blouse and jeans. Feeling very uncomfortable, I sat down and kept my knees from touching her.

"My name's Candy," she said, smiling. Bashfully I responded, "I am Jean-Robert." She poured beer in my glass from a pitcher, and brushed her leg against mine. She clearly made what I had heard people describe as "goo-goo eyes" at me. I couldn't believe it.

At times, she would touch my hand. I felt so flattered, yet still uncomfortable, believing deep inside that I was unworthy of this attention from so beautiful a young woman.

Shortly after midnight, I noticed some of the students beginning to leave. I was getting sleepy.

"Thank you for the beer. I'll see you Monday," I said to the professor. My glass was still half-full.

"You're welcome, Jean," he said, smiling. "We'll discuss that lesson on Monday."

As I headed to the parking lot, I heard Candy call my name. "John Robert!" I stopped. She was walking toward me and smiling. I thought maybe I had left my keys on the table and she had found them. I felt my pocket. Keys. *What could she want?* I asked myself.

"Will you give me a ride home?"

"Okay, but then you will need to give me directions back to Kennedy Boulevard."

"Sure!" she said and climbed in.

"Do I turn left or right?" I asked as we drove out of the parking lot.

"Turn right," she said and added, "When I asked for a ride home, I meant to your place, not mine."

"But why? Don't you think it's too late to study?" I said, thinking she wanted to review Monday's assignment about the Roman gods.

"Are you serious?" Candy asked, sliding closer along the bench seat. She leaned her head on my shoulder. I kept both hands on the steering wheel. Her blond hair smelled like honey.

"I like history," I said nervously. "Who is your favorite goddess? I like Venus."

"I hate history, but I like you. Do you have a roommate?"

"No," I said, all the while wondering why anyone wouldn't enjoy history. "I like history," I said once more.

"Are you some kind of a nerd?" she asked.

"Maybe I am." I didn't know what *nerd* meant.

"Do you have a girlfriend?"

"No." My mind was abuzz trying to figure out why such a beautiful white girl would want to be out with me past midnight. Nothing like this had ever happened to me before. No matter how hard I tried, I simply couldn't make sense of it.

"I like your accent. It's cute."

"Thank you," I responded. *Maybe that's it. It's my accent*, I told myself. Since I had come to the US, I had hated my accent. I always wished I had a British accent.

As soon as we stepped into my apartment, Candy pulled me to

her and kissed me gently on the mouth. The portrait of the white Virgin Mary on Florence's bedroom wall appeared in my mind and refused to go away. I felt trapped by Candy, as if under a kind of *vodou* spell. Yet I remained curious about the possibilities her affections implied. She looked around my austere rooms. In the living room were a TV tray and two lawn chairs. I had purchased them at a yard sale.

"Why didn't you get a furnished apartment?"

"You mean they rent apartments with furniture in them? I didn't know that."

"Are you kidding?"

"The landlord didn't tell me that."

"Where's the bathroom?" she asked.

"In the bedroom to the right," I replied. Candy went to the bathroom, and I sat waiting her return. I looked at my watch. It was almost one o'clock. "Come here, John," yelled Candy from the bedroom. Walking in, I gasped. Candy lay on my bed braless, in black panties. In her hand was the novel *Love Story*, which I had been reading. I had seen the movie and couldn't figure out why this couple had so many problems. I hoped the book would clear things up, that it would spell out the nature of romantic love, something I had never experienced, even remotely. Little did I expect that this very night, I was going to receive a "dose" of love more confusing than the movie or the book.

"So, you *are* a nerd. You read books. That is sooo cute," she said, waving the book at me and giggling.

"Yes, thank you," I said, still thinking *nerd* was a compliment of some sort.

"Do you want to go to bed with me?" she asked coyly. I thought "bed" meant "sleep." Seeing a beautiful, naked girl in my bed, I was anything but sleepy.

And Candy did look incredible lying there with her hair spread out on my only pillow. I was surprised at how much lighter the woman's body was than her face. I turned off the light and sat cautiously down beside her, holding my knees. I was nervous. "I can see me, but I can't see you," she giggled. I felt ashamed of my blackness, and, in the moment, longed to be white, white as she was . . . but with a nice tan. My heart pounded as I looked down at her. Candy sat up and unbuttoned my shirt.

"You're so shy. Nerds usually are. Why don't you get undressed for bed? Don't you like me?" she asked.

"Yes, I like you," I said. *Why does she care that I like her? I am a nobody*, I said to myself. No one had ever asked me that question. I still wasn't sure if she wanted to have sex, or just to sleep beside me. For me, it was as if Our Lady, the Virgin Mary, were in my bed and I were doing my best not to stare at her semi-nude body. She had been a kind of savior throughout my childhood. I remembered many moonless nights when Florence would send me to place sacrificial meals of roasted herrings and plantains at different crossroads, an old *vodou* ritual. Before I got there, hunger pangs would force me to eat the food. Afterward, I prayed to Our Lady, the Virgin Mary, to keep Papa Ghede, one of Florence's favorite *vodou* gods, from killing me for eating his food. My prayer had always worked.

Candy sat up and began kissing my chest, but I felt too ashamed of myself and too inferior to fully participate in the activity. I was more intent on removing the image of the Virgin Mary from my head. *Our Lady wouldn't want me to do this*, I thought. It was clear, even to me, that Candy was no Virgin Mary. She grabbed me by the shoulders and pulled me over on top of her. Soon there was no fighting it. I was under Candy's *vodou*-like spell.

To force Our Lady's image from my mind, I imagined myself parachuting out of a C-130. *One thousand, two thousand, Rip!* I thought, and the chute ballooned above me. It didn't work. There she was again, the Virgin Mother, this time standing on a cloud as I drifted down. Finally, I hit the ground, rolled, and the canopy dropped over me. With that, finally, Our Lady departed from my field of consciousness. She was gone. Without her protection, I was on my own.

After Candy fell asleep, I sat bolt upright on the mattress looking at her, unable to believe what had just taken place. I pulled the sheet over her and then folded my army jacket and used it as a pillow.

At daybreak I woke up. Candy was not in my bed. I walked into the living room and could see her leaning at the kitchen counter, eating a bowl of cereal. I kept trying to find the Virgin Mary in her face, but now it was impossible.

"Good morning," I said.

"Good morning. Will you take me home?"

"Okay," I replied. She faked a smile, and I regretted having slept with her. She must have had the same regrets. *I guess she figured out she doesn't like me*, I thought. I had known I was inferior. Why didn't she?

As I drove her home, she didn't sit close to me the way she had the night before. She sat close to the door, looking straight ahead. Neither of us spoke. I was overcome by feelings of inadequacy. Sweat was running down my back. When I turned into her street she said, "Stop here. My parents are racist, and I don't want them to see me with you." Her words stung me almost like a *rigwaz*. I stopped the car. "Thanks," she said, and got out. I watched her for a long time as she walked toward a large, two-story home. Not once did she glance back.

That afternoon, as I sat down to study, I felt a sudden itch like needle pricks in my pubic area. I jumped up and sort of squirmed around the room. The itching got worse as I moved about. I drove to the market scratching myself viciously. Oddly, when I stepped into the air-conditioned building, the itching seemed to stop. But on the way back home, it started again.

A week later, the itching had become unbearable. I scratched myself almost raw. I purchased rubbing alcohol, thinking it would cure the itch, but it only burned the raw skin, causing me to scream out in pain. A neighbor knocked on my door.

"Is everything okay in there?" he yelled.

"Yes," I shouted, "everything's fine."

Twice a day I repeated the alcohol treatment to no avail. Since an army nurse had rubbed alcohol on my skin before she gave me a shot, I assumed alcohol might kill any germs and cure the itch. At night, I could only find relief when I lowered the thermostat. During the day I filled the tub with cold water and sat in it for hours. I began to think I had developed an allergic reaction to the Florida heat. With that, I started thinking about going back to Seattle, where the weather was cool. I cut out the pocket-linings inside my pants and stopped wearing underwear so I could scratch myself more easily.

One afternoon in the school cafeteria, I ran into Mahmud, an Ethiopian I had met on registration day.

"Jean-Robert, how are you, my brother?" he asked. I liked his strong African accent.

"I am thinking of moving to Seattle or Alaska at the end of the semester. I am allergic to the Florida heat."

"I don't understand," he said.

"In the army I was stationed in Seattle, and then I spent a few months in Alaska learning to ski. I think my body became accustomed to the cool climate. Now I am allergic to hot weather," I explained.

"Is it not hot in Haiti, your homeland?"

"Yes, but I developed an itch that can only be cured by a cold climate. At home I sit in a tub of cold water to make the itch go away."

Mahmud exploded in laughter, and I wondered what could be so funny.

"Hey, man, I think you have crabs."

"I could see if there was a crab down there," I said. Again, he roared with laughter.

"Not that kind of crab, man. Crabs are tiny black bugs. Have you had sex recently?"

Why is he asking that? I wondered. "Not recently, two weeks ago."

"Well, man, she gave you the crabs down there."

"That's impossible. The girl is blond and beautiful," I said. Again Mahmud roared with laughter.

"How do I get rid of them? I looked down there and didn't see a thing."

"Buy a can of Black Flag and spray your pubic area. Then put on white underwear. After an hour, you'll see them. I suggest you also get rid of your mattress, man." I followed Mahmud's instructions and I saw dozens of tiny black bugs, each the size of a pinhead, in my underwear. In more ways than one, the experience with Candy was a defining moment in my evolution toward maturity.

If a beautiful white woman, who resembles Our Lady, can carry crabs, then I am not inferior, not to any race of people, or even to the Pope. No one is superior to anyone, unless he or she can walk on water. So my thinking went. My conclusions didn't make much sense, but neither did my one-night stand. I could feel myself coming of age in America.

I applied for a job in a restaurant called Mario's and was hired as a dishwasher with—I was told—the possibility of becoming a busboy and eventually a waiter. I liked working in restaurants. This way I could eat without having to cook for myself.

Several weeks later, I replaced the busboy, and then I was promoted to waiter. On a Saturday evening, my second day of waiting on customers, a well-dressed white couple was seated in my section of the dining room.

"Good evening, welcome to Mario's. I am Jean-Robert. I'll be your waiter this evening," I said, with my somewhat natural Haitian accent. I wore black pants and a white shirt, the restaurant uniform that I had been required to purchase with my own money.

"I like your accent. Where are you from?" asked the woman, who was visibly pregnant.

"I am from Haiti," I said, smiling naturally.

"We went on a Caribbean cruise for our honeymoon and stopped in Haiti," said the man.

"Did you like my country?"

"We did. But we saw a lot of poverty there."

"Yes, it's a very poor country," I replied.

"You speak English beautifully. How long have you lived here?" she asked.

"Six years. I am an American citizen," I responded proudly.

I took their orders and brought them their wine, then a salad. Each time I served them they smiled and thanked me. I liked these people. As I carried their entrees from the kitchen, the new busboy shoved the swinging door inward, knocking the tray out of my hand. Quickly, I grabbed a broom and swept the steaks mixed with broken porcelain into a dustpan and dumped them in the trash. Had this happened to me in Haiti, I would have picked the meat off the floor and waited for instructions. But since food was plentiful in America, I didn't see the need to jeopardize the couple's health.

"Will you be paying for those steaks?" asked the chef.

"No," I replied.

"I didn't think so." He took both filets from the trash can, rinsed them, and placed them on the grill. I was stunned, unable to understand why he'd have me serve these customers what he would never eat himself. The five kitchen workers looked on in silence. Then he put the same meat, with carrots, spinach, and roasted potatoes, onto new plates.

"Ready," he said, and rang a bell with his spatula. As I carried out the food, I was overcome by guilt. I placed the tray on a small stand beside the table; my hands trembled. The couple smiled at me.

"What was that noise?" asked the woman. My heart thudded.

"The busboy came in through the swinging door and collided with me," I stuttered.

"I hope no one got hurt," she replied, and we exchanged smiles again.

"No. We're fine." I took a deep breath and placed the plate in front of her, and the other in front of her husband. I watched as they each cut a bite-size piece of meat.

"Excuse me. Please don't eat this meat," I said as they lifted their forks. They seemed confused.

"Why?" asked the man. I glanced at his wife's pregnant belly, thinking a tiny particle of the broken glass might hurt their unborn baby. I took a deep breath.

"The filets could have pieces of broken glass in them. I hope you will not tell the manager." I had more complicated reasons to warn the customers about the meat. Deep down inside of me I felt this pleasant white couple was too superior to eat meat that had been swept off a filthy floor. In addition, I had promised myself to be a good citizen when I took my oath of citizenship. Because we had exchanged genuine smiles and pleasant conversations, I thought they would just pay the bill and leave.

"Where's the manager?" asked the man.

"He's standing at the bar, in the white shirt," I replied. The couple walked toward him, clearly angry. I stood beside the table, my heart pounding. He spoke briefly with my boss, who shot a stern glance in my direction. After the couple left, the manager signaled me toward him, slowly curling and recurling his index finger.

"You're fired, Cadet! Go home!" he said. I felt confused and betrayed, more by the couple than by the manager. A week later I returned to collect my last check. A note inside the envelope read: "$25.90 was deducted for two filets at $12.95 each." I could not understand why the cook and the manager, who were both white, valued the money more than the customers, who were also white. I continued to live under the strange illusion that white people loved and respected one another.

Soon I began to look for a new job as a waiter and listed Mario's as my previous employer on all the applications. When no one called me for an interview, I suspected that my previous boss was discouraging others from hiring me. So I began to lie on employment applications, stating I had no experience as a waiter. Once again, I was hired as a busboy with the possibility of becoming a waiter.

Before going to work at my new job, I decided to get a haircut. I went to a barbershop in a white section of town.

"Good morning," I said. The customers lowered the magazines they had been reading and stared at me. Suddenly an eerie silence filled the room, and I felt like a trespasser.

"May I help you?" asked a barber in a harsh voice. His tone surprised me.

"I am here for a haircut," I said smiling.

"I don't cut you people's hair. Don't you people have your own barbers?" he barked. I looked around. These people were from a hostile universe. What could I do? I turned around slowly and walked out, feeling very confused. In the army the barbers who had cut my hair were usually white men. Now, I had no other choice but to get haircuts in black barbershops where black men spoke badly of whites. I was beginning to suspect that the *blans* in the US might deserve some of the African Americans' ill will.

CHAPTER 7

I N JUNE 1977, a week after I graduated from the community college, I drove a few miles north to the University of South Florida, where I applied for admission. Several weeks later, a letter arrived from the office of Professor John Bell, an academic advisor in the Department of Social Sciences.

Once again, I wore my military khakis for my appointment with Professor Bell. Even at this late date, I had very few "dressy" civilian clothes, but mostly I liked showing my pride for having served in the United States military. The uniform always made me feel more confident.

"Good morning, sir," I said. He rose from his chair and shook my hand.

"Good morning, Jean-Robert. I detect an accent. Where are you from?" He pronounced my name correctly, as if he could speak French. I liked him instantly. He was dressed in a light blue shirt and tie with beige pants.

"I was born in Haiti, but the United States Army helped me become a citizen. I am an American now," I said. As I sat facing him, I couldn't keep my eyes off the framed photo on the wall behind his desk. In it, my new advisor was shaking hands with John F. Kennedy himself, my longtime hero. I could not believe it.

"Congratulations," Mr. Bell said, leaning forward.

"Thank you."

"How long were you in the army?"

"Three years."

Partly because I associated him with President Kennedy, Professor Bell stirred the same feelings of acceptance I had experienced with Mr. Rabinowitz at Spring Valley High. Not only that, but his handsome features, trim waist, and black hair reminded me a bit of Tarzan, except that he had a thick moustache. I could see that he was eyeing me intently.

"What did you do in the army?" he asked.

"I was an expert rifleman, a battalion clerk, and a paratrooper," I said.

"Impressive. Have you declared a major yet?" he asked, looking at my transcript. My eyes were glued to that photo.

"How did you know President Kennedy?" I asked.

"I was his ambassador to Nicaragua. He was a great man, JFK," he said.

"I know. He became a hero of mine, even before I left Haiti."

"So, what about a major, young man?"

"Well, I had decided on education, but I've changed my mind. I think I'd like to become an ambassador instead of a teacher." I think he understood the reason for my abrupt change of mind.

"I see. That means you want to study international relations, right?" said Professor Bell, half-smiling.

I was suddenly smitten with the idea of meeting important people and having an influence on history. "Yes, sir," I nodded. This seemed so much bigger a life's dream than becoming a teacher. Then he asked me an important question.

"Would you like to take French or Spanish?"

"French," I said, without a moment's hesitation. At last I would learn how to speak like the elites in my former country.

Professor Bell handed me his suggestions for my first semester's class schedule, and later I registered for the four classes. On the way to the bookstore, I ran into a former classmate from the community college. As we walked past the College of Education, he said, "Any loser can get into the College of Education. Teachers earn less than $12,000 a year."

"Well, thank God we're not in education," I replied, without telling him I had changed my major only moments before. I struggled for a moment with the sense of having betrayed my high school teachers, especially Mr. Rabinowitz, who had spent so much time teaching me English. But the picture of JFK in Professor Bell's office was now framed in my mind, as I imagined myself shaking hands with some future president or other heroic figure.

My French professor, Dr. De la Ménardière, taking attendance, called my name with a smile. He was white, bald, and in his seventies.

After class he approached me and said, somewhat slowly, in French, "'Jean-Robert' is a French name. Where are you from?"

"I am from Haiti." Aware of my severe limitations in French, I told him that I had grown up speaking only Haitian Creole.

"But I can see you understand French very well."

"Yes, sir, some, but I don't speak it."

"But we are communicating in French."

I realized that in Haiti, I had come to understand a lot of French expressions, but it would have been terribly presumptuous for a slave child to try to speak the inflated language of the wealthy and the middle class.

Like Professor Bell, Dr. De la Ménardière took a genuine interest in me, and I would often stop in his office for short visits. He told me that since his wife had recently died, he lived alone, and that he had a son named Christian who had left home.

"I'll clean your house on Saturdays in exchange for French lessons," I offered. He laughed heartily.

"When I was in Africa during the war, a young boy named Maurice made me the same offer. I wish I had adopted him," he said, shaking his head.

Dr. De la Ménardière accepted my offer and gave me directions to his house. Then he pulled a book from one of the bookshelves behind him. *Le Petit Prince*, by Antoine de Saint-Exupéry. In English, it's called *The Little Prince*.

"This is the most famous book written by a modern French author," he said. "I think you will find it very special in your life." I couldn't wait to start reading it. I knew it would help me in my goal to finally become fluent in French. And fluency would greatly increase my chances of becoming an ambassador to a French-speaking country.

"I'll see you Saturday morning at ten o'clock."

"I'll be there," I said, and left for the library to begin reading *Le Petit Prince*. In a French-English dictionary, I looked up the words I didn't know and took notes in preparation for my first lesson at Dr. De la Ménardière's house.

As many readers will know, *Le Petit Prince*, a kind of fable, begins when a pilot makes a forced landing in the Sahara Desert. As the pilot repairs the plane, a small boy, who had come to Earth from another planet, approaches him. I was fascinated by Saint-Exupéry's famous drawing of the boy. He was dressed like a prince with a sword in his hand. He asks many questions but ignores the various questions of the pilot. In the boy I saw myself, because I had lived as an alien in my childhood. Even then, in my reincarnation as an American, I often felt like a being from another planet. Even now, I sometimes feel that way.

In Saint-Exupéry's book, the little prince eventually meets a fox in a wheat field. "Come play with me. I am very sad," says the boy to the fox.

"I can't play with you. I am not tamed," replies the fox.

"What does 'tame' mean?" asks the boy.

". . . to create bonds," the fox replies.

"To create bonds?" asks the boy.

"To me you're only a little boy just like a hundred thousand other little boys. And I don't need you. And you also don't need me. To you I am a fox just like a hundred thousand other foxes. But if you tame me, we will need each other. You will be unique to me and I will be unique to you," replies the fox.

After the fox allows the boy to tame him, he shares a secret with the boy. "It's only with the heart that one sees clearly. What's essential is invisible to the eyes." A big smile spread across my face. *Now I understand how love works*, I said to myself. Had my father loved my mother, he would have seen something of her in me. He would have seen it with his heart. He would have raised me himself, rather than giving me to Florence. Or had Florence allowed herself to bond with me, I would have become unique to her, as the fox became special to the little prince.

When I went to Dr. De la Ménardière's house that Saturday, my first question to him was: "Am I right? Does 'to tame' mean the same as 'to love'?"

Dr. De la Ménardière lived in a three-bedroom ranch-style house that was located on the banks of the Hillsborough River. Spanish moss hung from the trees that shaded the back porch. After I cleaned the house, we sat there and discussed *Le Petit Prince* in French. He agreed with my notion that to tame and to be tamed indeed meant to love.

"I read the novel *Love Story* and it says love is 'never having to say you're sorry.' Did you ever tell your wife you were sorry?" I asked. He laughed.

"Hundreds of times," he said.

"Did you love her?" He looked at me oddly.

"You've never heard your father apologize to your mother?" he asked. My mind went blank. *What kind of question was that?* I was at a total loss for words. *Did anyone even give birth to me?* I wondered. Dr. De la Ménardière asked me to follow him to a tiny brick house in the backyard. He unlocked the door with an old-fashioned key and turned on the light. There were many shelves loaded with ceramic bowls, plates, and cups of all sizes and shapes.

"This was my wife's art shop. Every piece you see on these shelves, she made with her own hands. Her name was Joanne," he said. He took a cup from a shelf and gave it to me. "Look inside." In the bottom of the cup was a tiny ceramic frog. "Joanne loved frogs," he added.

"So, this shop is to you what the wheat field became to the fox?" I asked. Dr. De la Ménardière nodded and smiled with a sad look in his eyes. We returned to the porch.

"Tell me about your family," he said.

"They're in Haiti. They're fine. Are there alligators in your river?" I was trying to avoid the topic of family.

"I've seen a few over the years, but they don't come near the house."

After lunch, as I was about to leave, he handed me ten dollars. This became the routine.

One Saturday after lunch, Dr. De la Ménardière excused himself and went inside the house. He soon returned with a small wooden box and placed it on the table. Then he opened it and pulled out a stack of old letters tied with a faded ribbon. His hands trembled as he untied the knot.

"I'd like to share something with you," he said, and read the first letter to me. He became emotional, fighting back tears. He read a second letter. More tears. Then he explained. "These are from my best friend, the famous author Antoine de Saint-Exupéry. I too was a pilot. We flew together during the war. He might have been shot down over North Africa. Maybe he just crashed. His plane was never found."

I flashed back to my *restavek* boyhood, remembering my best friend, René, who disappeared after he had been beaten by the police. I felt like telling him about René but was too ashamed to bring up something as disgraceful as a childhood spent in slavery. In the following weeks, I would learn much more about Dr. De la Ménardière's life than he would ever learn about mine.

"Have you shared these letters with other students?" I asked.

"Not really. American students would not appreciate their significance."

"Why not?" I asked.

"I don't know. They're not as motivated as you are," he said. I could only smile.

I felt honored that he shared the letters with me. After I finished *Le Petit Prince*, he gave me *Vol de Nuit* (Night Flight) by the same author. The lessons continued for two semesters, and I became fluent enough to carry on pleasant conversations in French with my friend and mentor, Dr. De la Ménardière. *Le Petit Prince* became my favorite book of all time. Over the years, I have read it at least a dozen times, committing long passages to memory.

After a few months at the university, I rented a room in a townhouse closer to campus. Ross, my new roommate, was in his fifties. He was white. Late one evening, I noticed Ross reading a magazine, *Soviet Life*, at the kitchen table. My heart thudded. The Armed Forces Oath of Enlistment came back to me, "... I will support and defend the Constitution of the United States against all enemies, foreign and domestic."

I was so naïve about so many things. I liked Ross, but at that point in time, I became convinced that my own roommate was a domestic enemy of America. Because he was reading that magazine, I concluded he must be a communist, an enemy of my country. I had no idea that magazines like *Soviet Life* were available on newsstands. Later that night I lay awake weighing our friendship against my Oath of Enlistment, which I had taken with my right hand raised, saying the words, "So help me God." I recalled the film at Spring Valley High in which Kennedy collapsed in the back seat of his Lincoln convertible. I remembered the narrator mentioning that Lee Harvey Oswald, Kennedy's assassin, had lived and worked in the Soviet Union. In my mind, I would be committing treason if I didn't report what I was convinced of: that Ross was a Communist sympathizer. I wish I had read Twain's *Huckleberry Finn* by that time. At a crucial moment Huck decides that he would "go to hell" rather than turn in his friend, the runaway slave, Nigger Jim. And he *means* it. He really believes that he is hellbound for defying the immoral laws of his day.

After Ross left for work the next morning, I searched his room seeking more evidence. It wasn't hard to find. A pile of *Soviet Life* magazines sat right there on his nightstand. In the sincere belief that he could be a domestic enemy plotting to kill President Gerald Ford, I picked up the telephone and asked the operator to connect me with the FBI.

"Agent McCann speaking," said a voice.

"My name is Jean-Robert Cadet. I am an army veteran and a student at the University of South Florida in Tampa. I feel certain my roommate is a Communist."

"How do you know he's a Communist?"

"Well, for one thing, he has a stack of *Soviet Life* magazines in his room," I replied.

"What kind of work does he do?"

"He's a teacher."

"Does he conduct research at the university?"

"No."

"Give me his full name and I'll check it out."

I told the FBI agent everything I knew about Ross. I had the bizarre sense that, because of my army training, I would probably be given secret orders to "eliminate" Ross. By this time in my life, I had obviously watched too much bad television.

Even more bizarre, I *think* that I was prepared to carry out those orders when they came. I waited expectantly for weeks, but the orders never came. Eventually Ross moved out. Needless to say, we had grown distant in our friendship. I could not understand why this traitor had been allowed to get away, when the US Armed Forces had spent so many years fighting Communists in Vietnam and elsewhere.

The following semester at USF, I took a class that focused on Karl Marx. I was stunned to discover that Communism was primarily an economic system in which all property and means of production belong to the state. I was relieved that I hadn't gone to Vietnam and killed people over a competing theory of economics. I was also relieved that my friend Ross had survived my wacky chauvinism and my political naïveté. In the same class, I also learned a great deal about capitalism, taxes, and the welfare system. I could sense that my childish worldview was imploding with every new course I took and with each book I read.

My liaison with Candy had helped me mature relationally, and now I could sense myself growing intellectually and politically. My feelings of inferiority were no longer as severe as they had been when I first came to college.

During that semester, I moved into a one-bedroom apartment that was within walking distance of campus. Three apartments down the hall from me lived a beautiful African American woman who was also a student at the University of South Florida. I had noticed her on campus and I wanted to be her friend. I was especially fascinated by her because she bore a slight resemblance to the mulatto woman who had been assassinated by the Haitian soldiers in my neighborhood.

One day, not long after I had watched a movie on television in which some male character borrowed a cup of sugar from his female neighbor, I knocked on my own neighbor's door. I thought I had come up with a good way of meeting her. "Who is it?" she called through the closed door.

"I am a neighbor," I replied nervously. She opened the door just enough to see me.

"Yes?"

"Good evening. My name is John-Robert. I live three doors down from you. I was baking a cake and realized that I didn't have any sugar. May I please borrow a cup of sugar?"

"Where's your cup?" she asked. I hadn't even thought to bring one. But I was on a mission, so I plowed ahead.

"Oh, I'm sorry. May I also borrow a cup?"

Now the woman giggled. "Come in. I'm Gwen," she said, and went to the kitchen for the sugar. We talked for a few minutes, exchanging basic information. I tried to be suave like the guy in the movie.

Finally, Gwen said to me, "So, John-Robert, when the cake is done, you'll bring me a piece, right?" She handed me the sugar in a coffee cup.

As I walked to my apartment, I found myself panicking. I had never baked a cake. For the next month, each time Gwen saw me in the hall or the parking lot, she'd ask: "Where's my piece of cake?"

"I haven't baked the cake yet," I'd say. "But I will."

"Promise?" she'd tease. How could I make a cake? I didn't even have cake pans or a mixer.

"As soon as I find the right recipe, you'll have your cake."

Late one evening, Gwen knocked on my door and invited me to be the fourth player in a game of spades in her apartment. She seemed surprised when I told her that I had never played cards before. "Not even Old Maid?" she inquired.

"What's 'Old Maid'?" I responded.

"Never mind. We'll play a couple of practice hands. It's easy to learn," she assured me, and so I joined Gwen and two of her brothers in the living room of her apartment. Soon a man came in without knocking. He said hellos to the group. I assumed he was Gwen's boyfriend. She introduced him to me as Sam. I learned the rules of spades quickly, and we began the first game.

"I can't stand white people," Gwen said with contempt. The statement came out of nowhere. Apparently, we learned, something had happened at her part-time job, and she was really mad.

"Those motherf*****s always want to keep us down," her brother barked. Once again, I remembered those four domino players in Haiti, praising white people to high heaven. But I wanted to feel a part of the group, so I mumbled something inane, like, "Yes, white people are very bad." Deep down I had always been appreciative of the various white people who had taken an interest in me. Sometimes I reminded myself that, after all, I was half white myself. In my mind, the white people Gwen and her brothers often talked about were anomalies, few in number, and—as I always assumed— uneducated.

As Gwen dealt the cards, a football game between orange- and green-helmeted players came on the television. I had sometimes watched this crazy sport on TV when I was in the army. To me, being from Haiti, soccer was "football." I often thought this American game should be called "handball," because the ball is touched with the hands much more often than it is kicked. At this point, my understanding of American football was limited, at best. I could only identify the quarterback, the running back, and the receivers. I noticed Gwen's brothers and Sam directing their attention to the TV when the offense of the orange-helmeted team came on the field. For no reason but color, I preferred the green helmets. I liked it when the quarterback of either team launched the ball to a speeding receiver. At one point in the game, the green-helmeted quarterback threw a touchdown pass to a receiver in the end zone. I cheered. Gwen's brothers and Sam looked at me suspiciously.

"Who you rooting for, brother?" Sam asked.

"The green helmets."

"Say what?"

"The green helmets," I repeated.

"They're playing against a *brother*, man, a black quarterback." I couldn't understand why the quarterback's race mattered more to my new friends than the color of the helmets. *Perhaps they know the black quarterback personally*, I thought, which in fact one of them did. Suddenly I felt out of place in Gwen's apartment, as if I had disturbed everyone's evening by cheering for the wrong team.

"Well, I like both quarterbacks," I said, trying to make things right.

"You're an Uncle Tom?" someone remarked. I had no idea what that was, and didn't want to ask. I thought it might mean something like "Uncle Boogeyman." That was the way the words *Tonton Macoute* were translated in Haiti. The *Macoutes* were feared by everyone.

One Friday night, not long after that first card game, Gwen invited me to accompany her and Debbie, a friend, to a nightclub. It was the very same club where, months earlier, I had had the fateful meeting with Candy. As I walked through the doors, I noticed everyone in the room was black. It was confusing to me because the first night I had come to that club, almost everyone there was white.

"Where are the white people?" I asked Gwen.

"This is black people's night, Soul Night," she responded.

Gwen and Debbie went to the bathroom and left me to guard their seats at a table. At that moment, the tallest black man I had ever seen approached me.

"Hey little brother, which of the two ladies is yours?"

"We're all just friends."

"You mind if I join you? I'm Doug Williams."

"I'm John," I replied, naming myself in English, as I had been doing for many years. My friends soon returned from the bathroom. I could see they were flighty and excited by this unexpected guest. I soon learned that this huge man was the quarterback of the Tampa Bay Buccaneers, the orange-helmeted team we had watched. Doug stayed for a brief time, but before leaving he handed us three tickets to the following Sunday's game. He gave the girls his telephone number. I wrote it down too.

So that Sunday afternoon I went to my first American football game. The logo on Tampa Bay's helmets was an orange buccaneer holding a knife across his teeth. I immediately preferred the other team's logo, a blue lion, my favorite animal and color. So I silently rooted for the Lions, who went on to win the game. That night, from my apartment, I telephoned Doug Williams.

In my own ungraceful manner, I complimented the man. "I liked your long passes, even though the Lions returned two of them for touchdowns."

"Thank you, little brother. I appreciate your interest in my game." He seemed sincere in his appreciation.

During the next few months, I learned from Gwen and Debbie that my new friend, Doug Williams, routinely received hate mail, and sometimes nooses in the mail, simply because he was one of the first black quarterbacks in the National Football League. *Those people must not be college graduates*, I thought. More and more, I found myself becoming a devoted football fan. I came to appreciate the difficult positions black quarterbacks found themselves in, and I always rooted for their success, regardless of the team colors or logos.

Over the years, Gwen and I continued to be platonic friends. We would often play cards on Friday nights in her apartment. My failure to provide her with the piece of cake was often one of the jokes in our laid-back conversations. She was probably the closest friend I had made in all my time in the United States. I continued to be an adoring fan of Doug Williams long after our little friendship faded, and even after he became, in 1988, the first black quarterback to win a Super Bowl.

During my senior year at USF, I joined the Model United Nations Club on campus. I chose to represent China. The club met once a week to discuss the world's problems, such as poverty in Africa, the Cold War, and political instability in the Middle East. Child slavery in Haiti had always been on my mind, but I was too ashamed to place it on the agenda for discussion. I simply couldn't deal with my personal shame. If I could have washed my past away with a magic cleanser, I would have done so. I still find it incredible that, twenty years after graduating college, I would not only embrace my history of domestic slavery but would find myself denouncing the *restavek* system at the United Nations in Geneva, Switzerland, and before the Congress of the United States.

I never told Professors Bell or De la Ménardière, or anyone else, about my *restavek* past for fear that they'd think less of me. Each time they'd ask about my family, I always responded with some generalization like, "Everyone's doing well, thank you." During one of those conversations in Professor Bell's office, I discovered that only a very few well-connected people became US ambassadors. I thought about switching my major back to education, but I didn't want to disappoint Professor Bell, who, with that bemused look of his, had spent so much time answering whatever questions came into my head.

During my college years I could feel myself becoming more and more "Americanized." But there were many things, large and small, from my Haitian past that would often reassert themselves, almost by instinct. For instance, as I moved about the campus, I often chose to urinate in some inconspicuous outside place, usually behind a tree or a dumpster. One day, while peeing behind a large tree, I was startled by a voice behind me. "What the hell are you doing?" I turned my head around to see a campus police officer. Frightened, I tried to zip my pants, but I couldn't stop urinating. The officer drove me to the police station on campus, filled out a report, and gave me a written warning. A few months later I was caught again, this time behind a dormitory. Campus police took my name and radioed the station. When they noticed that I was too shaken to speak, they let me go. I liked peeing outside, and I still find the taboos against it to be a bit phony, or mannered. I guess some habits die very slowly.

One morning in October 1978, I attended a lecture given by the ambassador of India regarding his country's policies toward the United States. During the lecture, I kept looking over at my mentor, Mr. Bell, with admiration. When it came time for questions, I raised my hand.

"Your Excellency, why does your country spend so much on its military and so little on the poor? Don't you think if India were to join the SEATO alliance, it would save enough money to combat poverty?"

"SEATO is not a good option for India," he responded, and quickly took a question from someone else. Professor Bell looked at me with that half-smile of his and nodded. I always felt that my inquisitiveness and enthusiasm for knowledge made him proud of me.

In June 1979 I graduated with a double major in international studies and French. At last, I had my BA, but I was almost out of money. I had stopped working during the previous few months to concentrate on my final exams. I needed to find a job, and find it quickly.

Driving through town, I spied the United Parcel Service building and stopped in to apply for work. I was hired as a delivery driver provided that I pass the physical. The interviewer sent me to a clinic with a note that I handed to a nurse. She filled out a form and then escorted me to an examining room. The examination was intrusive and unpleasant, but I got the job.

At United Parcel Service, I was issued brown uniforms and a

locker. During the first week, Bill, my trainer, drove, and I delivered the packages when he stopped in front of customers' houses. The following week he sent me out alone on the same route. Each evening, I returned with half of the packages undelivered. "If by Monday you come back with the van half-full, I'll have to let you go," said my boss in a harsh tone. I could not sleep, wondering why I was so slow to deliver the packages. On Monday evening I was fired. For the first time in years, I felt those old feelings of self-hatred and failure.

Days later, walking with Gwen, I complained to my friend that the numbers on the houses should be large enough to be read from across the street. "They're large enough," she said and read the address from where we stood. I went to investigate. The closer I got to the house, the more visible the numbers became. At that moment I realized I needed glasses. It had never occurred to me to have my eyes examined. In my college classes, I had always sat in front because I could not read the board from the last row.

I scheduled an eye exam and was given a prescription. Wearing glasses was like having new eyes. I went back to see my former boss at UPS.

"Sir, your doctor made a mistake. He examined my rectum instead of my eyes. I was slow delivering the packages because I needed glasses to see the house numbers. Please give me a second chance," I begged.

"I don't give second chances," he snapped. I was surprised and very disappointed. But he was white, so I tried to make excuses. *Maybe he's ill. More likely, he's not well educated*, I thought. My high school teachers and college professors had always recognized my efforts and encouraged me to try again when I screwed up.

I was evicted from my apartment, and for a week I slept in my car until I explained my embarrassing situation to Gwen, who allowed me to sleep on her living room couch for a time.

Gwen told me I should put together a résumé for prospective employers. I had no idea what a résumé was. She explained it all to me, how you must create an outline of your life. I knew my military and college records were exemplary, but I had very little record of my strange and spotty work history. Despite Gwen's explanation, I still had no idea how to do a résumé for myself.

One day, with nothing but time on my hands and fifty bucks in my pocket, I made a strange, spur-of-the-moment decision.

I bought an atlas, climbed in my car, and headed north, all the way to the town in New York where I had gone to high school. I felt an urge to try to visit the classmate who had permitted me to sleep in his room after Lise had thrown me out.

When I arrived in Spring Valley, I parked the car and walked the old streets. In a way I felt as if I had come home. In some ways, this small city had been more of a home to me than Port-au-Prince had ever been.

On Main Street, I saw a sign in a storefront that read: "The Word Factory." I was intrigued by the name and walked in. I approached a pleasant-looking woman who was sitting at her desk.

"Good morning, ma'am. What kind of business is the Word Factory?" I asked.

"We're a résumé service, young man," she replied. My eyes must have lit up.

"That's very interesting. I need a résumé, and I don't know how to do it. How much do you charge for a résumé?"

"I'll interview you and write your résumé for 200 dollars."

"Gosh!" I said. I was astonished at this price.

"Well, how much do you have?" she asked.

"Not very much. Could you write my résumé, and I'll pay you after I get a job?"

She burst out laughing at this odd request, and I had to smile, too. In my heart I knew that I would honor my debt. But how could this stranger know my heart? I thanked her and started to walk out the door. Her voice from behind called me back in.

"I'm Linda Morris. What's your name?"

I told her.

"I'll tell you what, Jean-Robert. You seem to have an honest face. I'll write your résumé if you do some work for me," she offered. Incredibly, she then handed me the keys to her car. She gave me directions, handed me some packages, and sent me on a series of errands. After being treated with suspicion for much of my life, I was amazed at this display of trust and generosity. *This woman must be very well educated, like the professors at my university*, I said to myself.

Because I had left the area following high school, it took me a while to find some of the streets on the woman's list, but I was determined to do right by her. I completed the list and drove back to the shop.

When I walked in the door of the Word Factory, I heard Linda Morris and a man arguing with each other in the next room. The door was ajar. I peeked in.

"I can't believe you gave some young guy the keys to our new car," said the man, throwing his arms in the air. Meekly, I opened the door.

"Excuse me, Linda, I'm back," I said. Silence filled the room. The man turned and let out a sigh of relief.

"Look at him," my benefactress said. "I told you he had an honest face." She introduced him as her husband, Marty, a local high school teacher. I was upset to think that Marty would assume I had stolen the car. At the same time I could see that his anxiety made sense. How could he know that I would never purposely violate any laws, or that I had taken an oath to be a good citizen?

At my appointment the next day at the Word Factory, I gave Linda a list of clerical jobs I had held in the army, and she made the résumé sound as if I had been the commander of my unit.

When I had earned enough to pay for my résumé, Linda told me to keep the money. By this time, Linda, Marty, and their beautiful teenage daughters were treating me almost like a member of their extended family. When Marty asked where I was from, I answered, "Brazil." I was beginning to suspect that claiming Haitian nationality was not a good thing to do in the United States at this time. Certainly, I thought, they never would have welcomed a former child slave into their home. How wrong I was. Many years later I discovered they had suspected the truth of my background but kept it to themselves. Their feelings toward me didn't change, and to this day, we are close friends.

With the money I had earned, I returned to Tampa and—using Linda's beautiful résumé—quickly landed a decent job at a shipping company.

My bizarre childhood experiences played out in many areas of my life at that time, as they still occasionally do, even now. Any time the boss, a man in his mid-sixties, called me into his office, I would panic, certain that I had done something wrong. Often, my boss would give me purchase orders to process and say, "I want you to smile when a client walks in. Their business is our bread and butter."

"Yes, sir," I said. I tried, but I wasn't very good at it. I had not done much smiling in my life. A few days later my boss walked in with a Japanese client, and I faked a smile, baring my teeth in a kind of grimace. After the client had left, my boss asked to see me.

"Jean, can't you look natural when you smile?" he asked.

"Yes, sir," I said, faking a better smile.

"I want you to practice smiling in a mirror," he suggested.

It took me a few weeks to master the art of faking smiles. I understood that this is an important social skill. At the same time, it requires one to smile at a great many people to whom one doesn't really feel like smiling.

One day I walked into the lunchroom where my fellow workers were singing "Happy Birthday" to our receptionist, a young, friendly white woman. I joined in, and after she blew out the candles, I kissed her on both cheeks.

"Happy birthday, Jeanette," I said, smiling. She froze. Every jaw dropped and silence filled the room.

"Holy shit!" said a baritone voice. Everyone was staring at me.

"I am so sorry," I said, and I left the lunchroom wondering why everyone had reacted as if I had committed a crime. *What's wrong with these white people in Florida?* I wondered. I had kissed Linda Morris and her daughters good-bye on the cheeks at the Word Factory, and her husband didn't behave like these men.

Soon after, my boss called for me to come to his office. I began to sweat. Once again, I felt as though I were about to be severely whipped.

"Why the hell did you kiss the receptionist?"

"I am sorry, sir. In Haiti friends often wish each other a happy birthday with a kiss on the cheeks. Even guys do it to other guys."

"Consider yourself lucky," he said. "If you had kissed one of the guys, he probably would have killed you. You're not in Haiti, son. Remember, this is America, *and* you're in the South," he said.

Holy Jesus, I said to myself as I left the office. *How could I be so stupid?* It was a lesson I had learned a hundred times since I had come to America, but this was the first time someone spelled it out so clearly.

I sat at my desk, trying to understand what exactly was so special about the receptionist, who always smiled at me when I entered the lobby. I thought she was my friend. After that kiss, the men started taunting me, calling me "Hot Lips" and "Romeo." No matter how much I tried to be a "normal American," I seemed to be trapped by my background and by the color of my skin, neither of which I could change. I felt embarrassed, isolated, confused, and out of place. I wondered if I ever would escape these horrible states of mind.

CHAPTER 8

UNABLE TO TOLERATE the ongoing taunting, the nicknames, the lack of depth in any of my relationships, which were now almost exclusively work related, I quit my job at the shipping company. Once again, quite impulsively, in the fall of 1982, I headed out of state, this time for Southern California. Maybe I had listened to the song about "California Dreaming" and dreamed that it might be a place of escape from that horrible sense of not fitting in, of not being "normal." Perhaps mostly, I was longing for something real to do with my life, something that had meaning. And where better to look for the real than in Hollywood?

During the long drive, I kept having fantasies about meeting Lucille Ball when I got to the West Coast. After all these years, I was still a huge fan of hers. Lucy's comical expressions and crazy methods of solving problems always made me laugh. If I met her, I mused, maybe she would be another mentor, teaching me how to "lighten up" regarding my own problems and self-image.

It took me six days to reach Los Angeles, where I eventually landed a job as a driver at a Ford dealership, driving clients back home when they brought in their cars for service. I didn't meet Lucy, but I did encounter a number of other less familiar movie stars.

One day, I took a thin, forty-something woman home from the shop. At her home, I was surprised to see Robert Blake, the star of

Baretta, one of my favorite detective shows, feeding two horses in a corral near the house. *Wow!* I thought. *This is about as close as I will ever be to the rich and famous.*

One afternoon, driving down Century Boulevard after I had dropped off my last client, I saw a large sign atop a two-story building that read: "Control Data Technical Institute." Curious, I went in to see what it was. The receptionist, a blond woman in heavy makeup, greeted me. "May I help you?" Her plastic smile seemed glued on.

"What courses are being offered here?" I asked. She handed me a brochure. I scanned it quickly and decided to sign up for several computer courses. Because of my military background and lack of income, I received a full scholarship, and I began attending classes three nights a week. This way, I was able to continue working at the car dealership.

After completing the computer programming courses, I was hired by a data processing company as a computer operator. I found an apartment near my workplace in Santa Barbara. My boss, Mr. Carter, trained me on an HP-3000, a computer that was bigger than a refrigerator.

Driving home from work one Saturday afternoon, I noticed a sign that read "Avocado Farm." It was pointing down a dirt road. So I drove onto the farm, where, to my absolute amazement, were a number of guinea fowl, scratching around among some ordinary chickens beside one of the barns. I couldn't believe my eyes or my luck. It was as if a chunk of Haiti, a delicious chunk, had fallen in my path. As I mentioned earlier, the guinea hen was Papa Doc's personal symbol. Even more important to me was the fact that these chickens represented a level of wealth and comfort that I had always been denied. On the rare occasion that Florence cooked one of these delicacies, I was always given its feet to gnaw on, and the scrapings from the empty pot. I licked my lips. Never mind the price, I had to have one of these birds.

"How much is the gray bird with the white dots?" I asked a dark-skinned man who was working there. I didn't know the English word for guinea hen.

"Sorry, sir, they're not for sale," he responded. His accent was Spanish.

"Why not?" I demanded.

"People don't eat them in this country," he said.

"But they taste better than chickens, or turkeys," I said. He shrugged his shoulders and grinned. I think he knew what I was talking about.

"I haven't tasted one of these birds in years. Please sell me one . . . please," I begged. He looked left and then right.

"Okay, give me five dollars. The chickens are only three dollars," he whispered.

"I understand. But I want one of those."

He guided the flock into the barn and came out with one of the prize birds. He then tied its legs together with a piece of string and handed it to me. "Put it in your trunk, *rápido*," he said, "I don't want my boss to see."

I gave the man five dollars. I was so excited about my luck. Already I was imagining a festive meal in my little apartment. Then I purchased some avocadoes and drove off with the guinea fowl fussing inside the trunk. I remembered day-dreaming that I had the infamous dictator "Papa Doc" himself tied up in my trunk.

I kept the bird tethered in the bathtub that night and slept like a baby. The next morning, I set a pot of water on the stove to boil and brought the guinea hen outside in order to kill and clean it. I carried a sharp knife in a large paper bag.

"What kind of bird is that?" yelled a white woman beside the swimming pool. She came running up to my back porch and insisted on petting the guinea hen. I was clutching the bird in my arm as if it were a little puppy.

"It's a *pintade*," I said.

"A what?"

"I don't know its name in English. In French it's a *pintade*."

"How come its feet are tied together?" she asked.

What could be more obvious? I thought, but responded that I didn't want it to escape.

"What are you going to do with it?" she asked.

How dumb could this woman be? "It's my dinner," I said, smiling. Four other neighbors gathered around to look at the guinea hen, all of them white people. I looked around the group for a moment, expecting them to disperse now that they had seen the pretty hen.

They didn't budge. I figured they wanted to watch. A gasp went up from the group when I pulled the knife out of the bag and, with one sweep of my arm, decapitated my prized *pintade*, letting its blood spill onto the grass. I noticed a profound silence. I glanced at each of the five people, their eyes all as big as turkey eggs, their jaws open. I smiled stupidly and stuffed the dead bird into the brown bag.

"Oh, my God," one of them screamed, as if I had killed her family pet. Stunned at their reaction, I headed back to the porch.

I heard one of the group shout, "Somebody should call the police."

They were all in a tizzy. "Did you see what he did?" a woman screamed. "Did you see what that man did to that poor bird?" I rushed back inside with the beheaded guinea hen still thrashing around in the bag. I locked my door. My heart was pounding as if it wanted to fly out of my chest. *What the hell was that all about?* I said to myself. There was nothing to do but begin plucking the carcass in the kitchen sink, and try to forget about the crazy ruckus outside. It wasn't long before I heard a loud knock on my door.

"Who is it?" I asked.

"Open up. It's the police." I began to shake as if the *Tonton Macoutes* themselves had come for me. I broke into a cold sweat. Slowly I opened the door and saw two officers in blue uniforms. They looked like robots, their eyes concealed behind dark sunglasses.

"We received several complaints that birds are being killed in this apartment. What kind of birds are you killing in here, sir?" he asked.

"I am preparing a *pi-pi-pi-pin-ta-ta-de* for my di-di-dinner," I stuttered.

"A *pin* what?" asked an officer.

"A *pin-ta-ta-ta-de*."

"What's a peen-peen-ta-ah-ad?"

"A type of chicken, sir."

"So, where is it?"

"It's in the ki-ki-kitchen sink." The officers came in and looked in the sink.

"It's not a hawk, or an eagle, is it?"

"No, sir, it's a *pi-pin-ta-de*."

"How do you spell whatever you're saying?"

"P-i-n-t-a-d-d-dee-e. It's French," I said, trembling in fear and wondering why everyone was so concerned about a guinea hen. He wrote the word in a notepad.

"May I see your driver's license?"

"Ye-yes, sir," I said. He radioed the station and described me, "Black . . . foreigner . . . five-seven or eight." He gave them the number on my Florida license. Then he described the guinea hen, "Head, separated from body, spotted feathers, some missing from the body, black beak."

His partner went outside and soon returned with a Polaroid camera and photographed the dead hen in the kitchen sink.

"You know, Mr. Cadet, it's against state and federal laws to kill certain birds," he said.

"I am so sorry, officers," I said.

"Ignorance of the law is no excuse," he snapped. "I'll take some feathers to the lab and get in touch with you."

For hours afterward I was still shaking in fear. But I managed to cook the guinea hen in a delicious Haitian-style sauce. I sliced the avocados and fixed some rice and beans. The rich aromas caused me to salivate. Even after the trauma, my food turned out to be delicious. Each bite of *pintade* brought a little smile to my face. I concluded that the meal had been worth all the craziness. Maybe.

I never heard from the police officer, but after the incident, my neighbors rolled their eyes and looked away each time they saw me.

The following week, I was by myself in the office at work when someone phoned and asked to speak with a computer operator.

"I am a computer operator," I said, somewhat proudly.

"I am the manager of Compu-Data. We're three buildings down the street. I understand you people are using the HP-3000. We've just purchased one. Would you be interested in teaching our employees how to run it during your lunch hour? I'll be happy to compensate you for your time."

"Sure, I'll help you, but you don't need to pay me anything. It's probably only a matter of adjusting the printer."

"Can you come at noon?"

"I'll be there." My own boss had not yet arrived.

I went to Compu-Data with my sandwich, and Mr. Sims, the manager, escorted me to their computer room. I conducted a forty-five minute class with two of the employees. Mr. Sims asked me to return the following day to show two more staff members how to use the machine. The teaching experience felt empowering for me. Later, after work, I returned to Compu-Data to see how things had gone. I spent an hour supervising their employees as they ran the new system. The manager was very grateful for my help.

The following Monday, using a harsh voice, my boss called me into his office. I panicked. He waved a check in my face.

"This $250.00 check, from my competitor, is addressed to you. What the hell is going on?" he asked.

"Last week I trained their employees on the HP-3000 during my lunch hour and after work." I was baffled.

"Sign this check over to me," he said.

"But why?"

"You've earned it on my time."

"I am so sorry, sir. But I was on my lunch hour. I didn't take a minute of your time."

"Sign the check," he yelled. I endorsed the check and handed it to him, feeling as if I had been robbed.

"Good," he said. "Now, you're fired."

"Please give me a second chance," I begged.

"Disloyal employees don't deserve second chances," he said. I felt numb and totally confused, especially considering he had invited me to his birthday party, and I had shared pizza and laughter with him and his wife. How could I have been disloyal? I didn't give out any company secrets. Anyone could have taught Compu-Data's employees how to operate an HP-3000. I felt deeply hurt. Feelings of emptiness and injustice that had consumed my childhood washed over me once again. I had genuinely admired this boss.

Despondent over another bad turn of events, I loaded up my car and headed back across the country to Tampa. At least there I knew Gwen, the young woman whom I had befriended. I could count on her for a place to stay.

The hut in which I was born—my mother's house. I discovered it in 1999.

In 1999, I visited my mother's grave.

My aunt Anacine, whom I met in 1999.

I am pictured standing before a collapsed building as workers searched for bodies two months after the earthquake. Photo by Carl H. Vilfort.

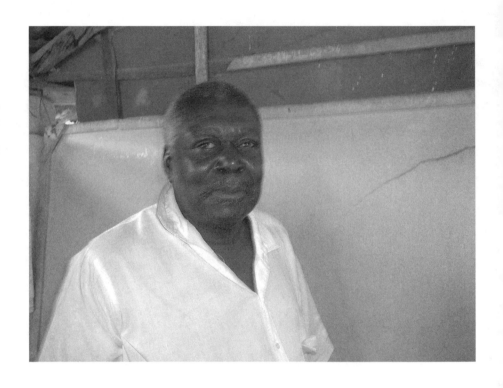

Maitre Jean Charles, the Haitian teacher who took me in for free.

Mr. Max Rabinowitz, the high school teacher who helped me get into the welfare system in New York. We have become good friends and see each other a few times a year. Photo by Phyllis Rabinowitz.

Loudy, ten years old, hauling water for those she serves.

*I reconnected Loudy, on the right, with her biological family
and enrolled her in school in October 2010.*

Mimrose is slaving while other children play. Mimrose was a wedding gift.

Mimrose at school.

*Speaking to an eight-year-old going to fetch water with
a five-gallon bucket weighing forty pounds.*

Addressing the International Labor Organization.
Photo by Doris Charollais. Courtesy, Terre Des Hommes Suisse.

Doing a radio show on the plight of children in domestic slavery.

Raising awareness in Haiti with a billboard campaign:
"Respect children's rights. / Let me go to school, too."

CHAPTER 9

I GOT BACK TO Florida in time to get a job substitute teaching in the summer of 1985 at King High School in Tampa. From the beginning, I liked so many things about being a teacher: the upturned faces of the kids, their readiness to learn, my various duties and responsibilities as a teacher, even the familiar classroom smells, but especially the opportunity to substitute now and then in my favorite subject, American history. I had cherished every minute of my own education, even in the primitive classrooms of Haiti. Now I had this small opportunity to give something back. I was thrilled to see myself functioning as a high school teacher. But the situation was short-lived. As the summer session was coming to a close, I found myself wishing I had followed through with my initial plan to become an accredited teacher.

I had been sharing a two-bedroom apartment with a USF student who had just moved out. I needed a new roommate to share the rent. As luck would have it, Gwen Cardell, my old platonic friend, was able to move in with me.

That August, I drove back to the University of South Florida, where I had graduated in 1979, and spoke with an academic advisor in the College of Education.

"I'd like to teach either secondary French or American history," I told the woman. She looked at my transcript.

"Since you have taken so many French classes, you'll need just two semesters of education courses to get French certification," she said.

I asked her to enroll me in the requisite French classes. "Next year I'll work on my certification in American history," I said. As usual, I couldn't wait to get back to school.

In my program I was the only black among the two dozen students seeking certification in Spanish, French, or German. As usual, I was totally on my own in the effort to secure my future. As my classes met during the day, I searched for evening work. During the second week of October 1986, I interviewed for a waiter's position at an upscale Italian restaurant on Tampa Bay Boulevard. The manager was a well-dressed, middle-aged white man.

"Where are you from, Jean? I notice an accent."

"I was born in Haiti, but I am an American now," I said proudly.

His reaction was instantaneous. "Haiti? Isn't that where AIDS comes from? How bad is the epidemic there?" he asked. The news at the time was full of reports about AIDS, many referring to the disease being transmitted by "people of Haitian descent."

"I don't know, sir," I said, feeling embarrassed that he had brought up this odd accusation about Haiti, one that would never be borne out in fact.

He persisted. "You know who Rock Hudson was, don't you?"

"Yes, sir, I read about his death in the newspaper a few days ago."

"He was a great actor, a real star. *McMillan and Wife* was one of my favorite TV shows, and I liked him in *Dynasty* too. And now he's dead," he said, shaking his head.

"I'm sorry," I said, as if my being Haitian had contributed to Mr. Rock Hudson's death. It had been fifteen years since I left Haiti.

"Well," he said. "You'd have to start as a dishwasher and work your way up to waiter."

"How long before I could be a waiter?"

"At least six weeks. First you'd move up to busing tables. It pays minimum wage plus 10 percent of the tips. When you become a waiter, you'll get a buck and a quarter an hour plus tips. You'll make a good living."

"I could start this afternoon," I said, thinking that every night I'd at least get a free meal.

When I reported to work, I noticed that all the waiters were young white men in their twenties. Immediately, I had doubts about the manager's promise to promote me. By this time, I had lost many of my romantic illusions about the beneficence of white people, and about the quaint notion of economic justice for all.

After four weeks, two waiters quit and were replaced by two more white men. I questioned the manager.

"Excuse me, sir. I remember you said new employees must start as dishwashers, but the new guys are waiting tables."

"Well, son, you don't have any experience waiting tables. The new guys have worked in fine restaurants as waiters for many years. It wouldn't be fair to start them at the bottom, would it?"

"No, sir, I guess not." I thought of telling him that I had been a waiter at Mario's but was afraid he would call my former boss and learn about the incident with the broken glass. After eight more weeks of dishwashing, I approached the manager again.

"Sir, I've been washing dishes for more than two months. When will I start busing tables?"

"Listen, son, everyone knows that Haitian boat people brought AIDS to this country. I'd lose my customers if they knew the waiter serving them was from Haiti."

"But I am an American citizen. I even served three years in the army. I'll show you my Honorable Discharge and certificate of American citizenship," I said, hoping that that information would make me more American than Haitian in his eyes.

"My customers will not be served by Haitians. It's not good for business."

"Well, then, I'm quitting."

"You can't quit until I get another dishwasher," yelled the manager. At the end of the week, I returned to collect my final pay.

"Get out of my restaurant, you AIDS-carrying nigger," said the manager, literally throwing the check in my direction. His accusation knocked the breath out of me. I had heard that word countless times, but I had never been called "nigger" to my face.

"Stupid ass," I mumbled as I picked my check off the floor and turned to leave. I said it loud enough that I was certain he heard me.

"Call the cops!" he yelled at a waiter. Petrified at the thought of encountering the police, I ran outside, jumped in my car, and sped off. Down the street from the restaurant I pulled into the rear of a McDonald's parking lot. I sat there, almost in tears. "Maybe I should go back to the army," I said to myself. I hadn't thought of that in years. "Yes, I'll go back to the army. That's what I'll do."

The next morning, as I was literally heading out the door of my apartment to visit a local recruiting station, the phone rang. It was the manager of a Holiday Inn restaurant inviting me to interview for a waiter's position. I made the appointment. "If I don't get this job, I'll return to the army," I told myself.

At the Holiday Inn, the manager, a Caucasian in his early thirties, introduced himself, but I didn't bother to get his name. I was only going through the motions.

Immediately, the inevitable question came up. "I notice you have an accent. Where're you from, John?"

"I'm from Martinique, sir," I said nervously. To avoid being linked with AIDS, I felt I had no other choice but to lie.

"Where is that?"

"It's a French territory in the Caribbean," I said.

"French, eh?"

"Yes, sir," I said.

"So do you speak French?"

"Oui, Monsieur, yes I do." By this point I knew French almost as well as I knew Creole.

"Can you start tonight?" he asked.

"Yes, sir," I replied. And a thought flashed into my mind: *That's it. From now on, I am no longer Haitian.*

"You're hired. You'll get minimum wage plus tips."

"Thank you, sir."

I continued taking classes, and in January 1986 I finished the requirements for certification in secondary French.

Mrs. Charles, my academic advisor, gave me the telephone number of a teacher named Cynthia Nassano, who, she said, was willing to accept me as an intern. More than a bit nervous, I placed the call that same day.

"Hello, may I please speak to Cynthia Nassano?"

"This is she."

"My name is Jean-Robert Cadet. I'm from the University of South Florida. I was told you might be open to taking me as an intern."

"Yes, I can see you Monday morning." Then she gave me the directions I would need to find Hudson High School in Pasco County.

"Yes, ma'am, thank you. I'll be there."

"I detect an accent. Where are you from?" My heart thudded. *Here we go again*, I thought.

"I am from Martinique."

"Oh, then you're a native speaker. That's great. I'll see you at seven," she said.

Pasco County, an hour's drive from Tampa, was a small community where many of the residents were retirees. When I arrived at the school, I met Ms. Nassano in the lobby. She was thirtyish, quite attractive, pleasant, but businesslike. She greeted me with a handshake and asked that I follow her to her classroom. As we passed the administrative offices, she introduced me to the principal, who was standing in the hall, greeting students.

"Dr. O'Donnell, this is Jean-Robert Cadet, my new intern, from USF," she said.

"Good morning, sir," I said, and we shook hands. I smiled.

"Welcome!" He was a tall, friendly white man in his sixties. Partly because he had a doctorate, I liked him instantly. I wondered why he was running a high school instead of a department at a university.

Ms. Nassano introduced me to her students, all of whom were white. I could see them looking me over with obvious curiosity. She explained that I was from Martinique, a French-speaking island in the Caribbean. I felt a strong tinge of guilt about my fib, but I was happy with the new country of origin I had chosen. It would be years before I visited there, and years before I found a way to correct my lie.

Just after Ms. Nassano had introduced me to the class, Dr. O'Donnell's voice came over the loudspeaker system. "Please rise for the Pledge of Allegiance." Its last three words were my favorites: ". . . justice for all." I noticed, in the last row, a tall boy in a black leather jacket, still sitting and half asleep. I looked at him and shook my head, thinking how ungrateful he was. I whispered to Ms. Nassano that I would like to say something to the boy. She looked perplexed, but nodded her okay.

I walked to his desk and spoke very quietly. "Young man, I need to say something about your attitude toward your country. I believe you owe it a little respect. You don't know how lucky you are to live in a country where you have access to twelve years of free education. Starting tomorrow, I hope to see you recite the Pledge of Allegiance with your classmates." Perhaps because of my strangeness and my accent, he took the criticism well. "Okay," he mumbled.

After class, Ms. Nassano told me that it was good of me to speak to the boy. *She must be very patriotic, like me*, I thought.

The next morning, everyone in the class recited the Pledge of Allegiance.

A week later, during our planning period, Ms. Nassano told me a little about herself. She was born in Kentucky, just across the river from Cincinnati, Ohio. She had moved to Florida because of her husband's job. I felt guilty for having lied to her about my place of birth. So I thought it might ease the guilt if I told her something true about my past. "My mother died when I was four years old. She was black and poor. My father was white and rich. Since I was born black, he gave me to a family who beat me almost daily." Ms. Nassano looked at me with genuine concern. But my guilt feelings did not go away.

"I am so sorry, Jean. How did you come to this country?" she asked.

"The family I had stayed with brought me to their new home in New York to do housework and then they kicked me out." I zipped through my entire history in the United States in a minute.

"Wow!" she said. "That's some story." I liked her a lot. She seemed to be a good listener. After school on Friday, Ms. Nassano surprised me with an invitation to come to her home for dinner the following night. I gratefully accepted the invitation. Now I liked my supervising teacher even more.

I was still beaming inside when we walked together to our parked cars. It had rained heavily earlier in the day. As we approached her car, I could see that it was sitting in a large puddle of water. "Oh, dear," she said.

As if by instinct, I did something really stupid. I attempted to pick Ms. Nassano up and carry her to her car. In Haiti I had often seen men carrying ladies through muddy puddles or streams. There was nothing dramatic or flirtatious in the gesture. It was simply my gentlemanly response to an unpleasant situation. As I said, it was stupid.

"No, stop! Put me down! What are you doing?" she yelled, looking around to see if someone had seen me try to lift her.

"I don't want your shoes to get wet. They'll be ruined. Get on my back. I'll carry you to your car," I insisted.

"No, Jean! You can't be serious. I am not getting on your back," she said, stepping into the puddle and hurrying to her car. Clearly, I knew I had done something that was out of line. "Over the top" is the expression these days. I expected her to turn around before she got in the car and cancel the dinner invitation. But she didn't. "I'll see you tomorrow night," she said. What a relief.

The next evening, I drove to Ms. Nassano's house. She introduced me to her husband and their two-year-old daughter, Katrina, who was standing near the table, sucking her thumb and holding a small blanket to her face. The girl was tiny, blond, and very cute. I smiled and made funny faces at her. She laughed, and I bent down, offering her a piggyback ride, which she gladly accepted.

A short time later, the school's Spanish teacher, Mrs. Jones, arrived with her husband. During the dinner Ms. Nassano's husband was very quiet. After dessert, I said my thank-yous and left the scene. I felt uncomfortable in the situation, knowing there was nothing I could do to ease those tensions.

Monday morning, during our planning period, Ms. Nassano apologized for her husband's lack of warmth.

"This was probably his first time having dinner with a black person," she said. After all these years in the States, I still didn't feel black.

"It didn't really bother me," I said.

"Things are not going well between the two of us." I was startled at her openness. I had always believed that most white people lived perfect lives, although of course I had read otherwise. And I had seen lots of movies.

"I am sorry to hear it," I said, adding, "I think he's lucky to have you." She smiled, and we exchanged a caring glance.

Not long afterward, Ms. Nassano surprised me once again. "Jean, I'd like you to call me Cindy. Okay?" I was a little hesitant. After all, she was my boss. "I'll try," I responded. As our friendship grew, the Martinique "fib" often weighed on my mind.

One Saturday morning in early May, Cindy called and asked if I could watch her daughter, Katrina, while she attended a daylong workshop in the Tampa area. I agreed, and she brought Katrina to my apartment. Gwen, my roommate, had just left for work. I spent the morning entertaining and playing with Katrina, who behaved as if she had known me all her life.

When Cindy came back for Katrina, Gwen had just returned from work. I introduced the two women, but Gwen acted very coldly toward Cindy. As Gwen walked back to her bedroom, I heard her mutter the words "white bitch" under her breath. I apologized to Cindy, who was as shocked as I had been to be labeled a "nigger." She told me not to worry about it and quickly departed with Katrina in tow.

"Gwen, why did you call Cindy a bitch? That was very rude." I pronounced "bitch" like "beach."

"I didn't call her a 'beach'; I called her a 'bitch.' I don't want white people in my house, they're nasty," she responded.

"Cindy is not nasty. She smells good," I said, thinking nasty was a reference to smell.

"I am talking about how they treat black people, not how they smell," she responded.

"I think you should write Cindy an apology."

"Over my dead ass," she snapped. "You don't know white people the way I do, Jean."

"Not all of them are nasty. Cindy's well educated," I responded.

"I don't give a shit about her education."

"Well, she treats me with kindness. Not many people have ever treated me better," I said.

That June, Cindy separated from her husband. She told me the marriage was over and she would be moving back to the Cincinnati area. As friends at first, she and I began to spend time together. She suggested that I apply to be her full-time replacement at the high school. I was really sorry that she was leaving, but elated at the possibility of having my own classroom and becoming a real teacher at last.

One day after school, as we were going over some lesson plans in her classroom, Cindy looked into my eyes.

"Jean, I think I am starting to fall in love with you," she said. Of course, the same thing had been happening to me. But the very first thought that popped into my mind had to do with the Martinique lie. My thinking went: *You shouldn't love me. I'm a liar. I lied to you about my place of birth.*

"I think I fell in love with you too. It happened a long time ago for me," I said. Right there in the classroom, we embraced and kissed. I recognized that moment as probably the happiest of my life. In a way, I didn't want to believe that an incredible woman like Cindy Nassano could actually love me. But I felt her love in every pore of my body. And that feeling was the polar opposite of everything I had ever known. I ached to tell her that I was really born in Haiti, but the words would not come out. *I don't need to tell her the truth*, I thought. *After she leaves Florida, she'll probably forget all about me.* I was wrong about that, and the Martinique lie would later come back to haunt me.

Several weeks later the school year ended, and Cindy came to my apartment to say good-bye. She brought Katrina along. Her car was packed with their belongings. Because of the situation with Gwen, Cindy didn't come in. We stood in the front yard, kissing and promising to write to each other. Katrina gave me a very special hug. As they drove off, tears ran down my face. I was all but certain that I would never see her again. Days later, a letter from Cindy arrived in the mail. She closed with, "I love you." I answered the letter immediately, racing to complete it so that I could tell her, "I love you too."

Almost every week a letter from Cindy arrived. I couldn't wait for noon on Mondays, the hour the mailman usually delivered the mail. Even before I opened it, the letter brought a smile to my face, as if its sweet contents were leaking out of the envelope and comforting my deepest soul. Wow! I was in love! I felt like the fox in my beloved book, *The Little Prince*. It seemed as if I had finally been tamed.

In late July I received notice that I had been hired as Cindy's replacement. The news was bittersweet. It meant that she and I would not see one another for at least an entire school year.

In September the semester began. My students, all Caucasians, looked at me with the same curiosity that I had experienced as Cindy's student teacher.

"I never knew that black people could speak French," said Terrie, a bright, uninhibited young lady. I smiled and directed everyone's attention to an atlas in their texts and pointed out African and Caribbean countries where French was spoken. At the end of the first week of school, I conducted a quiz. When the students had completed it, I asked if there were any questions. Alison Madison raised her hand.

"Yes, Alison?"

"Mr. Cadet, this isn't about the test, but I was wondering. What does your hair feel like? I've never touched a black person's hair." Everyone giggled nervously and waited for my response. I recalled how much I wanted to touch my father's smooth hair as he drove me to Madame Laroche's house.

"Well, Alison, if you are that curious about my hair, why don't you come and touch it?"

"Are you serious?" She smiled. The silver braces on her teeth lit her face. Her sense of curiosity reminded me of my own when I was her age.

"It's only hair. I promise that it won't bite." The class laughed, and a few other girls followed Alison to my desk and felt my hair with their fingertips.

"It's a little coarse," a voice said.

"Okay boys, don't be shy," I said. "You may touch my hair too if you like." The boys looked at one another, grinned, and remained seated.

News traveled very fast, and girls in subsequent classes had the same request. I obliged them. Over the course of the semester, a number of students told me I was their favorite teacher.

On the Friday before winter break, many students, especially the girls, brought in gifts and piled them on my desk. I tried to teach the lessons I had planned, but it didn't work. The kids were too excited. It was my first time experiencing Christmas, and their generosity had a strange effect on me. I found my mind wandering back to my boyhood, walking the streets of Port-au-Prince on Christmas mornings with a bucket, looking for a yard with a running faucet. I knew about Santa Claus, but it was clear that he didn't like us *restaveks*.

Until that day at Hudson High School, Christmas had meant less than nothing to me.

After the last class period, the students spilled out, wishing me Merry Christmas and Happy New Year. Minutes later, Alison returned, carrying a black boom box with a red bow tied around its handle.

"Merry Christmas, Mr. Cadet. I'm giving you the biggest gift, because you're my favorite teacher."

"Thank you, Alison. I am overwhelmed." And I truly was. My voice cracked. When Alison left the classroom, I began sobbing uncontrollably. Her gift had released a lifetime's worth of emotion.

When school resumed after winter vacation, I helped organize a French club. Mindy, a senior, was voted club president. Each month her class prepared French pastries and sold them in the cafeteria to raise money to promote French culture in the school. Since I had learned to cook as a boy and had worked in many restaurants, I prepared *coq au vin* and *poulet Cordon Bleu* for the junior and senior classes. We invited the administrators. The students decorated the classroom and brought in side dishes and desserts.

Dr. O'Donnell, the principal, and the administrative staff were very supportive of me. When they saw me in the hallway, they would either ask: "When's the next lunch?" or "Is everything okay?" To my surprise, when I was called into the office I never felt as though I were being summoned to be whipped.

During the last semester, I assigned *Le Petit Prince* to my seniors. I knew they would enjoy reading it as much as I had, especially considering that they were quite accomplished in French.

In one of our classroom discussions, I asked the students an important question. "How would you say Saint-Exupéry defines love in this book?" The students looked at me with a blank expression on their faces.

"I didn't see the word 'love' anywhere," Jonathan answered. Everyone agreed with him that "love" was not even mentioned in *Le Petit Prince*. *They are so accustomed to being loved, they cannot recognize it in the dialogue between the fox and the little prince,* I thought.

Like the fox, I was becoming more and more accustomed to the strange reality of being "tamed" by someone who loved me. The letters from Cindy continued to arrive, and I answered each one of them. Occasionally we talked on the phone. She was living and working in Cincinnati. She suggested that I come to visit her and Katrina over summer break. As the school year dwindled down, I found myself counting the days until I could see the woman I loved once again.

CHAPTER 10

O N T H E L A S T day of the school year, one of my favorite students, Alison, handed me a wallet-sized picture of herself. On the back she had written: "You are really a different teacher. Have fun with everything. Good luck. Love, Alison."

Later that day I asked her, "So tell me, how am I different?"

"You are just different, that's all," she smiled. I tried to coax the reason from her, but to no avail. She, too, was different, special. I loved Alison's soul, her center, which I felt was much wiser and more mature than her years. But, as a teacher, I didn't see myself as different. I was simply trying to emulate the best models and mentors from my past, always trying to be as prepared, enthusiastic, and creative as I could be. At this time in my life, I saw teaching as a self-enriching responsibility. I tried to see each of my students as someone who might go on to be a teacher herself or himself.

"You have a nice summer, Alison. Thanks for being such a great student," I said. Several other students had given me their pictures, but I cherished Alison's the most. To this day I still have it. I guess she was what I had been so many times: "teacher's pet." Because of students like her, I worked hard at becoming an even better teacher. Maybe I wanted to have an entire classroom of "pets."

Early that summer, I packed up my courage and drove to Cincinnati to visit Cindy. I brought along my prized boom box, energized with a new set of batteries, to play cassette tapes as I made the long drive. Early in the trip, I put in a Beatles tape and cued up my favorite song, "The Ballad of John and Yoko." In what can only be described as a state of euphoria, I sang along with John. I found myself singing so loudly that I wondered if other motorists on the freeway could hear me. I didn't care in the least.

> The man in the Mac said,
> "You've got to turn back."
> You know they didn't even give us a chance.
> Christ, you know it ain't easy.
> You know how hard it can be-e-e-e.
> The way things are goin',
> they're going to crucify me.

It was my favorite song ever. I played it over and over. Little did I sense that there would be more than a few crucifixions (some of them self-inflicted) waiting for me at the end of my drive.

Cincinnati is a medium-size city in the southwest corner of Ohio, just across the Mason-Dixon Line, which follows the Ohio River, separating the North from what used to be the Confederate South.

As I drove into the parking lot of her apartment building, I saw Cindy looking out of the kitchen window. She and Katrina came to the door as I carried in my suitcase. I don't know which of us three was the happiest, but it was a lovely reunion after all those months.

The mother and daughter lived in a small, two-bedroom apartment in a predominantly black neighborhood of the city.

As I sat on the couch, Katrina came and stood facing me.

"You want to play a little game with me?" she asked. I smiled. It was a déjà vu moment, as if the Little Prince were speaking to the fox.

"Sure! What game would you like to play?"

"Candy Land."

"I don't know how to play Candy Land."

"I'll teach you."

We sat on the floor playing Candy Land. Her laughter was infectious. I couldn't remember the last time I had laughed like a child.

Maybe never. We rebonded quickly and were soon pals, as we had been in Florida.

A few days later, Cindy suggested that I apply for a teaching position in Cincinnati. "The pay is better here than in Florida," she said. For reasons that had little to do with economics, I took her advice and sent my résumé to several school districts around the city. During that summer, we lived together almost like a family, but I was careful to maintain a slight emotional distance from Cindy. Part of it came out of my fear of relational love. But mostly it had to do with the lie I had told her on the first day we met.

In my mind the lie had become more than simply about my place of birth. It had a lot to do with *the nature* of my birth country. Being from Haiti carries none of the romance associated with the other Caribbean isles. Then, as now, Haiti had a bad reputation, part of it richly deserved. Most Americans knew one thing about Haiti: It was/ is the poorest country in the Western Hemisphere. I felt almost as if I had failed to inform Cindy that I had once been an ax-murderer.

Through those first weeks I helped Cindy care for Katrina, reading to her often and teaching her fractions, sometimes using slices of pizza or pieces of candy as illustrations. I bought her a bicycle with training wheels and played with her at the park. After a few weeks, to my surprise, Katrina began calling me Daddy.

"Sweetie, don't call me Daddy. Okay?" I said.

"Why? Don't you want to be my daddy?"

"I'll just be your friend. You already have a daddy," I said. She pouted for a bit but continued calling me Daddy.

About a month into the summer, Cindy and I were sitting on the couch in the living room. "Jean," she said, "We need to talk." My heart thudded. *What could this mean?* I thought perhaps she had discovered the Martinique lie, which I often wrestled with while going off to sleep.

"I can't continue living with you this way. It's like we're married, but we're not. You know I love you, but, if we're not going to get married, maybe it's better that you leave." This was not what I had expected. In some ways it seemed worse.

"This takes me by surprise," I said. "I need time to think about it."

Cindy's gentle ultimatum weighed heavily. Not because I didn't love her, but because I was afraid of losing her. My failure to tell her about my true childhood loomed like a wall between me and the woman I loved. "Life is so incredibly complicated in America," I thought, not for the first time, or the last.

The following day, Cindy took Katrina to visit her mother in Northern Kentucky. With a huge burden on my heart, I gathered my belongings, packed them into my car, and headed south toward Florida once again. Throughout the drive, Katrina's voice echoed in my head, "Daddy, you want to play a little game with me?" Again, I recalled the fox in *Le Petit Prince* telling the boy, "You will always feel responsible for what you've tamed." I felt as if I were carrying Katrina inside of me. I felt responsible for her, and responsible for Cindy, as well. I had never experienced such complicated feelings before. In the absence of any parental guidelines, I was running on instinct, which is to say, *running away in fear*.

When I reached Tampa the next day, I phoned Cindy. "Where did you go, Jean? I looked in the closet and your clothes were gone. Katrina thinks I chased away her daddy. She's been crying all day, and so have I."

I desperately longed to tell Cindy the truth, but I could not make the words come out of my mouth. "I am in Tampa. I needed to talk things over with a friend." This was true, but I knew there was no one who could help me move through this emotional impasse. "You really want me to come back?" I asked her, "After all this?"

"I want that very much, but only if you're open to getting married," she said.

Later that day, in a dazed stupor, I purchased a ring. Clearly my instincts were working to protect me. Then, less than twenty-four hours after arriving, without touching base with any of my friends, I climbed back into my car and headed north, toward something I had never known in my entire life: home . . . family . . . and love.

When I arrived at the apartment, I apologized that I had left without telling them. I begged Cindy's forgiveness, then Katrina's, then Cindy's again.

When things settled down, I took Katrina's hand and approached her mother. With the other hand I pulled the ring from my pocket. I knelt on one knee and asked Cindy to marry me. "Of course I will," she said. I should have been the happiest man in the world, but the lie still loomed, more dreadful than a *rigwaz*, over my soul.

In early August 1988, I received a call from the Cincinnati Public School District inviting me for an interview. I was ushered into an office where two women, an African American and a Hispanic, were waiting.

"Welcome," said the African American. "I am Mrs. Rogers, Middle School Principal, and this is Mrs. Fonslow, District Foreign Language Coordinator."

"Good morning, I am Jean-Robert Cadet."

Mrs. Rogers, in her mid-fifties, was dark-complexioned with short hair. I was a bit put off by her. I soon realized that it was because she closely resembled Florence.

Mrs. Fonslow, also in her fifties, was short and round.

"Tell me about yourself," said Mrs. Rogers.

"I've just finished my first year of teaching in Pasco County, Florida. And prior to that, I spent three years in the military, where I became an American citizen. I paid for college with the GI Bill and majored in international studies and French."

"What made you go into teaching?" asked Mrs. Fonslow.

"I had a wonderful teacher in high school and wanted to follow in his footsteps."

"We desperately need black role models on our teaching staff. Our student population is about 75 percent black and 25 percent white. We have 55,000 students in the district. A great many of our black children are from single-parent families with no father figure at home," Mrs. Rogers said.

I nodded my head in feigned understanding. In truth, I was shocked to hear that my skin color was more valuable to her than my teaching skills. I also didn't understand why she thought it was important that I know about the racial makeup of the students. When I had interviewed to replace Cindy at Hudson High, race was never mentioned. Maybe because there were so few black students in the school. The interview seemed to go well, but it was hard to get my head around this new situation.

Because of my own experiences, I could not see any correlation between a student's home life and his or her success in the classroom.

I had succeeded at school despite having been a child slave without any home life at all. I saw each of these two environments as distinctly separate from the other. Of course, I couldn't have been more mistaken.

"You'd be teaching sixth grade social studies and Ohio studies at the Academy of World Languages. All sixth grade classes must be taught in French. It's called total immersion. We want our students to be fluent in the target language," said Mrs. Fonslow.

"One minor problem, though," Mrs. Rogers said. "The books are in English. You'd have to translate your lessons into French. At the Academy of World Languages, we also offer Chinese, Japanese, Arabic, German, Spanish, and Russian." I was impressed to hear that black and fatherless children were provided such extraordinary educational opportunities. But I had doubts that I would be the right person for the job.

"I am not certified to teach either social studies or grade six. My certification only covers secondary French, grades seven through twelve, and history."

"Don't worry. You'll do just fine. We'll give you all the support and resources that you'll need to succeed," replied Mrs. Rogers.

"Are the students fluent in French?" I asked.

"Not all of them. Some have never had French, but we believe that the more they are exposed to the target language, the faster they will learn it," said Mrs. Fonslow. Since I had spoken no English when I came to America, Mrs. Fonslow's explanation made sense to me. The interview ended. I was hired for $24,000 a year. I was happy, and so was Cindy.

In early September, I embarked on my new teaching career at the Academy of World Languages. My first class was World History. Upon entering the room, I noted one black girl among twenty-five white students. They were all casually dressed in new clothes and shoes. They looked so small, compared to my high school kids in Florida. The young people appeared confident, well equipped with school supplies, and ready to please their teacher.

"Bonjour," I said.

"Bonjour," everyone answered in unison. Their enthusiasm brought a smile to my face.

After that class, I collected my briefcase and walked across the yard to my second period World History class. There I was surprised to find only African American students. They seemed tired, lacking both school supplies and enthusiasm. They were casually dressed in faded clothes that needed to be ironed. Their tennis shoes looked worn out.

"Bonjour," I said with enthusiasm and wrote my name on the chalkboard. No one answered.

"You speak French, don't you?"

"Man, we don't speak no French," boomed one boy.

"My name is not 'man.' It's Mr. Cadet," I replied, pointing to my name on the board.

"Whatever."

"What is your name?"

"Donald Scott," he mumbled.

"Donald, I would like to be called Mr. Cadet. Am I understood?"

Immediately, I regretted having taken this job, fearing that I would be ineffective with students who were the same color as I. "How am I going to teach these students world history in a language they don't understand?" I pondered. I was grateful now that our book was in English.

Those first weeks of teaching were fraught with difficulties and anxieties. But they were dwarfed by my other anxiety. Many days, returning home from school, I could think of nothing but the Martinique lie. More than once, I would find myself alone with Cindy on the couch or in the kitchen, and I'd say something like "I have something to tell you."

"What is it?" she'd ask, and I'd tell her some crazy story about something that had happened at school.

"I thought you were about to tell me something important," she'd say.

"That was important to me," I'd fib, and then I would busy myself with schoolwork or with Katrina's activities.

At school one day in November, I was writing on the board when I sensed someone was misbehaving in class. I turned suddenly and caught a glimpse of Donald Scott showing his penis to the girl next to him. "What the hell are you doing?" I yelled. My anger startled everyone. Donald pulled his shirt over his unzipped fly. Normally, I would not have said "hell." It wasn't much of a swear word, but it only came out of me when I was shocked or angry. Ever since I had seen the *restavek* girl being punished with the hot pepper, I had become very protective of little girls. As I was writing a discipline referral in order to send Donald to the office, a school security guard entered my room. "Mrs. Rogers wants to see you right now!"

Mr. Martin, the assistant principal, followed the guard into my room and sat at my desk to take over the class.

I panicked, but I thought once I told Mrs. Rogers what the boy was doing in class, she'd be on my side.

Walking into the principal's office, I saw the school janitor, a gray-haired black man, sitting in a chair facing Mrs. Rogers's desk. His brow was sweaty, as if he had been running. Mrs. Rogers pointed to a chair next to the janitor.

"Sit down, Mr. Cadet. Mr. Kline told me he heard you screaming 'hell' at the children while he was in the hallway. Mr. Kline, please tell me again what you heard Mr. Cadet say in class?"

The stern expression on Mrs. Rogers's face made me very nervous. My mind traveled back to my boyhood as a *restavek*, standing in front of Florence, the dreaded whip in her hand. My stomach churned.

"In all my twenty-two years of cleanin' schools, I never heard no teacher yell at no children like dat. I tell you, I was sweepin' the hall near the bafroom and I heard him yell, 'What the hell you doin'?'"

"Donald Scott was showing his penis to the girl next to him as I wrote on the board." My voice cracked.

"I don't care what Donald was doing. You can't use that kind of language in the classroom." Her words shocked me more than Donald's action.

"Amen," said the janitor.

"That kind of language can destroy children's self-esteem," said the principal.

"Yes, sir, it sho can," responded the janitor.

"It was just a spontaneous reaction on my part. I have never seen a student, or anyone, do that before."

"I don't think you are the role model that I thought you were when I hired you," Mrs. Rogers said.

"No, sir, them small children is innocent," said Mr. Kline.

"I am sorry," I said, wondering why in the hell something like "hell" was taboo.

The bell rang, and—still glowering—Mrs. Rogers dismissed me. I rushed to the bathroom in the nick of time. This kind of stress always affected my bowels. When I entered my next class, I was still in shock.

During my planning period I saw a letter in my mailbox and opened it. I was stunned. It was a reprimand for shouting "hell." Teaching my subsequent classes was all but impossible. I could not concentrate on the lessons I had planned.

Driving home after school, I wondered if Cindy had ever been reprimanded for anything. She was in the kitchen making dinner.

"How was your day?" asked Cindy.

"It was fine," I said. I couldn't bring myself to tell her what had happened. A shell of isolation had been forming around me. I could feel it getting thicker and thicker.

When the school year ended, I found a memo in my mailbox that said my services would not be needed for the next school year. I was happy that I would not be returning to a dysfunctional situation like that.

My end-of-year evaluations from the academy were rated "marginal." I took comfort in looking back on those I had received from Hudson High, which were all excellent and affirming.

CHAPTER 11

IN EARLY JUNE OF 1989, a year after I had moved to Cincinnati, Cindy began to plan our wedding. I suggested that we simply elope to Las Vegas. I had heard that couples could get married in their cars as if they were buying fast food. I made no secret that I wanted to avoid the embarrassment of not having any relatives among the guests, but Cindy insisted on a small wedding to be witnessed by her family and a few close friends. I conceded.

Days later, we applied for a marriage license at the county courthouse and stood beside each other to fill out the application. Once again, I thought of telling Cindy the truth about my place of birth, but I was still unable to get it out. On the line for place of birth, I wrote—what else?—"Martinique."

We arranged for a Christian minister to perform the wedding ceremony in a small reception hall. One of Cindy's brothers had befriended me a year earlier, and he agreed to stand by my side as best man. Cindy's younger sister would be the bridesmaid, and Katrina the flower girl. Less than a dozen guests were invited. We hired a caterer to set up a table of food in the same room where the wedding ceremony would take place.

On our wedding day, July 14, 1989, I drove Cindy and Katrina from our apartment to the hall. I wore a blue suit, and Cindy was in an ankle-length white satin dress. Katrina wore a cute "little-girl" gown. When we arrived, the caterer, an African American woman, was setting out the buffet fixings on a long table. At the end of the table sat a small three-tiered cake. I stared at it in a kind of stunned disbelief. I had been to one other wedding in this country and had seen the little bride and groom figurines standing atop a large cake. But in our case, the observant caterer had painted the groom's face with some kind of dark brown coloring. Something seemed so wrong in this. The guy on the cake was me, of course, but he was also obviously *not me*. I was the black man who was marrying the white woman, but that black man was somebody other than whom he had made himself out to be. He was a liar with a false identity. I could almost hear him shouting at me: "Don't be an impostor. Tell Cindy the truth. She thinks she's marrying a man from Martinique, not a former *restavek* from Haiti."

During the ceremony, I felt sweat running down my back, though the room was pleasantly cool. The whole event was somewhat excruciating for me. We said our vows. The minister said the crucial words, "Now I pronounce you husband and wife. You may kiss the bride." Cindy and I faced each other, there in front of her family and friends. We kissed and I looked into the eyes of the woman I loved, who was now my wife. But I kept hearing the tiny black groom's voice in my head, pleading with me in Creole: "You have given her *pawol nèg* [literally, a black person's word, a lie]; now give her *pawol blan* [the truth]. For the love of God, man, tell her the truth." I wanted to tell the little man to shut up and leave me alone, but I knew that he was right.

After the ceremony, the guests toasted Cindy and me with champagne, and we all ate from the lovely buffet table. Toward the end of the evening, the caterer served the wedding cake. Cindy and I did the traditional thing. We smooshed the cake into each other's mouth. Everyone laughed, even I. We all ate and drank and celebrated the coming together of this unusual couple. But no one had an inkling of the real extent of our differences—except for me. In my heart, I felt anything but celebratory. When the guests had gone, the caterer placed the leftover cake in a bag along with the figurines for us to take with us.

We had decided not to do a honeymoon, so we went back to our house for the wedding night. That night, as Cindy readied Katrina for bed, I found myself in the kitchen putting various things away, including the leftover cake. I held the wedding figurines in my hand, and the groom spoke to me once again.

"You're a liar and an impostor." It was almost as if I could see the little figure's mouth moving. I responded under my breath, "It was her idea to get married, not mine. If I tell her the truth, she'll think I am a liar." With a fury that I had seldom ever exhibited, I threw the figurines into the trash, pushed the waste can under the sink, and slammed the cabinet door shut.

Although that particular moment would have a lot of competition, I think it was probably the lowest point in my adult life. I felt trapped in a web of lies that I had spun myself. Sick with remorse, I made my wedding bed on the couch, and as I lay down, I heard the distant voice of the little groom under the kitchen sink speaking to me again. "Cindy has never lied to you. Why don't you tell her the truth?"

I went back to the kitchen and took the garbage outside with the little groom still taunting me. "Liar," he said.

"Shut the hell up," I yelled, as I threw the bag into the dumpster. I walked slowly back into the house and lay down once again on the couch. A while later Cindy came into the living room. She stood there for a long moment, staring at me in disbelief.

"What the hell are you doing?" she screamed in a kind of whisper, so Katrina wouldn't hear.

"This is totally wrong. We should not have gotten married," I responded, tears welled up in my eyes.

"Are you nuts? Jean, what is your problem?"

"The wedding was a mistake. I think we should get it annulled," I said.

"I don't believe this. This is way too much. I am going to bed."

Cindy slammed the bedroom door hard behind her. I went to the door and pressed my ear against it, hoping that she wasn't crying. If she was, I couldn't hear it, maybe because I was in tears myself. I couldn't stop crying. I climbed onto the couch, certain she would be asking me to leave.

Early the next morning, Katrina woke up and came in the living room with her blanket, sucking her thumb. The hair on the back of her head resembled a bird's nest. I had slept only a smattering of minutes. As I fixed Katrina breakfast, Cindy came out of the bedroom. She looked drained. I felt dreadful.

"Good morning," I said. She glanced angrily at me.

"Morning," she mumbled. My heart was beating as if I were still a little boy, living in a kind of unending dread.

This time, I was sick with worry. Would Cindy ask me to leave? This thing called love was still a confusing mystery to me. I wished that I could turn my love off like a faucet and become numb to all these complicated feelings. Because it hurt me so much to see Cindy in pain, I began to make amends as best I could. I cleaned the apartment, fixed dinner, and participated in the games she often played with Katrina. Slowly the tension began to dissipate, much like fog in the morning.

But the lie remained, keeping me separated from this wonderful woman.

Around the first week of August, two weeks after the wedding, I got a call from Mr. Bill Edwards, the principal of the Academy for the Performing Arts. He asked me to come in for an interview. This time I didn't try to imagine what the neighborhood or the school was like. I knew. The building was a historic and very old high school, box-shaped, with ornate cornices that gave it the appearance of a museum. It was located in Cincinnati's blackest ghetto. Mr. Edwards greeted me with a loose handshake. He was tall, pear-shaped, and in his late fifties. He seemed likeable, for a principal.

"Everyone calls me Mister E.," he said.

In his office was a piano. A portable air-conditioning unit was humming softly in a window.

"Tell me about yourself, Mr. Cadet."

I went through a brief capsulation of my work history since arriving in America, while Mr. E. perused my résumé.

Finally, Mr. E. leaned back in his chair, rotating it slowly from side to side. He looked at me intently.

"I need someone to teach two levels of French and four social studies."

"Yes, sir," I said. "I could do that."

"How do you handle discipline problems?"

"It depends on the seriousness of the situation. I would give a warning for talking too much or coming to class unprepared. If the problem persists, I would telephone the parents or assign detention."

"Good answer," he said. "The mission of this school is to provide students with the very best education while focusing on the performing arts. Some of our graduates have made it to Broadway and into films," he said proudly, like a father bragging about his children's success. He took a deep breath. "Sixty percent of our students are black and forty percent are white. We have 1,500 students here, and 60 teachers." I was impressed, but once again the ratio of black to white students meant nothing to me. By the end of the meeting, Mr. Edwards said I was hired, and he assured me that his door would always be open. I could come to see him at any time.

At home, Cindy was happy for me. We both felt that I would be teaching in a much better school environment than the previous one.

Near the end of summer, we purchased a small, two-story house in a suburb. During the weeks prior to our move, I had come to a hugely important decision. On the very day of our move-in, I acted on that decision.

As I was loading books into an empty bookcase, I retrieved my passport from a secret compartment in my suitcase and carefully inserted it between several of Cindy's reference books, which I had grouped on the shelf, similarly to the way they had been placed in the bookshelf at our apartment. For reasons even I don't completely understand, I was unable to summon the courage to come out with the truth about my shame-filled past on my own. But I was determined to tear down the wall that was standing between us as husband and wife. I knew that Cindy would sooner or later find the passport and discover my horrible secret.

For the first few months after we moved in, I lived in a state of unremitting anxiety about the moment she would pull a favorite book from that shelf and discover my passport and read that my place of birth was Haiti. But as the months rolled on, I forgot that it was there in the bookshelf, ticking ever so quietly, like a time bomb.

By the time of our move, Katrina was five years old. She attended an elementary school in the suburban school district close to our new home. On our first Christmas together as a married couple, Cindy took the family to visit her parents in Kentucky for dinner. The house was full of relatives when we arrived, and more were still coming. Because I grew up seeing everything in terms of superior and inferior, I assumed love amongst relatives was much stronger or better than a love born out of mutual friendship like ours. *I wish I could have this better kind of love. Family love*, I thought.

As I looked around at all the family members gathered near the tree, a weird thought crept into my mind again and again. *Where do I rank on the list of the people whom Cindy loves?* I wondered. Because she often spoke to her mother on the phone, I put her mother, Jean, on top of the list, along with Katrina. I placed her father second, her sister third, and her brothers fourth. *Maybe I am between a third cousin and a nephew.* No matter how hard I tried to understand it, I just didn't get how love worked. *Maybe if Cindy loves too many people, she'll have less love for me*, I thought.

As we drove home that night I began to test her.

"Suppose we were in an airplane with your immediate family, and the pilot says someone has to be thrown out; otherwise the plane will crash. Which one of us would you throw out?"

Cindy had become aware long before (no doubt the afternoon I tried to carry her across the puddle in the school parking lot) that my thought processes were not the same as most people's. She looked over at me for a long moment. "I am not going to play this ridiculous game."

"Ah ha! I know the answer. So, you would throw *me* out, right?" I could see Cindy was getting upset. I continued pressing the issue. "Let's say I was in the plane with you and your cousin, Paul. Which one would you throw out?" Staring out the windshield, she crossed her arms, as angry as I had ever seen her.

"Right now I would pick *Hitler's* third cousin to stay in the plane," she muttered. She was really mad. So I went along with the joke. "But what if it was Hitler's *fourth* cousin?" She stared out the window.

No one would dare suggest that I didn't come to my insecurities honestly. For a time I lived with a recurring thought: *Maybe if I had met someone who had grown up with no one to love*, someone like myself, *then I would have been first on her list.* But, over a long period of time, I learned so much more about love by simply feeling the reality of Cindy's love for me, especially her incredible *patience* with me, and with my strange mental "processes." Over time, the idea of there being some kind of competition for love just faded away.

A month after Christmas, I returned home from the grocery store and found Cindy leaning against the wall in the dining room with my passport in her hand and a blank expression on her face. My heart leapt into my mouth.

"Who in the hell are you? Your passport says you were born in Haiti." She sat down at the table. Her shoulders seemed to collapse around her. I put down the grocery bag and pulled a chair up beside her.

"I didn't think you would have accepted an intern from Haiti. When you asked where I was from, I panicked and said 'Martinique.'"

"I don't give a damn where you were born. Why should I?"

"You have no idea what I had been through in Tampa, until I landed that job at Hudson High. Being black was a burden. Having an accent was a burden. And being Haitian was the biggest burden of all, because Haitians and AIDS were so inseparably connected. The only place *anywhere* that being a Haitian and a black man didn't seem to matter was in the army. It was horrible." Cindy leaned back and looked at me. The anger in her face was dissipating.

"Please forgive me," I said.

"I do. I guess I do. I'm just trying to understand. All this time, you didn't tell me," she shook her head.

"I simply could not bring myself to tell you that the first moment of our relationship was built on a lie. The best I could do—honestly, the only thing I could think of—was to leave my passport where I knew you would eventually find it. I am so sorry."

She leaned against me, and I put my arm around her shoulders. "Of course, I forgive you. How could I not forgive you?" she whispered. I felt the wall tumbling down. I began to quietly sob.

"Thank you," I said finally, with as much depth and intensity as I could utter those two words. Then I hugged her more tightly than I ever had. This was so different from the night I walked out of Florence's house, but for the second time in my life, I felt truly emancipated.

The new school year began in late August. Mr. Edwards called an assembly in the auditorium. "When you are in this building, you will conduct yourselves in the most respectable manner. You will treat each and every staff member with courtesy and respect, and, if you don't . . . let me be blunt . . . you will be thrown out. Any staff member may question you at any time, and anywhere in this building. You are the reason why we're here. If you resist us and our concern for you, you will be thrown out. You are all artists. That means you must learn to appreciate and respect each other's work. We are a family, and this is your home away from home."

As I listened to Mr. E.'s speech, my feelings toward him bordered on hero worship, and I couldn't stop smiling. He sounded like JFK speaking short, rapid-fire sentences! *This man knows how to run a school*, I thought.

One Friday afternoon in mid-January 1990, I showed a short film about the passage of laws by Congress to my American history class. The room was dark, and someone from the office came in, handed me a folded sheet of paper, and left without saying a word. I opened it and saw that it was a message for Judy Brewer, a white student. Without reading its content, I gave her the note. The film ended, and a student switched on the light.

Seconds later I heard the voice of Judy Brewer. "How dare you open my mail? Don't you know it's a federal offense to open somebody's mail?" The whole class seemed shocked by her tirade.

"Young lady, you have no right to scream at me," I said. Judy continued raising her voice to impress her peers. After class, I placed a call to Judy's mother, and she agreed that Judy should serve a thirty-minute detention in my room after school.

After the last period ended at 3:20, Judy came in and moved to the last seat while I stayed at my desk, grading papers. Twenty minutes went by, and I told Judy to go home. She picked up her book bag from the floor and walked out.

"Have a nice weekend," I said. She didn't reply. "Judy, I am being nice. You were supposed to stay for thirty minutes. I'm letting you go early."

"Well, do you want me to stay for another ten minutes?" she snapped.

"No, Judy, I don't want to punish myself any more than I have to," I said.

At school Monday morning, I saw a white woman standing near the library. She was tall and appeared to be in her late forties. As I approached her to say good morning, she brandished her index finger and shook it violently at my nose.

"What did you do to my daughter?" she screamed.

"What did I do?" I asked nervously.

"You know what you did, and I don't have to tell you," she thundered.

"No, ma'am. I have no idea what you're talking about. What did I do?" I asked again.

"You know exactly what you did to my daughter," she repeated. I ignored her and went to my room, heart still pounding.

During my planning time, a security guard with a walkie-talkie came in. "Mr. E. wants to see you in his office," he said.

I knocked and entered. Mr. Edwards was calm. As I stood facing him, my stomach churned.

"Take a seat," he said.

"Mrs. Brewer, Judy's mother, was in my office early this morning. She said that Friday afternoon during detention, you fondled Judy's breasts and put your hand between her legs." I took a deep breath. My throat felt dry.

"I did no such thing."

"Mrs. Brewer said that Judy would not lie about something like that," he responded.

"She lied. I stayed behind my desk grading papers the entire time she was in my room."

"Was the door open?" asked Mr. E.

"Yes," I said. Mr. E. took a deep breath.

"The School Board has been notified. I have to follow procedure. There will be an investigation," he said.

"I didn't go near her. I hope you believe me." Mr. E. did not respond. To me, that meant one thing. I rose slowly and left his office in a daze.

I returned to my classroom and sat pensively at my desk, looking at the students. The gnawing feeling of fear, so familiar from my childhood, returned. I wondered if they knew that I cared about them and their education. Of course they couldn't know that my dream was to follow in Mr. Rabinowitz's footsteps and make a difference in young people's lives.

"Read the first three pages and answer the questions at the end of the chapter," I said, burying my face in my hands and peeking at the students between my fingers. They looked back up at me, thinking I was being funny. I wished I could have simply told them the story of what had happened. They would take my side, I was certain. They would understand that this was anything but funny.

"You guys are not working," I said.

"You usually assign these questions for homework," said Albert.

"Never mind what I usually do," I snapped. After class, Sarah, a white girl, approached my desk.

"Are you okay, Mr. Cadet? You look worried," she said.

"I am all right, Sarah. Thank you for asking."

At lunchtime, I sat in the workroom with my face on the desk, eyes closed and thinking of every moment I had spent with Judy in detention.

"What's wrong?" asked Joy, a colleague. I took a deep breath and explained that a white girl had accused me of molesting her during detention.

"Don't worry. Everything will be okay, but call the union representative immediately," she suggested.

I phoned the union representative, who told me to wait for the outcome of the investigation. Later I was surprised to see Judy show up in class. I couldn't teach. It was as if my tongue were stuck in my throat.

At home I laid out the incident to Cindy. She was upset, and I felt that she had made a bad mistake in marrying me. And I should have followed my instincts. I could see that the accusations weighed as heavily on her as they did on me. I remembered when she told me about announcing to her family that she would marry me. Everyone knew what an interracial marriage in the United States would mean. She laughed in recalling that her father had said that someone ought to knock some sense into her head. "You're asking for a difficult life, young lady," he had concluded. A difficult life indeed. Once again, I thought of fleeing to Tampa and getting a divorce, hoping that this might let Cindy off the hook.

"How can a student do something like this to her teacher?"

"Judy was upset with you, and she knows how to hurt a black man," said Cindy.

"Don't black men belong on this planet?" I said. She didn't respond, but she came over to me and held my head to her bosom. Her heart was beating fast like a muffled drum.

I spent many sleepless nights thinking of outcomes that were all too possible: losing my job, of course, but also losing my teaching license and being branded a child molester for the rest of my life. I could only assume that even jail was a possibility. I trembled with anxiety each time I saw Mr. Edwards in the hallways. Judy was very quiet in class, avoiding eye contact with me. On Friday morning, I found a note from Mr. Edwards in my mailbox, requesting to see me during my planning time. I was nervous, expecting to be fired. The secretary told me to wait in Mr. Edwards's office.

I sat heavily in the chair with my arms supported by the armrests and my eyes fixed on the pastel portrait of a young African woman on the wall opposite me. I stood up. The suspense was too much to bear, so I began to pace back and forth. After several incredibly long minutes, Mr. Edwards walked in, holding a can of Coca-Cola.

"How are you doing, Mr. Cadet?" he asked with concern.

"How should I be doing, sir?" I replied, straight-faced. He sat at his desk and placed the Coke in front of him, then leaned forward with his hands folded and fingers intertwined.

"I have good news for you. Judy came to see me this morning. She said that she wanted to get back at you for giving her detention. She felt that you had no right to open her mail. I've already contacted Judy's mother. She didn't have anything to say." I let out a huge sigh of relief. "Thank God," I breathed. Then, as I gathered up my sense of personal honor, I made a decision.

"Mr. Edwards, I want Judy and her mother to come to this office and apologize to me in your presence." He pursed his lips and nodded up and down, as if he had foreseen how I would react.

"Jean, I am asking you as a friend to let it go. These things have a way of reaching the media. And that wouldn't be good for the school. We depend on donations to keep the arts programs going. Bad publicity might shake donors' confidence in our school."

"But don't you see, sir, I could have been ruined. You have no idea what I've been through."

"Jean, listen to me. If your house had been burglarized and the police caught the thief, I don't think you'd want him back in your house, would you?" he asked.

I didn't quite get the analogy. "No, I wouldn't. But this is different. I would have gotten over a robbery. I don't care much about things. Judy shattered your confidence in me when she made the accusation. You probably thought that I was a child molester. My reputation is all I have in this world," I said, tears streaming down my face. I thought of telling him that although Cadet was a borrowed name, I would never do anything to damage it, but I knew he wouldn't have understood.

"Jean, I am asking you as a personal favor. Please let it go. Honestly, I did not believe Judy's story," he pleaded.

I wanted to say, "Then why didn't you tell me so?" But, out of respect for authority, I held my tongue.

As I walked out, Mr. Edwards reached out and shook my hand with a worried look in his eyes. During my lunch period, I returned to the teacher's workroom and told my colleagues that Judy had confessed. They were very happy but not surprised. Later that day, Judy was absent from my class. She had transferred to another school.

At home, when I shared the news with Cindy, her face lit up, and she hugged me. "I am so sorry that this happened to you yet again," she whispered. The stress I had been under for so many days didn't completely go away. I often picked fights with Cindy, each time almost challenging her to divorce me. "This marriage was a big mistake," I yelled one afternoon. She cried and suggested that we find a marriage counselor. Seeing her in such pain made me feel guilty. We did see a counselor, and things settled down.

In April of that year, Cindy told me she was expecting. Soon there would be a sibling for Katrina. I had very mixed feelings about bringing a child into this world. My child. *What does being a parent mean?*

The question kept recurring to me. *What is a father?* I had absolutely no memory of being parented. None. And now I was going to be one. I had engendered a child. The thought of it was almost terrifying. But I managed to repress most of my fears and anxieties. I began to look forward to meeting my own child, and I often wondered if his or her pigmentation would affect every aspect of his or her life.

CHAPTER 12

I N EARLY JUNE 1990, I enrolled in a master's degree program in French literature at the University of Cincinnati. My goal was to improve my teaching skills and earn additional money to help finance the education of our children. In late August I returned to teaching, with a class schedule that was the same as the year before.

One morning in September, a photographer entered my classroom and snapped several pictures of me. The students looked inquisitive, and I wondered why my photograph was being taken without my permission. The man thanked me and left. Later I saw the principal in the hallway near his office.

"Mr. E., a photographer came to my history class today and took several pictures of me."

"Yes, Jean, the Board of Education wants a black male role model with a nice appearance to feature on its new calendar. I couldn't think of anyone else but you to recommend." I looked at him in amazement. *What nerve*, I thought, but as usual I was unable to vocalize my irritation. He could see that I wasn't happy. "Don't worry. It's an honor," Mr. E said. "It's for public relations purposes only." I was amazed: *How can he say I am a role model when six months ago he offered no support when I was accused of molesting a teenager?* I wondered if he understood what a *role model* really is. Or maybe I didn't understand. In this culture, a role model seems to be anyone who looks the part.

On a bitter cold day in the middle of the school year, I took Cindy to the hospital after her water broke. We had already learned after a mid-term sonogram that the baby would be a boy. Cindy had picked the name Adam, and I chose Bradley as his middle name, making his initials ABC. We thought it was cute, especially with the two of us being teachers.

I was permitted to stay in the delivery room, helping Cindy through the birthing process. Adam weighed nine pounds. The delivery nurse wiped him clean and placed him in my arms. I was aglow. "You're going to Harvard, young man," I whispered to him. Cindy laughed. We were both so happy. Adam was the most beautiful baby I had ever seen, with Caucasian features and thick, black hair. His skin was almost as pale as Katrina's. I thought he resembled my father, but not me. "If only Philippe could see his grandson," I told myself.

I left the hospital walking tall and went home to prepare for my classes. After school the next day, I returned to see Cindy and Adam, who was in a bassinet beside Cindy's bed. The label on the bassinet read, "Race: White." Soon, a nurse came in. She looked at me.

"Are you the baby's father?" she asked.

"Yes, I am," I replied.

"Oops!" she said. And with a magic marker, she crossed out "White" on the tag and wrote "Bi-racial." *Two hundred years after slavery, they are still using the "one-drop rule,"* I thought.

Mr. Edwards, the principal, did not return to the performing arts school after winter vacation. We learned that he had suddenly resigned. Mrs. Mack, my department head, told me that Mr. E. had been accused of having inappropriate contact with several boys at the school. I was devastated and confused. I could not imagine that well-educated people, in this society, were capable of such crimes. I had never quite forgiven him for failing to come to my defense. *Maybe he didn't do it,* I found myself thinking. *Maybe he was as innocent as I had been.* Then another thought came. *Or maybe he had projected some of his own guilt onto me.*

The assistant principal started serving as acting principal, and an interviewing committee was created to begin the search for a new principal.

During the first week of February, Black History Month, teachers received instructions from the Board of Education to teach and encourage racial tolerance and equality. As I walked the hallways, I heard teachers lecture about Frederick Douglass, Sojourner Truth, Jackie Robinson, Rosa Parks, and Maya Angelou. In one classroom I saw students watching *Roots*. In another class, a white girl was reading *Harlem*, by Langston Hughes.

I even heard the "I Have a Dream" speech coming from one of the classrooms. I couldn't help standing for a while outside the open door. Once again, I was mesmerized by the melodious voice, the cadenced delivery, and the deep emotion of Dr. King. When the recording ended, I moved on to my destination, the school cafeteria. And there it was. The same paradigm I had observed the first time I heard that speech. Black and white students were still sitting mostly at separate tables. This time I understood some of the ironies that come with Black History Month.

Mrs. Mack, who was a member of the interviewing committee for the new principal, asked me if I would meet and escort interview applicants to the conference room during my planning periods. The first candidate I greeted was white and in her forties. She wore a blue skirt and pink blouse. Her hair was in a ponytail. She introduced herself as Mrs. Clinton. We shook hands and exchanged smiles. I escorted her to the conference room, where she was warmly received by the committee—three white males, two white females, and one black female.

After school, I approached the lone black member of the committee.

"What do you think of Mrs. Clinton?" I asked.

"She's definitely a strong candidate, has lots of experience, smart, but she's white."

"What?" I asked. I was flabbergasted yet again.

"She's white."

"What difference does that make?"

"The School Board is not interested in rebuilding the school's image with a white principal. The Edwards scandal is still fresh in the public's mind."

"Then why are we wasting time interviewing white candidates when they don't stand a chance of getting hired?"

"For insurance purposes, in case we can't find a qualified black candidate," she replied. I found the logic bewildering. I had been in this country for twenty years, dealing with race issues on a very personal and regular basis, but I was still unable to make good sense of it all.

Days later, I greeted another white applicant, a Mr. Bauer, in the lobby. He was tall, handsome like JFK, and in his forties. He wore a dark blue suit. As I gave him a tour of the building, he asked about my accent and national origins and about the subjects that I taught. I liked him immediately. But I couldn't escape the feeling that something almost sinister was going on. I thought of letting him know that he had already been profiled, and that he wouldn't be hired because of his race, but I changed my mind. Filling him in on the "realities" of our search process could create a furor, and I would be in the middle of it. I realized that the whole thing was an elaborate dance. My role was to waltz the candidates into the ballroom. Period. Perhaps I was finally learning the racial ropes.

Later that day, I asked Mrs. Mack her impression of Mr. Bauer.

"He's young and has the incentive to do a good job. Unfortunately, again, he's white," she said. I couldn't believe that I was hearing this from the head of the history department, who happened to be Jewish.

"I think the newspaper ad for principals should say, 'White candidates need not apply,'" I said.

"Are you serious?" she asked.

"Just kidding," I said. But I hated being even a small party to this deception. Racially, there was a reverse cruelty to the hiring process. After I had escorted the third victim, a white man, to be interviewed, I took myself out of the cynical game. I told Mrs. Mack that I would do no more escorting of candidates who didn't have a chance. Needless to say, she wasn't pleased with my decision.

The school year ended in early June without a new principal being hired. No wonder. I still found it hard to believe that the hiring committee was a group of professional educators.

At the end of July, before the start of the new school year, I telephoned Mrs. Mack to find out whether a principal had been found.

"Yes, we've hired someone. Her name's Dr. Eldridge. She seems very nice. She directed an arts school in St. Louis. She has all the qualifications we've been looking for. And, Jean, are you ready for the big plus?" She asked with excitement.

"I think I have an idea," I said.

"You're right. She's black. Isn't it wonderful? Her very presence will help restore the school's image and sense of purpose," she said.

"I hope so."

"You're so cynical, Jean. This woman's sophisticated. She's in her late sixties, but looks fifty. She's spry and strong. We'll all get along with her just fine."

"Is that a guarantee?" I asked.

The 1991–1992 school year rolled by without any major incidents for me. My students tested well and I was enjoying a new kind of comfort level at the performing arts school. In June, I looked back on the year with a kind of amazement. *That's the way school is supposed to be*, I said to myself.

Perhaps I had spoken (to myself) too soon. In early September of the following school year, a week after school started, an African American girl student came into my history class, handed me a late-admittance form, and took the last seat in the back. I could see the girl was dealing with a major acne problem. Immediately, she lowered her head as if hiding behind the boy in front of her. I smiled, recalling my first day at Spring Valley High School. I distinctly remembered sitting in the last seat in the corner of the room, trying to hide behind the boy in front of me. But I guess I forgot how much I had wanted to blend in at the time, to be anonymous.

"Tamika, will you please take a seat in the first row? Don't hide yourself. You're a beautiful girl," I said, hoping to give her a little confidence. She smiled and moved to the second row. I handed her a book and began the lesson.

The next day, as I began my first-period class, a security guard came into that class and told me to report to Ms. Kelly, the assistant principal. I panicked, trying to figure out what I might have done this time, so early in the year. In Ms. Kelly's office was an African American couple waiting to see me.

"Mr. Cadet, this is Mr. and Mrs. Johnson. They are concerned about a comment you made to Tamika yesterday," said Ms. Kelly.

"What comment?" I asked.

"Did you tell Tamika to sit up front because she was beautiful?"

"Yes," I said, "but I didn't use the word 'because,'" almost thinking the parents had come to thank me for caring. But I was confused by the stern expression on their faces.

"See, he admits it," snapped Mr. Johnson.

"That was very unprofessional of you to tell Tamika to sit up front because she was beautiful," said Mrs. Johnson. I was astounded.

"Isn't 'beautiful' a compliment?" I asked.

"Yes, but not from a male teacher to a female student," said the assistant principal. I was totally confused and speechless. I took a deep breath.

"Mr. and Mrs. Johnson, would you have been happy if I had told your daughter she was ugly?" I asked. Every jaw dropped. The assistant principal asked me to return to class. Once again, I worried about being fired. During lunch that day I told a male colleague about the earlier meeting.

"Don't you see," my friend explained. "Telling a girl she's beautiful could be interpreted as a sexual advance." I was still confused.

"Aren't we supposed to care about them, and to help build their self-esteem?"

"Sure," he said, "but not in *any way* that could possibly be misinterpreted."

I was grateful for the advice, but I seemed to face an almost impossible balancing act. In Tamika's case, the issue became moot. The Johnsons had her removed from my class.

I spent the rest of the school year selecting my words very carefully. I often put my hands in my pocket to avoid congratulating anyone with a simple pat on the back. To me the classroom environment became tense and artificial, a human minefield, with angel-faced students who were like dangerous objects that could explode at any moment. But even more dangerous, it seemed to me, were many of the adults in these students' lives, their teachers and parents.

During the 1994 school year, I began hearing rumors of looming cutbacks due to a failed tax levy and the district's huge budget deficits. I worried about losing my job, even though I was almost never absent, and a high percentage of my students always passed their ninth grade proficiency tests. I had learned that teachers were retained based on seniority rather than their performance and attendance, which made little sense to me.

My son Adam breezed through infancy and toddlerhood. Shortly after his fourth birthday, he began asking me about his grandmother and grandfather from my side of the family. I wasn't ready for that line of questioning.

"I don't have a mommy and daddy," I said.

"Why not?" he asked, and I quickly changed the subject. Days later, he looked up at me from a puzzle he was working on. "Daddy, where do your mommy and daddy live?" *He's like the Little Prince*, I thought. *He'll never give up on a question.*

"They're in Haiti," I said.

"Where's that?"

"It's an island in the ocean. I was born there."

"Why don't they come to my birthday party?" Again, I steered the topic toward something of more immediate interest. How could I explain to a young child something as unthinkable, not to mention *terrifying*, as the childhood I had lived through, and the fact that I never had parents? Then a new idea popped into my mind. Maybe I could tell Adam the story more carefully, more gently even, if I were to write it down. Then I could give it to him when he was older.

Almost immediately, I began to write a memoir of the events of my childhood in the form of a letter. I sat at the dining room table and opened a new spiral notepad: "Dear Adam. It's time that you know the true story of your Daddy's life." And then I plunged in. "My mother died when I was four years old." Immediately, as if I had turned on the tap outside Florence's house, the memories started flooding in upon me. I wrote something nearly every day. Some days, I would write feverishly for three hours straight, losing all track of time. Many of the pages were water-marked with tears.

In late May of 1995, I was in the middle of a history lesson when a security officer came into my room. "You need to report to the principal's office," he said. What could I have done? Nothing came to mind, but by now I was programmed to expect the worst. By this time I had learned never to warn students before calling their parents about behavior problems. I had avoided ever being alone in a room with a female student. I had stopped saying "boy" when talking to a black kid, and had kept my hands by my side like a robot whenever a female student hugged me, which happened more than a few times.

I knocked on the principal's door and walked in.

"Mr. Cadet, according to the School Board Office your teaching contract may not be renewed next year because you're not certified to teach American history," she said. Even though the news was bad, I let out a huge sigh of relief. Innocent of all charges!

"Well then, I'll be happy to teach only French classes," I replied.

"That is not going to work, Mr. Cadet. We will be reducing our workforce and cutting back on foreign languages," she said.

"Then I'll take classes this summer to fulfill the requirements for American history," I offered.

"If you still want to work in the school district, you can call the Board Office after you're certified in American history," she said.

"Thank you, Dr. Eldridge," I said. After less than a year, many of my colleagues, black and white, already despised her. As I walked back to my classroom, I pondered, *Why did she need to interrupt my class for this? She could have told me after school.* It was obvious to most of the teachers and staff that our protracted selection process for principal had been seriously flawed.

That summer, I enrolled at the University of Cincinnati, taking two of the three history courses to fulfill the requirements for certification in American history. Because schools had always been my refuge, I enjoyed being in the classroom, either as a student or as a teacher. One of my courses covered plantation life in the antebellum South, and the other dealt with slave societies in Hispaniola. I knew I would ace that course. I was already something of an expert. Haiti and the Dominican Republic had been called "Hispaniola" before the nineteenth century.

During that summer semester, I discovered interesting details about my birth country that I might never have come to know on my own. I learned how the French masters had used dogs to hunt down and recapture runaway slaves. Maybe this was why Haitians are so prone to mistreat their dogs. Maybe something deep inside our cultural makeup *remembers* the viciousness of those long-ago growling, snarling beasts that had been accomplices to the French in terrorizing my ancestors.

And I learned how it was the habit of those same French slaveholders—when runaways were captured and returned to their estates—to cut off one or both of the ears of their delinquent, black chattel. There was a part of me that felt grateful, and even a bit amazed, that I still had both my ears. To this day, I shudder when I recall Florence threatening to cut off my ears for this or that infraction. Why did she sometimes use *that* particular threat? Clearly, it had come down to her as part of the system that the powerful employed to control the weak. No doubt, as a young person she had heard her neighbors, or her parents, use the same threat against their *restaveks*. In these more modern times, few owners of child slaves would have acted on the threat. They didn't need to. We children *believed* they would do it. Something deep inside us *knew*—viscerally—that such an act of violence had been carried out many times in the past. Not only that—I was aware that if Florence, in a rage, had decided to exact that particular punishment, she could have done so. There was no one, nor was there any social or legal structure, that would have protected me from her wrath. Even today, families can do as they please with their *restavek* slaves. And that's what they do.

In one of my classes, the professor made a statement that he might have found in any of the history texts about that region: "After the Haitian blacks successfully revolted against their French overlords, the institution of slavery ended forever on the island."

I raised my hand.

"Excuse me, sir. Not to contradict you, but slavery never really ended in Haiti. It evolved into another form. Today the slaves in Haiti are children. They call them *restaveks*."

"Where have you read about that?"

I didn't answer the question directly.

"Actually, I am writing about it at the moment. I'm from Haiti myself." By this point I had no problem revealing my true nationality.

"Good for you. I look forward to seeing it when it's finished," he said. I nodded.

I figured he thought I was referring to an essay I was writing for class. In fact, I was talking about the letter I was writing to my son.

Over a long period of time that letter grew into something else, something beyond even the graduate school essay on *restaveks* that earned me an *A*.

Published in paperback by the University of Texas Press, the long letter, now in book form, was titled—not surprisingly—*Restavec*. Later, under the same title it would be published in French, then even in Haitian Creole. My letter to Adam would become a letter to the world.

The summer session ended. I made the Dean's List and registered for the last course to fulfill the requirement for certification in American history, to be held that fall. My work on "the letter" proceeded day after day.

In my final semester at the university, I found myself immersed in Chinese history, taught twice a week during evening hours by an extraordinary professor, himself Chinese, named Mann Bunn. During the day I worked as a substitute teacher and sent my résumé to suburban schools, hoping to work for a principal more like the one who had been my boss in Florida.

Some of my classmates complained to each other about Dr. Bunn's heavy Chinese accent, but I understood him quite well. I knew the situation from the other side. Some of my own former high school students in both French and American history had complained to their parents about having problems with my accent to justify their low grades. I remembered calling one parent whose child had received failing grades in both classes. We chatted for a few minutes.

"My son said that your accent was so strong he could hardly understand you. But I understand you perfectly. Obviously he was making excuses," the student's mother had said. I admit to having been startled by the woman's honesty.

My college classmates also complained about the course's reading assignments. "Why do we need to learn about the plight of rickshaw men in the 1900s?" they would whine. "This is stupid."

To me, the story of the rickshaw men was crucial. I came to admire their strength and resolve. They were Chinese citizens who, as a class, were treated as subhuman by their fellow countrymen. How could my fellow students miss the fact that these men were iconic, heroic symbols in the struggles of the working class?

In our textbook, a rickshaw man who had been cursed by a well-dressed student responded: "How can you curse me like that? Even though I pull a rickshaw, I am still as much a human being as you, a gentleman. In school, don't they teach you about equality?"

After I read the quote, my mind, of course, wandered back to my boyhood in Haiti on so many of our so-called "Independence Days." Slaves from Africa had freed themselves in the early days of the nineteenth century. Everyone in Haiti was now supposed to be equal. I remembered us *restavek* children fetching water all day while our owners and their children ate their traditional *joumou* (freedom soup) as they listened to "Papa Doc" carrying on endlessly, lacing his polemics with cultural lies: "Liberty, Equality, Fraternity." What good were these flowery abstractions? Such virtues were nonexistent in Haiti's class-based society. And for us *restavek* children, the words should have been replaced by more basic values: "Food, Clothing, Education."

I found myself wishing that I had had the courage and wisdom of that illiterate rickshaw man when I was a boy. I wish I had been empowered to scream at Haitian adults: "How can you enslave us children? You're exploiting us because we're small and powerless, and our parents are not here to protect us. In school, didn't they teach you about equality?" Had I raised these issues, no doubt, I would have been beaten raw. Or worse.

In mid-December, as the semester was ending, I happened to be walking with Dr. Bunn to his office when he stopped in the hall to speak to a colleague. "This is Jean-Robert Cadet, my star pupil," said Dr. Bunn. For some time afterward, I couldn't stop smiling.

CHAPTER 13

IN EARLY JANUARY 1996, after a year and a half of writing and revising, I finished the letter to my son—three hundred double-spaced pages long. Adam was my reason for engaging in this process, but I realized early on that there were other energies at work, driving me to spend so many often pain-filled hours getting my "miserable life" down on paper. All along the way, I knew that I was engaged in a most healing experience.

I asked Cindy if she would like to read my "letter." Over the years, I had already shared many painful pieces of my childhood with her, but here it was, rolled up into a sequential ball, the twelve years as a *restavek* in Haiti, as well as some related material, as I carved a new life for myself in the US of A. My wife, who during our years together had dealt with so many of the *effects* of my abused and truncated early years, sobbed again and again as she encountered in print the events that had inspired my various behavioral "issues." When she had finished the long read, she said something that took me totally by surprise.

"I think this should be published," she suggested. "Really, Jean, I think other people should read about your life."

I reacted instinctively. "No, it's much too personal. Who wants to read about my horrible childhood? I just hope Adam will read it someday," I said. Then Cindy said something that really knocked me over. Her question would change the direction of the remainder of my life.

"Don't you think your story could make the plight of *restaveks* known to a lot more people? And then maybe—just maybe—something will be done about their situation?" Her idea forced me to think. I still had many ambiguous feelings. *Why should I expose so much pain, so much nakedness, to the public?* I thought.

After much soul-searching, I decided to take a stab at realizing what Cindy had proposed. Maybe I owed something to my own modest story. It might be a traumatic read for someone brought up on love and care and personal security here in America, but it did have something of a happy ending. I had succeeded against heavy odds and had—more or less—turned my life around. Maybe I did owe something to all those Haitian children still trapped in the brutal system that had made a nightmare of my childhood. I took some strange comfort in the fact that, like so many similar memoirs, it would probably not find a publisher anyway.

After more than a few rejection letters from publishing agents, I visited my Chinese friend, Dr. Bunn, at the University of Cincinnati. I thought he might be a good person to speak with regarding my manuscript. He was glad to see me when I showed up unannounced in his office.

"I have a manuscript about my childhood in Haiti. Would you be willing to read it and tell me what you think?" I asked.

"Sure, I'd be glad to read it, but I am on my way to China," he said. "Look, I will take it with me, and let you know what I think of it when I get back," he said. I handed him the manuscript, feeling more than a little uncomfortable that a friend would be reading about my childhood spent in domestic slavery and social isolation. It was several months later when I received his response in a letter. "I liked the manuscript, and asked Dr. Ann Twinam, a history professor, to read it. She liked it as well. Call me as soon as possible." I placed a call to Professor Bunn, and he asked to see me the next day.

When I showed up at his office, he took me into a conference room down the hall, where I met Dr. Twinam. A short while later the dean of the history department walked in. "This is Jean-Robert Cadet; he was a slave in Haiti," said Dr. Twinam. The word "slave" hit me like a grenade. I had just written a book about my experiences with child *slavery*, but—even in my mind—that term was something of an institutional abstraction, and an anachronism. I had never in my life been introduced as a *slave*. The word was so real. It sounded horrible, impossible to imagine, even to me. Had I *really* been a *slave*? Was that *really* the defining word about who I was, about *me*? After all these years, I hadn't come to grips with this most degrading reality. *I, Jean-Robert Cadet, had grown up a slave.* If shame could kill, I might have died on the spot.

Fortunately, I was immediately liberated from these negative feelings by the next thing out of Dr. Twinam's mouth.

"Jean has written a wonderful manuscript. It's the kind of material I need to supplement my courses in Caribbean history. I think it should be published."

The next day, Dr. Twinam wrote a letter on my behalf to the University of Texas Press, and within days, I received a call from the press requesting a copy of the manuscript. Soon a contract from the University of Texas Press came in the mail along with a check. Cindy beamed as she looked over the contract. We both knew this was all because of her.

In mid-August, I found a part-time teaching assignment at a suburban high school, not far from my house. There were just a handful of minority students on campus. Most of the white kids, it seemed, had never been taught by a non-Caucasian. Some referred to me as "the black teacher."

In February 1998, my autobiography, *Restavec*, was published. The *Cincinnati Enquirer* gave it a good review, and Barnes & Noble, the largest retailer in the area, scheduled a book signing. Cindy sent invitations to her friends and relatives and to our colleagues. When I arrived for the signing with Cindy, Adam, and Katrina, I saw a large table in the middle of the store with a stack of my books and a large poster that bore my picture and the front cover of my book. Cindy, choking with emotion, put her arm on my shoulder.

"How should I sign the books?" I whispered to Cindy.

"With best wishes," she said. My wife is always so practical and matter-of-fact.

As I sat for the book signing, I saw a long line of Cindy's relatives coming toward me with smiling faces. Jean Nassano, my mother-in-law, arrived with a bottle of champagne to toast my success. Although some members of Cindy's family had already read the book, I worried they would think less of me, knowing the details of my background. After all those years, it remained difficult for me to accept the obvious: that I had been in no way responsible for the way I had been treated as a child and adolescent. With the publication of this book, I recognized that my strange life, with all its pain and indignities, had at last been validated, in an almost miraculous way. Here it was; here *I* was, in print, in bookstores, in libraries, my story in black and white, *nèg* and *blan*.

A few weeks after the book signing, I was surprised, and a bit over-whelmed, to receive a phone call from a producer at National Public Radio who asked if he could interview me about my book. After the conversation, still shaking with excitement, I put the receiver down. I couldn't believe it. *Holy cow!* I thought. *Cindy had been right from the very beginning. Maybe my story could have an impact on child slavery in Haiti.* Days later, the NPR interview took place in a studio at a local university. I was told that it would be aired the following day at a given time.

I always kept a radio on my classroom desk, which I sometimes listened to during free periods or after school. When the broadcast time rolled around during my third-period class, I told the students that I had been interviewed on a national radio program and asked if they would like to listen to that conversation with me.

"Why would a radio station be interested in you?" one girl asked, a legitimate—and not unkind—inquiry. I still wondered about that myself.

"Well, as you know, I wrote a book about the story of my life, and I guess they liked the story."

"What's so special about it?" she pressed.

"Listen, and maybe you'll find out."

When the program began, the students listened intently. I could see that they were almost wide-eyed in disbelief. For me, the moment had profound implications. It was the first time I had ever made my story known to a classroom full of young people. More important perhaps was the internal reality. For the first time I felt more pride in my past than shame.

"You never had parents?" one student asked.

"Well, of course I did, but I have no memory of them. I was taken away before I was old enough to remember."

"Who raised you?" asked a girl.

"I had no one I could count on, so I raised myself. If you really want to know about me, you could read my book. It's not a very long book." With that, I quickly began the day's lesson. I still found it embarrassing to be exposed like this, and I didn't want to waste class time speaking any more about myself. In the weeks that followed, two students told me that they had read *Restavec*. They even asked me to sign their copies of the book.

In early July of 1998, I received an invitation to speak about my book at the Broward County Library in Fort Lauderdale, Florida. In attendance were many Haitian immigrants. In the question-and-answer session after my presentation, a number of these people spoke up, somewhat defensively, it seemed to me.

"Not all Haitians mistreat their *restaveks*," one woman said. "We had a little boy staying with us. We sent him to school. He was like a member of our family."

"If he was treated like family, he was not really a *restavek*," I responded. "Where is he now?"

"I don't know, but he became a mechanic." I thought about pointing out that had the boy really been like a member of their family, they wouldn't have lost track of him.

Another man raised his hand.

"Child slavery in Haiti is caused by the poverty, pure and simple, and until that problem is solved, nothing can be done for these children."

I had heard this argument many times before. I responded, "Those who enslaved me were not poor. They were quite simply cruel and inhuman, and clearly that is the way most Haitians treat their *restaveks*." The man nodded his head, appearing to accept the validity of my point.

Later on in the Florida trip I was interviewed by the *Miami Herald*. The following day, an article about me appeared in the newspaper, one that would soon find its way to Haiti.

CHAPTER 14

IN MID-JUNE 1999, I boarded an American Airlines flight from Cincinnati to Port-au-Prince. In a gift box I was carrying, I had placed my book, *Restavec*, a copy of my master's degree, and a photograph of Adam, then eight years old, wearing his soccer uniform. The primary purpose of this "vacation" was to locate my birth father. Somewhat desperately, I wanted to prove to my dad that I was worthy of his respect and even—perhaps—his love. It had taken more than twenty-five years to ready myself for this journey into my own history as a child of Philippe Sebastian—and as a child of Haiti.

As the plane circled Port-au-Prince, I looked down from my window seat and noticed several huge slum towns of rust-roofed shacks along the shorelines. The mountains towering over the city looked scorched and lifeless. They appeared to have always been in this condition. The truth is, like much of the countryside in Haiti, they had been mercilessly defoliated over the years, without any substantial replanting. The plane finally eased its way down onto the lone runway of Haiti's threadbare airport. My heart was pounding as the plane roared to a stop and taxied toward the terminal. Although there was little love lost between this strange island nation and me, I realized that I had come "home" at last.

The stairway used by the passengers to deplane piggybacked on the same 1960 Ford pick-up truck that I had climbed as I boarded the Pan American jet to America in 1969. Now the truck was a dull orange. The sun, brighter and hotter than I could remember, glared off the silver body of the plane as I stepped onto the tarmac. A tropical breeze carrying some vaguely familiar smells swirled around me.

Outside the airport, gaunt-looking men swarmed the travelers, begging to carry their bags. A policeman chased a crowd of beggars with a stick, but they returned when he went to unsnarl a mini traffic jam. The vehicles, mostly 4 × 4s, were dented, dusty, and pointed in every direction in the unlined lot. As they came and went, thick black smoke shot out of the tailpipes. Taxi drivers did their best to secure a fare. Using Creole for the first time in years, I asked a yellow-shirted taxi driver the price to Route Bourdon, a twenty-minute ride.

"Thirty US," he said.

I hadn't forgotten a skill I had learned with pennies as a child. "Twenty US," I countered.

"Twenty-five US," he bartered, still sizing me up.

"Forget it," I said, and began walking away.

"Okay, let's go."

I followed the driver to a parking lot across the street, and he opened the back of a Nissan 4 × 4, placing my bag on a dusty tire. I got in the front seat and we headed away from the airport's mayhem.

"Could you please turn on the air?" I requested, without even thinking. I guess I had become accustomed to the luxuries that accompanied a middle-class US lifestyle.

"You must have left Haiti a long time ago," he said with a grin.

"Yes, a very long time ago. Is this your car?" I asked.

"I rented it for the day," he said, as we joined the traffic jam on the airport road. "I'm trying to survive. You know how it is?"

As we moved toward our destination, it seemed that people and cars were heading in every direction, like ants in a broken colony. The population had exploded dramatically since I left Port-au-Prince. Electric wires dangled from light posts; the streets were trash-strewn and in major disrepair. *At least*, I thought, *Papa Doc kept things clean and orderly in the sixties.*

I didn't need to be told that the plight of poor children and *restaveks* remained largely the same as it had been under the Duvalier regime. I could see it with my eyes. All over Port-au-Prince, kids in tattered clothing were fetching water or walking children in uniforms to or from school. In bygone years, the *restaveks*, whom I identified as the most shabbily dressed of the children, had slaved for the wealthy or the upper middle class. But now most of them were "owned" by Haitian people who were themselves living in the firm grip of poverty.

As we reached Bourdon Boulevard, the street where I had lived with Florence, I experienced a flood of memories. My first thoughts were of the murder of the mulatto woman by soldiers wearing the guinea-fowl shoulder patches. As we drove by the woman's house, I found myself singing some of the words to her favorite song. The house itself was now hidden behind other structures, and its low iron fence had been replaced with a twelve-foot-high wall.

I had the driver turn down Madame Laroche's street. All I could think of was the night she beat me in my wet clothes. The neighbor's words echoed in my mind. I hadn't thought of them for years. "When you're done skinning him, send me his hide to make a drum." These memories were as vivid as if it all had happened yesterday, yet I remained completely detached from them. *This thing happened here*, I might realize. But I felt nothing about whatever it was that had happened. I cared without caring, felt without feeling, if that makes any sense at all. Madame Laroche's house, too, was now hidden behind walls. The neighborhood had become wealthier, and this is what people with possessions need to do in order to keep themselves relatively safe: build walls.

After edging up the street toward what I hoped was still my father's house, I told the driver to stop. I got out. I couldn't believe my eyes. The house was dilapidated, some of its windows boarded up, the front porch almost in ruins. After paying the driver, I walked into the yard, still shaking my head in disbelief. This I did care about. I had deep and complicated feelings about my father. I always will. *He must be gone*, I thought. I had been preparing myself for that likelihood.

Then a young man in his twenties came out of the kitchen to meet me.

"Bonjour," I said.

"Bonjour," he replied.

"Does *blan* Philippe still live here?" I asked, my heart bursting with anxiety.

"He died last year," he said, looking me over intently. "He told me about a son living in the US. Are you him?" He asked. My heart sunk like a stone in a well. I was hugely disappointed, but felt no sorrow. *What in God's name am I doing here?* I asked myself. I felt as if my adult soul were evaporating in the heat. Then a new reality bore down upon me. *A year too late,* I thought. My father had managed to avoid me one last time. This time for good. Those horrible feelings of abandonment descended on me once again. Now they could not be fixed, or reversed.

Finally I looked at the young man. "Yes, I am Philippe's son." I spoke these words slowly, aware that they were dripping with cynicism. "Who are you? How did my father die?" I asked.

"They call me Westner. He had cancer."

"Do you live here?"

"Yes, I took care of Monsieur Philippe while he was sick, and now I am caring for his brother, Monsieur Daniel."

"How did you care for my father? What did you do?"

"The things you do before a man dies. I fed and bathed him," he said. *Perhaps,* I thought, *if I had been here and given him baths during his final days, we might have bonded as father and son.* But then an alternate reality crowded my thought process. *It probably would have been worse,* I realized. *If he had rejected me now, it would have been so much worse.*

"His brother, Monsieur Daniel, is inside," the young man said. "Would you like to speak to him?"

"Yes, thank you," I said, still dealing with the devastating news. But I didn't *really* need to see my uncle. I had wanted only to see my father, and to feel connected with him for one tiny moment of my life. I followed the young man inside, and he pointed to a doorless room.

"Before I go in there, I'd like to see my father's room," I said. The man pointed to a closed door. I opened it and walked in. The young man went back outside. The room was all but empty. The walls were bare and dirty. I looked around for something that belonged to my father, something I might take back home with me. I was hoping that such a talisman might make me feel, at long last, as though I had

had a real parent, one that existed, like everyone else has. In a closet I saw a green ledger and old receipts scattered about. I opened the ledger and ran my fingers across the entries penned in black ink. His handwriting was so much different than mine. "Oh, God, Papa," I whispered, tears running down my face, "I wish you had recognized me. I needed you so much. Can you understand me? I still feel so lost, Papa, like I don't belong anywhere." I tore a single page from the ledger, folded it carefully, tucked it in my shirt pocket, and then walked toward the room where I would meet my uncle.

In a small bed I found an elderly white man, fully clothed, lying on his back and staring at the ceiling. His white hair was wet with sweat. His face was gaunt and unshaven.

"Bonjour, Tonton [Uncle] Daniel," I said. The word "uncle" felt strange rolling off my tongue. "I am Jean-Robert, Philippe's son, come from America." He turned his head slowly toward me.

"Philippe never mentioned a son named Jean-Robert," he said, almost angrily. I realized that he must be senile. If the young man Westner knew of my existence, Philippe must have told his own brother.

"It's because he gave me away when I was very little," I said.

"For him to do that, you must have been a very bad child," he responded, his eyes narrowing. The old man's words were like the sting of a bee. Although momentarily furious, I knew those words described my own deepest sense of myself, a subconscious feeling that would probably never go away completely.

I walked away from the old man without saying goodbye. In the yard I said my thank-yous to Westner and started walking toward the main road. I was in a kind of punch-drunk haze. In five minutes' time, a huge piece of my life had evaporated. Mixed with the stale, pungent air of my native country, I could almost taste my despair.

Walking up the busy road toward Petionville, I saw dozens of boys in tattered clothes wiping car windows in the slow moving traffic, trying to earn a bit of money for food. Under "Papa Doc" Duvalier, street boys earned their little monies selling slingshots and kite strings. Because of political instability after the Duvalier regimes, the baseball factories had totally disappeared.

I approached a vendor selling secondhand clothes.

"How long have you been selling these 'Kennedys'?" I asked.

"We don't call them 'Kennedys' anymore," she replied with a grin, adding, "Now we call them *pèpè*." Later I learned that this was a new Creole word for something of no value, junk. But they weren't really junk. They were valuable for those who needed them. I still preferred thinking of them as "Kennedys."

"Thanks for setting me straight," I said, and then hailed a taxi to take me to my hotel in the wealthy suburb of Petionville. This much had changed. I was no longer dirt poor in Haiti.

As the taxi wound its way toward my hotel, I was shocked to see the mountains above Port-au-Prince disfigured by shantytowns of cinder block boxes mixed in among the walled estates of the rich. Many of the shacks were unfinished and ash colored. From a distance they resembled clusters of tombs with holes to slide the coffins in. Clearly, they had no running water, no sewage system, and, of course, no electricity. "Maybe this is the way it should be," I thought, "the poor living right in the face of the rich."

The next morning, Friday, I decided to travel out to Petite Rivière, the town I had visited as a child, my "hometown." With Philippe dead, I hoped to find relatives of my late mother, or at least some personal fragments of my early childhood to carry home with me, like the pages from my father's ledger. And something else that had become very important to me: *Maybe someone will remember the real date of my birth.*

I had always felt strange when someone asked me my birthday. "Honestly, I have no idea," is what I wanted to say. Instead I would rattle off the birthday that had been imposed upon me, February 15.

Before going to the bus station, I stopped at a store to purchase bottled water to drink during the trip. As I paid the cashier, a woman with very black skin, I noticed several tubes of skin-lightening cream on a shelf behind her. I remembered Florence, thirty years ago, washing her face twice a day with chilled water, believing this would lighten her complexion.

"Does that skin-lightening cream really work?" I asked the cashier, pointing to the boxes of cream.

"Yes, it does. People buy it all the time."

"Do you use it?"

"I do," she replied almost proudly.

"Was your face blacker than it is now?" I asked. We Haitians speak with one another very directly. A question that might seem rude to Americans is usually handled matter-of-factly. In the States everything one says these days must be "politically correct."

"Yes, it was," she answered.

I glanced at her in her low-cut dress and could see that the cream was as ineffective as Florence's chilled water, because her arms and shoulders appeared to me to be the same dark chocolate shade as her face.

The "bus" I boarded to Petite Rivière was a large truck, brightly painted with lavish designs, its roof stretching over the front cabin. Benches had been welded into the bed for people to sit on. "Saint Joseph" was written above its windshield. Almost all the buses had spiritual names.

After a six-hour ride on horrible, dusty roads, the bus stopped at a large charcoal market. This was Petite Rivière. It seemed that nothing had changed here in thirty years except for the scattering of motorcycles that now served as local taxis.

I had decided I would walk to the Ecole Maitre Jean-Charles, where I had gone to school for a few months. I recalled that my tuition had never been fully paid. If the teacher was still there, I planned to give him a year's worth of tuition. I guess I had forgiven him for the severe beating he had administered so long ago. When I got to the school, the students had already gone home. I opened the gate.

"Onè!" I yelled. It was the traditional greeting in the countryside, meaning: Honor.

"Respè!" (Respect), shouted my old teacher Maitre Jean-Charles, as he hobbled out of his house. His hair had gone gray. He was an old man. I couldn't believe that I was now taller than he.

"Bonsoir, Maitre Jean-Charles."

"Bonsoir."

"Do you know who I am?"

"No, who are you?"

"A long time ago, they called me Jean-Robert Cadet?" His eyes seemed to light up, and then a grin spread across his face.

"Where have you been? I asked many students to find you."

"I returned to Port-au-Prince, and then I was sent *à l'étranger* [abroad]."

"Ah," the old man nodded. "That is why I felt you were now a *blan*."

"Why did you accept me gratis?"

"No one had ever offered to clean my yard in exchange for education. I always thought you were special. After all these years, you came back to see me."

"Here, this is my gift to you for taking me in as a student." I handed him seventy US dollars and a flashlight.

"Mèsi! Mèsi! Mèsi anpil!" He was literally shaking with excitement. Tears were rolling down his face. I smiled. I had given him a huge amount of money for rural Haiti. My gift contained a bonus, as his tuition at the time had been $5.40 for a year. I thanked him again and went on my way. "At least there is one person who remembers me," I thought.

Walking northward, I felt a drop of water, warm like spit, splash on my neck. Then it began to rain hard. Instinctively, I started to run. It was almost funny. Where was I running to? There was nothing around to shelter me. Drenched and out of breath, I finally stopped.

The road was muddy and the air smelled like fresh dirt and cow dung. I could hear crows cawing and bickering from the treetops. The road led me to the river Estère, where I had swum with Louis on my previous visit. I stared at the river in shock. It was brown and murky from soil eroding off the treeless mountains. The last time I had seen it, the river had run clear and clean, perfect for a thirst-quenching drink or a swim.

The metal supports for the bridge were still standing where I had seen them last. The rain finally stopped. Standing there on the bank, I watched three men with unsheathed machetes and a woman approaching the opposite bank. Before crossing the river, the men removed their pants and sandals, held them and their machetes on top of their heads, their free hand hiding their genitals. The woman raised the skirt of her dress to her chest and followed the men across the muddy river. It was as if an old movie were replaying in front of my eyes.

"Bonswa," I said, using the Creole instead of the French.

"Bonswa," they replied in unison.

"Is Grand Hatte far from here?"

"It's a good little walk ahead," replied one of the men.

"Mèsi."

Because my clothes were still wet from the rain, I crossed the river fully dressed, fighting the currents and avoiding slippery rocks in the riverbed. I didn't even bother to take off my shoes. I held my backpack high over my head.

The trail leading to Grand Hatte was busy with men and women going south toward Petite Rivière. Darkness began to fall, and I felt a bit of panic, wondering where I would sleep in case I couldn't find my relatives. I saw an elderly man smoking a pipe on his porch and approached him.

"Onè," I said.

"Respè," he answered.

"Did you know a woman who had a child many years ago by a *blan* who owned a coffee factory in the area?" I asked. He looked me up and down.

"Are you the child?"

"Yes, and I am here looking for my mother's relatives."

"The yard you want is up the road across from a *mapou* tree."

"Mèsi." I breathed a sigh of relief. A short walk later I stopped under a massive tree on the roadside. The tree's canopy had kept its floor dry from the rain. I went into the yard and saw two huts and a kitchen shack.

"Onè," I called.

"Respè," answered a woman, coming out of the kitchen.

"I am looking for the family of a woman who had a child by a *blan*." An elderly man with white hair came out of a hut and looked at me for a long moment, and then a toothless grin spread across his face.

"Alfrenold, is that you?"

"My name is Jean-Robert now."

He explained that Alfrenold was the name my late mother had given me. I stepped closer to him, and he put his arm on my shoulder. A crowd coalesced around us in a matter of seconds. Or so it seemed.

"They call me Dwèt. Henrilia was your mother. I am your uncle, the late Henrilia's brother," he said proudly. "You must have been living across the sea." Haitians can almost smell a foreigner, even if he is black and speaks Creole.

"Yes, I live across the sea now."

A young woman in her twenties came and inspected my face. "You are my uncle!" she exclaimed, and wrapped her arms around my waist. "I am called Henrilienne. My mother, Yaya, was your sister. She named me after your mother. She told me about the scar beside your mouth. Yaya passed two years ago. Come, let's go to see your mother's yard," she said.

The crowd led me to a yard with a small, grass-roofed hut. My lips were quivering, and tears streamed down my face. In a spontaneous ceremony, they walked me around the grass-roofed hut three times, clapping and singing, "Thank you, God. Thank you, Jesus, grand master in the sky, for sending Alfrenold back to us." The more I wept, the louder they sang. Afterward I said goodnight. Everyone said, "We'll see you tomorrow if God wishes." Then they all moved off, except Henrilienne.

I stood at the threshold of the hut, looking in. I could not believe that I was standing in my mother's home, where I had lived as a toddler. I closed my eyes, smelled the air, and tried to recall being in this tiny room, much smaller than my kitchen at home. In my mind I created an image of a small child walking behind his mother and holding the tail of her dress. I almost felt like a child again, probably for the first time since I had left Haiti. But I was unable see my mother's face, even when I imagined myself being fed at her breast.

The walls of the hut were made of mud mixed with grass. On a small table stood an oil lamp fashioned from a tin can. Under the table was a five-gallon plastic bucket for drinking water. In a bamboo basket were pots, wooden spoons, dented aluminum plates, and cups.

Henrilienne lit the lamp. From its bright orange flame snaked a thin plume of black smoke. Soon, someone brought in a lumpy grass mattress that had been borrowed from a neighbor and placed it on the floor. My pillow was a blue corduroy sack stuffed solid with rags and tied in a knot at the top. I changed into dry clothes and spread the wet ones out to dry on the cactus fence outside the hut.

"How did my sister die?" I asked.

"She was sick for a long time," said Henrilienne.

"But sick from what?" I probed.

"We don't know, uncle. She was very sick when she died."

"Do you know how I got the scar on my face?"

"I do. Your mother went to pick corn in the garden and left you in Yaya's care. While Yaya was in the kitchen, you ran after your mother and bumped into the sharp edge of a corn leaf. Yaya said she heard you cry, but your mother reached you first. You were bleeding and she was so upset. Your mother beat her severely. She felt that your mother loved you more than her because your father was a *blan*." Tears welled up in my eyes. I whispered to my dead sister, "I am so sorry, Yaya." If the love my mother had given me was as tangible as a medallion, I would have gone to the cemetery and placed it on my sister's grave. That moment there in my mother's house was fraught with an almost exquisite despair.

"Oh, God, why did you put me in this mess?" I said in English. Then I breathed a pain-filled sigh that seemed to hang in the air much like the plume of smoke rising from the tin lamp.

Henrilienne took my hand. "I am so sorry, uncle. My mother always talked about her little brother who had gone away forever."

"Did she ever mention the date of my birth?"

"Non."

"Did she say how old I was when I went running into the corn field?"

"Non."

"How old was Yaya when this happened?"

"She said that she was ten or twelve years old."

"How old are you now?"

She thought for a moment. "I am in my twenties."

"Do you have a birth certificate?"

"Non."

"Can you read?"

"Non." She lowered her head shamefully.

"The yard is very small," I said.

"It used to be a lot bigger. When your mother died, a portion was sold to cover the funeral expenses. When Yaya died, I sold a portion. The rest now belongs to you."

"Thank you," I said, overcome with bittersweet emotion. "But I will not be needing it."

Henrelienne placed a tin can beside the mattress.

"You can pee in this, uncle," she said, smiling as she left.

"Sleep well, niece," I said.

"See you tomorrow if God wishes." She lay down on a mat near a corner of the hut. Before I blew out the lamp, I checked my watch. It was only nine o'clock.

As I stretched out on the strange mattress, mosquitoes buzzed around my head. It had been many years since I had dealt with mosquitoes. A short while later I noticed a somewhat round shadow on the wall by my feet. I thought perhaps it was cast by the moonlight shining through cracks in the door. I closed my eyes, hoping to fall asleep, but the thought that my mother loved me more because I was fathered by a white man kept running through my mind. Minutes later, I opened my eyes and saw that the odd shadow had moved closer to the floor. I shined my flashlight toward it and saw hundreds of tiny black spiders in a tight formation. I jumped up and lit the lamp. The spiders retreated up the wall to the grass ceiling. "Don't worry, uncle, they don't bite," said Henrilienne. For a long while, I kept the flashlight aimed at the ceiling, but eventually I turned it off and fell sound asleep.

At the first hint of daylight I was awakened by the crowing of roosters, and shortly thereafter I heard a murmur outside the door. I put on my sandals and went out. Before me were dozens of men, women, and children in tattered clothes. Many of them had been part of the improvised procession around my mother's hut the night before.

"Good morning, everyone," I said.

"Good morning; how are you?" they asked in unison.

"Mwen pa pli mal, non [I'm not too bad]," I said, beaming. For the moment, it felt so good to be surrounded by my "relatives." This was in fact the closest I would ever come to my own birth family.

The people on my mother's side have so much love for me and can see that I am a part of their blood, I thought. Each person told me his or her name, and how he or she was related to me. I was gushing with internal pride.

"They call me Amelia. I am the child of the child of your late uncle on your grandmother's side," said a woman. "I come to see what you bring me," she added.

"I am the child of your late mother's niece on the side of your late grandfather," said a man holding a machete. I tried to picture in my mind an extended family tree. "I come to see what you bring me," he said, echoing the first woman. And so it went.

After listening to this chorus of introductions, I excused myself, went back in the hut, and took from my backpack two hundred US dollars' worth of Haitian currency. The wad was thick as a deck of cards. I went back outside. The people, their eyes big and bright with anticipation, charged forward, pushing each other aside.

As I distributed the money, I noticed that the shoes and wet clothes I had spread to dry on the cactus fence the night before were all missing. I assumed Henrilienne had brought them inside.

After I gave the last of the Haitian dollars to a great aunt, twice-removed on my mother's mother's side, I asked Henrilienne if she had brought my shoes and clothes inside.

"Non," she replied.

"Has anyone removed my shoes and clothes from the cactus fence?" I shouted to the crowd.

"Who could have done such a thing? Jean-Robert came to see us, and someone took his wet clothes and shoes from the fence. Se pa serye sa. Se meshanste [That's not fair. That's mean]," said Henrilienne. A collective murmur filled the air. Those who were genuinely upset crossed their arms, supporting their chin with the palm of their hand. I felt compassion and empathy because of their impoverished life, but no real connection to them as "family." To these people I was, understandably perhaps, little more than a rich foreigner.

Because I was bent on determining my true date of birth, I went to see Dwèt, my late mother's brother. He was in his yard sitting on a straw mat under a mango tree. He greeted me with a toothless grin.

"Good morning, nephew," he said. "How was your night?"

"Bonjou, uncle," I said. "My night was not too bad, thank you. But I'm curious. Are you able to remember my date of birth?" He thought for a moment.

"I know you were born during the mango season, probably

between June and August, but I can't recall the year," he said. Then he called his niece. "Henrilienne, take Alfrenold to see Mrs. Jo, the midwife. Mrs. Jo delivered almost everyone in Gran Hatte."

Henrilienne led me to a hilly trail, and we entered a small yard. Inside were a straw-roofed hut, a coconut tree, and a kitchen shack.

"Mrs. Jo," she said loudly.

"I am in the kitchen," answered a voice that was sweet, old, and rusty. We stood at the threshold and saw Mrs. Jo squatting at a tree-rock-stove and fanning the fire with her straw hat.

"Mrs. Jo, this is Alfrenold, the late Henrilia's son," said Henrilienne. Mrs. Jo looked up. Her eyes, teary from the smoke, were sunk deep in their sockets. A toothless grin spread across her wrinkled face.

"This is a miracle! Alfrenold, is that you? Oh, oh!" she said. Pushing down on her knees as if they were arm rests, the woman rose to look at me, shaking her head over and over. I reached for her hand, which felt almost skeletal.

"I've come to ask if you remember my date of birth." She thought for a moment.

"Oh yes, it was during the mango season. I don't remember the month. But your birth was easy. Some are very hard. Henrilia called you *Ti-blan* [Little white boy] when she first laid eyes on you. I cut your umbilical cord and babysat you many times. When you cried I pacified you with my own *tete*. You loved it," she said, palming her left breast. I smiled. "Wait! I'll show you something." She went into her hut and returned with a knife that was worn and old. "I cut your umbilical cord with this." And then, almost in the same breath, "Can you give me a little money, Alfrenold?"

"I don't have any more money. I gave it to my relatives. When I come back, I'll bring you something."

"Thank you," she said. As Henrilienne and I were heading back to my mother's hut, a young woman approached me.

"Mrs. Silencieux sent me to fetch you."

"Who's Mrs. Silencieux?" I asked.

Henrilienne responded, "She's your aunt, your late mother's sister." I was surprised and eager to meet her. We followed the woman a good distance, and then into a large yard. Sitting in the shade of a mango tree was a dark-complected, elderly woman smiling at me.

Her hair was tied up in a colorful scarf. I knew intuitively that this old woman resembled my own mother. For the first time, in that moment, I had a sense of my own mother's face.

"I am your aunt, Anacine. You still have that scar. I remember how upset your mama was the day you got cut by that corn leaf."

"Bonswa, ma tante," I said. *Tante* is the word for aunt.

"Bonswa, my child," she answered, and wrapped her arms around me. *Finally*, with this aunt, I felt a connection that I could not explain, even to myself. After I learned of my father's death, this was the one thing that I had been hoping for. I rested my head on her shoulder, closed my eyes, and breathed in the natural smell of her skin. I knew that this was as close as I would ever come to experiencing my mother's presence, to feel her long-ago love for me.

"Would you like a cup of milk?"

"Oui, ma tante. Mèsi, ma tante." I was neither hungry nor thirsty, but I wanted to partake of something from her house. She went into the kitchen shack and returned with a cup of hot milk. I took a sip.

"Ma tante, it's very sweet," I said.

"I put in extra sugar because I love you very much," she said, and I smiled. I took another sip, and then gave the rest of the milk to a little girl who had come into the yard.

Anacine and I sat down in the shade. I held her left hand, looking at its dark lines.

"Ma tante, do you know my date of birth?" She closed her eyes, trying to remember something that happened long ago to my mother.

"You were born during the mango season, between June and August. Earlier, during the coffee season, we saw that the *blan* went to Henrilia's house often. But when her stomach was big with you, he stopped seeing her. She loved you like the two eyes in her head." Tears welled up in my eyes.

"Do you know where my mother is buried?"

"I am an old woman. I don't remember so many things, but my son will know." With that she called out, "Rodrigue, Rodrigue."

A middle-aged man appeared in the door of the house next door. "This is your cousin Alfrenold, from across the sea. He wants to find my sister's grave."

"I will take him there, Mama."

I greeted my cousin and followed him on a long walk. Henrilienne stayed behind. He asked me many questions about the United States. I told him that there wasn't really any money in the streets.

Finally, we came to a small cemetery on a hillside overlooking a dry creek bed. Rodrigue stood beside an unpainted concrete tomb. In Haiti, the entire tomb is exposed, like a little house. "This is it," he said. The word *Henrilia* was hand-scrawled awkwardly across the face of the tomb. Neither the date of her birth, nor of her death, was written anywhere.

For the first time since age four I was physically close to my mother. So I spoke to her. "Good morning, Mama. This is me, Alfrenold, your son. I was given the name Bobby, and later Jean-Robert Cadet. I came to see you, and I can almost picture you in my mind. I think you look exactly like your sister, Anacine." I whispered all of this in Creole. My eyes were still puffy from having shed so many tears the day before, but I sobbed once again. "I love you, Mom. I love you." I said this in English.

"Why is there a bottle buried upside down in the tomb?" I asked Rodrigue.

"I think she liked cola, but I don't know what flavor," he said. I could feel myself disengaging from the whole experience. It was almost too much for me, so I wandered around the cemetery, looking at the other primitive crypts. One was quite small. Inside was a wooden box whose lid had been smashed in, and on the nearby ground lay a child's pink dress with white ruffles. I moved closer so I could see inside the box. It was empty. I called to Rodrigue and he came to where I was standing.

"There's no corpse in the box."

"It's been stolen."

"Why would someone steal the remains of a child?" I asked. Rodrigue looked at me strangely.

"To use in a *vodou* ceremony," he said.

"Why did they leave the dress on the ground?"

"Leaving the dress here was a part of the ritual."

I suddenly felt even more uncomfortable. "Okay, let's get out of here," I said. Unlike most Haitians, I had never established a relationship with the Vodou religion and its many strange rituals. Today

Vodou is regarded as a legitimate religion, like any other. But I held the American view. I didn't want to know any more than I already knew about it.

As we walked away from the cemetery, I turned back around. "Goodbye, Mama," I said. There were no more tears.

At my aunt's yard I saw about a dozen people, mostly men, waiting in the shade of the mango tree. Some were barefoot, with machetes in their hands. "Bonswa, blan," they said in unison.

"Bonswa," I said. "But I am not a *blan*," I added.

"Ah, your father was *blan*, so you're *blan*," said a man in his thirties, smiling. "Last night we heard that you came from across the sea. We live a good walk from here. We couldn't come any sooner. They call me Saurel. I am the child of the child of your late uncle, Simeus," he added. I shook his hand, and once again each person explained how he or she was related to me. Of course, some of them were only too willing to claim a relation to the "rich guy" from across the sea. I had no way of knowing who was telling the truth. At one point, my aunt called me into the kitchen hut.

"These people came to get money from you, because they know you came from across the sea. They didn't bring you anything. Tell them you have nothing to give them. Otherwise, they will not leave."

I was astonished. "But what could they have brought me?"

"Eggs! They have chickens," she said. My mind went back to my boyhood in Port-au-Prince. I remembered eggs as delicacies that Florence never shared with me until I came to the United States.

I approached the men under the mango tree.

"I don't have any more money. I am very sorry."

They didn't seem to be bothered. "When you return again, don't forget us," said another man. The crowd trickled out of my aunt's yard.

Late in the afternoon, I went to bathe in a creek not far from Anacine's home. When I got to the creek, I found several women scrubbing laundry in their underpants. They were topless. I cast my gaze skyward to avoid looking at their exposed breasts. Perhaps a healthy dose of American Puritanism had seeped into my subconscious.

"Bonswa, Mesdames," I said.

"Bonswa," they replied in unison. I could sense they were smiling at the crazy foreigner.

Farther up the creek and out of sight, I climbed naked into the flowing steam. Unlike the river, this water, running from the mountainside, was cold and clear. I relished the experience. I understood that even something as simple as bathing outdoors was connecting me—physically and symbolically—to my roots in Haiti. Certainly, my mother had scrubbed my clothes, and me, near this very spot. I understood what I was engaging in my own ritual, a kind of adult baptism.

When I returned to my aunt's yard, I watched two boys, each using a pestle to husk rice in a mortar, like synchronized drummers hitting the same spot on their drums. Familiar smells of food wafted from the kitchen shack. I was intoxicated by the smell. Before sundown, Anacine served *lalo* (a spinachlike leafy vegetable), white rice, and red bean sauce. I found much comfort in the meal. Perhaps I had tasted this same food in my mother's milk, or when I was a toddler. After dinner I sat beside Anacine under the mango tree, holding her hand.

"Was my mother older or younger than you?"

"She was younger. Dwèt is the oldest."

"Was she darker than you?"

"She was."

"How did she die?"

"She had pain in her belly."

"Do you know how I got to Port-au-Prince?"

She thought for a moment. "After Henrilia died, someone took you to *blan* Philippe at the factory. He was about to leave for Port-au-Prince. He did leave and he took you with him. We believed he would take care of you, his own flesh."

I looked at her beautiful hands. "You have long fingers," I said. She chuckled.

"You're no longer Haitian with that accent of yours. You're a *blan* now."

"I am still Haitian."

"A Haitian would never say, 'You have long fingers.'"

"Why?" I asked, bewildered.

"Telling someone she has long fingers is like calling her a thief." I laughed heartily, and Anacine joined me. I probably had heard this expression as a child, but I had forgotten it.

"Do people from Port-au-Prince come here looking for children to stay with them?"

"*Non*, we are too far away, but I do know one woman who sent her daughter to Port-au-Prince to stay with someone."

"Is she being treated well?"

"I don't know. We never know these things."

"You are aware that most children like me who are taken to Port-au-Prince by strangers become slaves, no?"

"I know about this. I've seen some of them. I am glad your father took you to Port-au-Prince." I could have told her about my childhood, but there was no point. She saw only the good thing. I had been sent to America.

At bedtime my aunt lit a lamp on a small table and placed a plastic bucket beside my bed. We said our sweet "bonswas." As I lay down to sleep I began to sweat profusely as heat radiated down from the tin roof. The room felt hotter than any I had slept in since leaving Haiti. Every hour, a mechanical bird sprang out of a German cuckoo clock and cuckooed several times, while my aunt slept soundly in the next room. At sunrise, after very little sleep, I heard roosters crowing from treetops near and far. I fell asleep once again, but the strong aroma of brewing coffee awakened me for good. It was five o'clock, almost daylight. I walked outside with my toothbrush and paste. Brushing my teeth behind the house, I became aware, in a kind of epiphany, how the substance of my life had changed, down to the smallest details and rituals. Thirty years earlier I had used my finger and wet ashes to clean my teeth.

"Bonjou, ma tante," I said, as I walked back into the house.

"Bonjou, nephew." We grinned at one another, so happy to be family again. Coffee was served. Anacine had added lots of sugar in my cup. I thanked her for this little gesture of love. Anacine was the only relative who didn't ask me for money. I promised her there would be some the next time I came to Haiti.

That Sunday morning, I said good-bye to everyone in the vicinity and headed down the road toward Petite Rivière in order to catch the bus back to Port-au-Prince. As always, well-dressed folks were walking to church. Watching them struggle through the rushing water, I found myself again feeling very sorry for them, especially the women. *If only there were a bridge*, I thought. I snapped a picture of their crossing with a camera I carried in my backpack. Then I removed my sandals and pants and began fording the river myself. Once again, the chill of the mountain water made me gasp. I stepped on a slippery rock and went down, but still managed to hold my backpack in the air. The people laughed at me, and I shared in their laughter. Reaching the river bank, I dried myself as best I could, got dressed, and continued walking.

Because it was still early, I went to visit Fort Crête-à-Pierrot, where the hero Toussaint L'Ouverture had fought Napoleon's troops in 1802 during the struggle to end slavery and secure Haiti's independence from the French. Standing at the fort's entrance and looking in the yard, I saw goats and donkeys grazing on the shrubs. A man was defecating beside some rusted cannons that were lying on the ground. To me, this seemed like an insult to our national history. *Should I say something to this man?* I wondered. Fortunately, I remembered that I was in Haiti. This was the way things were, and I was reacting like an American.

Heading toward the market bus stop, I saw a group of boys kicking a dilapidated basketball in a dusty field. I stopped to see them play. I remembered the first time I had watched a basketball game in America. To this day I remember asking myself: *Why don't they kick and head the ball into the basket?* Until I fell in love with American football, I always thought that soccer was the only sport worth playing.

I noticed that only three out of the twelve boys wore shirts, none shoes. And one player was stark naked. When the ball went out of bounds near where I stood, I picked it up. It was stuffed with leaves and laced up like a shoe. The naked player came toward me, and I threw the ball to him.

"Mèsi," he said.

"Where are your clothes?" I couldn't resist asking.

"My mama's washing them. I didn't want to miss the game," he said, happily. "Lucky kid," I thought and left. For me, his luck was in having a mother.

The bus arrived, and I climbed aboard for the long ride to Port-au-Prince. The next morning, I caught my flight back to Miami, then on to Cincinnati.

Cindy hugged me as I came in the door. "How was your trip?"

"I didn't get to see my father. He died last year," I said.

Cindy could feel my disappointment. "I'm so sorry, Jean." she said.

"But I found my mother's relatives, including her sister, my aunt Anacine." I told her about Anacine always putting extra sugar in my coffee, and what that gesture meant to me. "*And* . . . I found out when I was born. More or less."

"When?" Cindy asked.

"During the mango season, between June and August," I said. "I guess that makes me six months older than I am. Or maybe six months younger."

"We're still going to celebrate your birthday in February," Cindy said. "It will be too confusing for the children if we switch." Of course she was right, and what difference did it make?

The trip had been a mixed bag, but definitely worth doing.

"I am so proud of you, Jean," Cindy beamed. "You faced a very painful history head-on. I just wish you had been able to see your father. He would have been so impressed."

"Maybe he would," I said. "Maybe."

After I processed my photos from the trip, I placed the picture of the women wading across the Estère on the nightstand next to my bed. Each night, before I fell asleep, I looked at the photograph. And each night I felt an urge to do something about that situation.

A month after returning to Cincinnati, I received a letter, post-marked Port-au-Prince. The sender's name was on the envelope: "Jerome Laroche," the son of Madame Laroche. I remembered him as a boy standing next to his sister in the doorway, watching and laughing as his mother beat me. I could still see his face, laughing as I screamed in pain. I opened the letter.

Dear Sir:

Two months ago, I was at the Miami International Airport, waiting for a flight to Port-au-Prince. I had been in Geneva, Switzerland, attending a conference on child slavery. I picked up a newspaper that someone had left in the chair next to me and saw an article about your book, *Restavec*. I took the newspaper home, and with my limited English, I thought that you might be Bobby, a boy who lived with my family about thirty years ago. Bobby was

eventually sent to New York. I found your address on line and decided to contact you. Are you that Bobby? If not, I am sorry for the inconvenience. But if you are, I'd like to stay in touch with you via e-mail.
Sincerely,
Jerome Laroche

He had included his e-mail address, and so I replied to him that day.

Dear Jerome:
Yes, I am Bobby, and glad to hear from you. How are you and your family? Please tell me more about the conference on child slavery. Hope to hear from you soon,
Bobby

In Jerome's reply the following day, he said that his mother had died of cancer ten years ago. He was married, with two boys, aged 13 and 15. He had studied civil engineering and had come to America in the mid-1980s. He had worked part-time as a security guard in a department store for a week, and then returned to live in Haiti. He was now employed by Foyer Maurice Sixto, a literacy center for children in domestic servitude. The center was financed by Terre des Hommes, a nongovernment organization based in Geneva, Switzerland.

Jerome had sent a copy of my book to Doris Charollais, president of Terre Des Homes, who would later play a key role in getting it published in French.

Early in the summer, a letter arrived from the United Nations in Geneva, Switzerland, inviting me to speak on behalf of Haiti's children in *restavek* and be part of a Working Group on Contemporary Forms of Slavery.

It was clear to Cindy and me that I was moving into a new role as a kind of ambassador representing child slaves in Haiti. I recalled that day, standing in the dean's office at the University of Southern Florida, when I first wanted to be "an ambassador."

A project that had started as an ambiguous but sincere urge to tell my life story to our only son appeared to be morphing into a narrative much larger than me or my family, larger even than the *Restavec* book. I still find it hard to believe that, in spite of the pain-filled process of first living it, and then of writing it down, my childhood memoir was becoming a kind of allegory about all Haitian child slaves, all those who are alive at this very moment, abused in this moment, unloved in this moment, forgotten, invisible, hundreds of thousands of them, suffering in ways the world can't imagine, right now, as you read these words.

The same thing may be true of *A Stone of Hope*, which describes my post-*restavek* life in the United States. This is obviously a very individualized account, in ways that are unique to me. Nonetheless I believe it is a story that mirrors psychologically the lives of most former *restaveks*, teenagers and adults who are attempting to make their way in a world they only partly comprehend, a world most of us call "normal," but which former slaves are ill-equipped to deal with. Whether they are living in the United States, Canada, Europe, or in Haiti still, each of these must confront his or her world, day after day, without ever having been shown *how to be, how to act, how to live*, without—during their most precious and formative years—ever having been shown even a dollop of respect, without having been "tamed" and taught by the power of love.

My first thought, as Cindy read the letter, turned toward the one who had inspired this moment: our son. "You know, Cindy, I think I would like to take Adam with me to Geneva," I said.

Cindy considered it for a brief moment. "That would be incredible, Jean." She beamed. "What a thrill for him."

In my e-mail reply to the invitation, I asked if Adam could accompany me. The response was positive and warm. He was more than welcome to come along.

When we arrived in Geneva, Doris Charollais and Myriam Riunaud greeted us warmly with three kisses on the cheeks. Both were in their mid-fifties. Myriam and her husband, Jean-Pierre, had a house in an upscale neighborhood in a small town in France near the Swiss border. I shared a room at the Riunauds' house with Adam. He stayed with either Doris or Myriam during the daytime while I attended various conferences on child slavery at the United Nations.

The room where I delivered my speech to the UN reminded me

of a picture from my high school history textbook. Each panelist was identified by a tag that bore his country's name. The desks were on raised platforms and equipped with microphones and headsets. In a small room with glass walls were interpreters who simultaneously translated the speeches. Sitting in that room, I saw my role even more clearly. Yes, in a very real way, I was a kind of ambassador, representing 300,000 *restavek* children, a group almost large enough to form a small nation. I felt humbled and proud to assume this role. I found myself wishing that some of my inspiring high school teachers and university professors could be here with me.

When my time came to speak, I was introduced by a man reading a concise abridgement of my life as a former child domestic slave who had written of his experiences in an "inspiring memoir" entitled *Restavec.* I was generously applauded.

"Good afternoon, ladies and gentlemen and distinguished guests. I am Jean-Robert Cadet, and I would like to thank the High Commissioner for Human Rights for the opportunity to take part in this twenty-fifth session of the Working Group on Contemporary Forms of Slavery.

"Since Haitian independence, the affluent have reintroduced slavery using children of the very poor as domestic slaves. *Restaveks* are treated worse than slaves, because they don't cost anything and their supply seems inexhaustible . . ."

After my speech, I was warmly applauded once again. Some in the group gave me a standing ovation. At this point, the Haitian ambassador got up to deliver what amounted to a rebuttal.

"My government lacks the financial resources to eliminate the *restavek* system," he began, "because it is too ingrained into the social fabric of Haiti . . ." He spoke these words to what was clearly an incredulous audience. There was no applause after the ambassador's speech. As the session ended, the audience gathered around me, extending formal and informal good wishes. Even the Haitian ambassador came and shook my hand.

"I am glad to meet you, Jean-Robert, and my heart was touched by your book," he said in French.

"Thank you, Mr. Ambassador. I am happy to meet you, too," I replied.

A tall, slim, and extremely beautiful woman, draped in a lavender silk shawl, approached me. I thought she might have been Ethiopian.

"Mr. Cadet, I believe you were chosen by God to speak for Haiti's *restaveks*," she said.

"God must have chosen the wrong speaker," I responded, "because those children are still in slavery. They don't have much time. They're growing up fast. Something must be done now. Universal education can free these children from servitude. The world has the resources to make it happen."

"Be patient, Mr. Cadet. You had my full attention," she said. The woman's words were encouraging, but I still have trouble seeing myself as having been chosen by God. Unless God has chosen me the way he picked Job.

At the end of September 2000, I stopped teaching to advocate nationally and internationally for the demise of child slavery.

I received a call from Kansas senator Sam Brownback's secretary. She said the senator would like to invite me to address the United States Senate Foreign Relations Committee about child slavery in Haiti. She asked that I write a forty-minute speech and mail a copy of it to her. She further explained that my travel expenses and lodging would not be covered.

With my being out of work, I knew this trip would be an added burden for our family. Nonetheless, Cindy encouraged me to do it. We were thrilled to think that the United States government might pressure Haiti's government to create and enforce laws against child slavery. I worked hard on the speech. The text was approved, and at the designated time I flew to our nation's capital.

Even more than in Geneva, I was nervous about my presentation. As soon as I entered the room where the committee would hear my speech, I came face-to-face with Senator Edward Kennedy of Massachusetts. I could not believe my eyes. I recalled trying to persuade René, my boyhood friend, that President Kennedy had been a real person. Now I was standing in front of his brother.

"Good morning, Senator Kennedy," I said, and shook his hand, somewhat vigorously. In a way, I felt as if I were shaking hands with JFK himself, who remains, even now, my greatest hero.

"Good morning, young man, how are you today?" he asked.

"Fine, thank you, sir," I said. "I am here to speak about child slavery in Haiti," I added.

"Good luck to you," he said. As he walked away, I smiled at the thought of how we Haitians had pictured his late brother personally packing up and sending off secondhand clothes to Haiti from the White House.

In the room where I spoke, I shared a table with Kevin Bales of the organization called Free the Slaves. Facing us were Senators Jessie Helms of North Carolina and Sam Brownback of Kansas. My speech was similar to the one I had given at the United Nations in Geneva, but its conclusion had to be different:

"I believe it is the moral obligation of this great nation to help Haiti solve the *restavek* problem. The United States government has the resources and the means, and Haiti is a neighbor only 600 miles from our Florida shores. In 1994, you sent troops to restore President Aristide, who had been deposed, and to give hope to a people who are accustomed to living under the iron fist of dictators, but that democracy will never take hold as long as 10 percent of Haiti's children are still living in slavery."

I was hopeful that the US government would soon address the issue of child slavery with the government of Haiti. I guess I had forgotten the US government's long, abusive history in Haiti, a history built on maintaining the status quo. I also could not know that the United States, which had deposed President Aristide once, would soon do so yet again.

Weeks after my speech, I sent a letter to Senator Sam Brownback's office asking that foreign aid to Haiti be linked to education and the elimination of child slavery; otherwise, I repeated, democracy would never have a chance to grow. He did not reply. My request was apparently ignored.

Soon thereafter, I received a call from one of the production assistants with the CBS news program *60 Minutes*. The caller informed me that the show's producer had read my book and was interested in doing a program on *restaveks*. I was thrilled, thinking that such an important program might go a long way toward compelling Washington to push Haiti to protect its most vulnerable children and prepare a plan for mandatory education.

"When would they like to leave for Haiti?" I asked, presumptuously.

"Well, we've learned that some Haitians in New York and Miami are keeping slave children in their homes. We thought perhaps you'd know some of them. We would not show their faces if they cooperate." I could not believe my ears.

"Why don't we go to Haiti?" I asked.

"I don't think the American audience would be very interested in child slavery that is going on in Haiti."

"If I knew that a child was being kept in slavery in America, I would call the FBI, not *60 Minutes*," I said. She never called me back. (It would be ten years later, in the period following the earthquake, that *60 Minutes* would cover the *restavek* situation, and me, on the ground in Haiti.) A few days after my conversation with the *60 Minutes* staffer, a woman from ABC's *20/20* called. When she mentioned going to Haiti to do a program on *restaveks*, I was much more hopeful.

"This is something we're thinking of doing in the next couple of months. Would you be willing to accompany us to Haiti?" she asked.

"Yes, definitely. I want to do everything possible to bring this child slavery business into public view," I said.

"We'll set up a date to meet in New York next month. I'll stay in touch by e-mail," she said. My hope was that, after Americans viewed the proposed program, they would write to their representatives in Washington, demanding that economic aid to Haiti be linked to universal education and to the elimination of child slavery.

CHAPTER 15

Not long after the initial contact with *20/20*, I received a call at home from Jerome Laroche, whose family I had lived with briefly as a child. He had moved to the United States once again. He said he was ill and staying with a distant relative who lived in Queens, New York. Over the previous months, Jerome and I had slowly moved toward a kind of friendship through phone calls and e-mails. I told Jerome that I was scheduled to come to New York in a few weeks for a meeting with the producers of *20/20*. I told him I would stop by for a visit at that time.

When I arrived at LaGuardia Airport, a chauffeured limousine took me to the ABC building. Two women and a man who were waiting in the lobby greeted me warmly. They were writers and producers of the news show. Because it was noontime, we went to lunch at a trendy restaurant, where we discussed, in some detail, their ideas for the project as well as the trip to Haiti.

"Everything is set, but the plan has to be approved by the executive producer, the man upstairs. He's like God," said the writer. *If he's like God, then he'll approve the trip*, I thought. My hosts promised to call me as soon as "the man upstairs gives it a go."

After lunch we drove back to the ABC building. My hosts went in and the driver dropped me at my hotel. That was that.

Later the same day, I phoned Jerome and said I would be coming to see him. He sounded very happy. The following day I took a taxi to Jerome's apartment in Queens. I knocked on the door, anxious to see my old "friend."

Although it had been many years since we had been together, I recognized the man who answered the door. He was tall for a Haitian and thin, with a large, distended belly. He sported a close-cropped beard. We shook hands and smiled at each other.

"Bobby, welcome, come in. It's been a long time," he said. I was immediately conscious of the fact that I was here in this house as Jerome's *equal*. The small living room had been furnished with a brown velvet couch and a matching chair, both covered in clear plastic. On the wall was a large gilded portrait of the Sacred Heart of Jesus in a gold frame. A giant-screen TV stood against the opposite wall.

"Sit down, Bobby," said Jerome, wincing in pain. "It's so good to see you again." His command of English was weak, so we spoke in Creole.

"What is the diagnosis?"

"I don't know yet. I need to have more tests."

"Did you go to a hospital in Haiti?"

Jerome chuckled. "In Haiti, people go to hospitals to die. Haiti is not really a country, Bobby. But you know that."

"So, you think Haiti got its independence too early?" I asked. He laughed again.

"That's a question I'm not smart enough to answer. Slavery was a very cruel institution, you know."

I stared at him. *Indeed I know, Jerome.* I knew my thought was an accusation.

"But I'm amazed at you, Bobby. How long did it take you to learn English well enough to have written a book?"

"I am still learning English, but I've had much more trouble trying to figure out the American mindset. My cultural faux pas are rarely forgiven. I really can't understand white people, Jerome, and most can't understand me. They can be so strange, depending on which state they're from. They can also be kind, but I think they're obsessed with sex and race."

"I always thought the *blans* were more evolved in their thinking," he said. "Especially in the educational sphere."

"I thought so, too. It's hard to believe whites made it to the moon."
We both laughed. "I once told a female high school student she was
beautiful, and her parents had her removed from my class. I swear I
will never understand this crazy culture. You're not even allowed to
kill a chicken in your own backyard in this country."

Jerome laughed.

"Who's going to try that?"

"Me, I tried. I did it."

"No, Bobby. You didn't?"

"It was a guinea fowl. You know how delicious they are. Before I
killed it, a white woman came out of her apartment and stroked it
like a puppy." Jerome exploded in laughter and slid off the couch.
Sitting on the floor, he took a deep, painful breath. I helped him
back onto the couch. We both were perspiring from all the laughter.
It had been many years since I had engaged with anyone who knew
both my background and my past. I felt so much at ease.

"Finish the story," he said.

"No, I don't want you to aggravate your condition," I said.

"I don't care. I want to hear what happened next," he begged.

I told him how the police came and couldn't figure the whole
thing out. That started him laughing and grimacing once again.

We settled into reminiscing about everything in Haiti, except
the thing that had lurked for so long in the back of my mind: those
beatings I had received from his mother. I wanted to know how he
could have laughed at something so horrible. Luckily, Jerome's host,
a Haitian woman in her thirties, came into the house wearing a white
uniform. She worked as a nurse's aide. We chatted briefly in Creole
before she disappeared into her bedroom.

Jerome got up from the couch. I watched him wince in pain,
holding his lower back with both hands, as he tried to keep his balance. Moaning like a woman in labor, he led me into the kitchen.
The sink was piled high with dirty dishes. Tiny roaches were crawling across the cluttered countertop.

I helped Jerome wash a few plates and silverware. He loaded the
plates with cabbage stew and some rice and beans that were sitting in pots on the stove. Everything was cold. He opened a small
microwave oven. I cringed to see it. Inside, it was coated with layers

of dried food. I heated the plates one at a time, and we sat down to lunch. Jerome lowered his head to eat. I thought it strange that he barely looked at me. Was he ashamed, perhaps, remembering that in Haiti I was not permitted at his family's table? More than likely, I was simply *hoping* that he would remember, and maybe feel some shame. Finally, I broke the awkward silence, asking about his sons. He told me their names and ages, but didn't say much about them.

So I talked about my kids: Katrina's academic successes and Adam's athletic skills, all the sports we played together—soccer, American football, basketball, tennis, golf, and baseball. I was proud of my kids. I didn't mind boring him with stories about their accomplishments.

That night, rather than return to my hotel, I slept on the couch in the living room.

The following morning, Jerome asked me to accompany him on a trip to the hospital for tests. His host had told him which bus to take into town. He received the test results that same morning. They showed that he had renal cancer, and probably needed a bone marrow and kidney transplant. When I explained Jerome's financial situation to the hospital administrator, she suggested that he apply for Social Security benefits, provided that he had worked in the United States legally.

Because Jerome had mentioned in his letter that he had worked as a security guard in a New York department store, I took him to the Social Security building there in Queens. As I walked in, I had that feeling of déjà vu. The office was similar to the one where Mr. Rabinowitz had sent me to get public assistance. I approached a woman behind a glass window.

"Good afternoon. I am here to help my friend apply for Social Security benefits. He doesn't speak English very well," I said.

"What's his Social Security number?" she asked. I handed her Jerome's card, and she pulled out his computer record. It showed that Jerome had paid a total of $2.35 in Social Security taxes in 1985.

"Where have you been all these years?" she asked. Jerome shot a glance at me, and I translated the clerk's question for him.

"In Haiti," he replied.

"In spite of his short work record, your friend is qualified for benefits, provided that he's not employed and has no assets," she said, and gave me a form to fill out.

"He has nothing. He'll be living with me in Cincinnati," I said, as I began filling out Jerome's application. I could see that Jerome understood what I had said to the clerk. His eyes widened.

I had told Cindy, as I was preparing for this trip, that I might invite Jerome to come live with us, since he was without family in the States. Clearly the woman he was staying with seemed overwhelmed with her own life and responsibilities.

"Sure," Cindy had said, "We'll figure it out if we have to." As always, she was gracious and generous.

A month later, Jerome arrived in Cincinnati. We gave Adam's bedroom to Jerome. I transformed a small office space into a room for the nine-year-old. I told him he could "camp out" while my old friend was with us. Adam found the situation—and our new housemate—an exciting change.

Jerome was accepted for treatment at Jewish Hospital, a few miles from our home. He continued with a dialysis program for months afterward. During one of his hospital visits for a series of tests, I told the attending physician that I was willing to give Jerome a kidney. He explained that Jerome's cancer would have to be in remission for five years before he could receive a kidney transplant. In the meantime, we were told, they would try a bone marrow transplant.

Jerome understood only a few words that I had spoken to the doctor. "What did you tell him?" he asked.

"I said I want to give you a kidney," I responded in Creole. Jerome looked at me and then lowered his head. His lips quivered and tears rolled down his face.

"Thank you, Bobby." His voice cracked.

"You'd do the same for me," I said.

Jerome's treatment began a few weeks later, following more tests. I filled out a number of legal forms, accepting full responsibility for him.

During this period, I received an e-mail from *20/20*. It read: "Dear Mr. Cadet, the trip to film in Haiti was not approved. Good luck on all your future endeavors, Bill." I was disappointed. "Well, I guess their 'man upstairs' doesn't feel that child slavery in Haiti is worth his effort," I said to Cindy.

"Don't be discouraged," she responded. "There will be other opportunities."

Several weeks before Jerome's scheduled bone marrow transplant, I went to Haiti to deliver a bunch of clothes and supplies I had collected for *restavek* children being schooled at the Foyer Maurice Sixto, the literacy center where Jerome had been working. This trip would also enable me to contact Jerome's family and carefully lay out his very serious condition and the terms for his treatment. My plane arrived late in the afternoon, and Jerome's sister, Marie-Claire, picked me up at the airport. She was driving a fancy Mitsubishi SUV.

"You're a godsend, Bobby," she said in French. "Thank you for taking care of my brother." She was fighting back tears.

"Jerome is doing well," I explained. "He will soon receive a bone marrow transplant. I offered him a kidney, but I imagine you'd rather give him one of yours," I said, using Creole instead of French.

"Oh, Jesus, yes. Thank you," she cried.

"The doctor said your brother will need to wait five years after the bone marrow transplant to receive a new kidney," I said.

As we approached her two-story, yellow and white cinderblock house, she honked her horn. The iron gate slid open. She drove in and parked in front of the porch. As I removed my luggage from the car, I saw a girl in a dirty, woman-sized dress pushing the gate shut. Then the girl went into a small, windowless room beside the house. *Oh my God*, I thought, *Jerome's sister has a restavek*. I was incredulous. No, I was beyond incredulous.

On the porch sat Jerome's father in a rocking chair. He looked thin and frail. As we shook hands, a toothless grin spread across his face. He smelled like urine. A boy and a girl came out of the house. Marie-Claire introduced me to her children. Maida, the daughter, kissed me on the cheek. I shook Marc's hand.

I stepped into a spacious kitchen with modern appliances and a large table.

"Make yourself at home," said Marie-Claire. I put down my bag.

"Celita," she yelled. Suddenly the girl appeared. Marie-Claire did not even think of introducing us. I made eye contact with the girl and smiled. She didn't respond. Haitians rarely smile at *restaveks*.

"Take the valise of the Monsieur upstairs and put it in Monsieur Marc's room," ordered Marie-Claire in Creole. "Oui," came the response. Always "Oui."

This is unbelievable, I thought. *All these years, nothing has changed.*

"Are you hungry?" she asked me in French.

"Yes, I'll eat something," I replied in Creole. I walked out onto the porch, where—through a kitchen window—I watched Celita setting the table. I felt like some being from another planet who was witnessing a grotesque cultural phenomenon. Yet everything about it was as familiar to me as my face in the mirror. Aware that the situation before my eyes was repeating itself all over Port-au-Prince and in many other places around Haiti, I felt hopeless and helpless. My advocacy work in the United States, meager as it was, seemed almost pointless. These were basically good people who were oblivious to what they were doing to this innocent child. Or maybe they simply didn't care.

Soon Marie-Claire called everyone in for a spaghetti dinner. Her husband, Samuel, had come downstairs and we were politely introduced. Right after we sat down, she launched into a chorus of gratitude.

"Thank you, Bobby, for everything you're doing for Jerome. What would I have done without you, my brother?" Marie-Claire gushed. I felt uncomfortable with her praise and even more uncomfortable to see Celita bringing water and food to a table with no place set for her. Marie-Claire seemed to have no recollection that her family's dinner table had been off limits to me when I was the resident slave child in her mother's house. My insides were boiling. I could hardly chew my food. In my mind I screamed, "Are you people some kind of parasites? Can't you see your own children in this little girl?"

By late evening, we all sat on the porch continuing the discussion about Jerome and his cancer treatment. I noticed Celita moving alongside the house with a dress in her hand, and then I heard water splashing on the cement. I knew she was taking a bath in the dark beside the reservoir. The family bathroom was off-limits to her, of course.

"Celita, did you feed the dog?" yelled Marie-Claire.

"Oui, ma tante [my aunt]," answered Celita.

"Celita, when you're done taking your bath, go fetch my comb and rollers," ordered Marie-Claire.

"Oui, ma tante," said Celita, robotically.

Maida sat passively watching her mother fuss with her hair. I felt helpless. *Both of these girls,* I thought, *one privileged, and one abused, are the victims here.* Moments later, Celita went upstairs and returned with a shoebox and handed it to Marie-Claire. Of course, the woman didn't bother to thank the girl, who disappeared into a dark corner of the house. I couldn't see her, but I knew that she was standing within the sound of our voices.

"Does it snow in Ohio?" Maida asked.

"Yes, but not as much as in New York," I said.

I wanted to ask Celita to sit with us. Marie-Claire would have reluctantly agreed to my request, but I was certain Celita would feel out of place, and there was no way to predict how Marie-Claire might treat her after I left.

The lights went out because of a blackout, a regular occurrence in Port-au-Prince. A generator from a house across the street came on, sounding like a tractor. Samuel flicked a special switch that turned on the lights, now powered by six storage batteries kept in a wooden box on the porch. At ten o'clock the family retired upstairs, leaving the girl to gather the cushions from the chairs and bring them inside. I stayed behind and helped her. "Mèsi," she said, afraid to make eye contact with me.

Her final task finished, Celita disappeared into that hot windowless cinder block box outside. I, Jean-Robert, the man, lay wakefully in a small bed in Marc's room. The *restavek* boy, Bobby, still alive somewhere inside me, finally fell asleep under the kitchen table.

Early the next morning, the scraping sounds of a broom on concrete awakened me. I looked at my watch. It was five o'clock. I got out of bed, looked down from the balcony, and saw Celita sweeping the yard in the gray, predawn light. Of course, everyone else was still in bed. The girl didn't see me where I was standing, and I couldn't stop watching her. The situational symbolism was obvious. I was observing myself. She was me.

After cleaning up the dog's mess, Celita washed the car. Then she drew water from the reservoir and carried it upstairs on her head in a bucket. I heard her flush the toilet and pour water in the bathtub.

When I came down for coffee, Celita was setting the table for breakfast. As everyone ate, the child stood near the doorway with her hands behind her back, waiting for requests. I had no appetite. After breakfast Celita cleared the table and carried water from the reservoir to the kitchen sink. She then washed dishes.

After breakfast, with no one around, I drew a bucket of water from the reservoir and started up the stairs toward the bathroom, only to meet Samuel coming down.

"Don't do that, Bobby. Celita will fetch your water. Where's Celita?" he yelled.

"Plait-il," answered Celita, who quickly appeared at the foot of the steps.

"That's all right. I am much stronger than Celita," I said, hoping he'd understand that men shouldn't allow little girls to carry their load. Celita reached for the bucket.

"That's okay," I said, and continued up the stairs.

The family had some business to do in town. When Samuel, Maida, and Marie-Claire got in the car to leave, Celita was there to open the gate. They drove off, and the young girl pulled the gate shut. Marc had already left for school.

After I got dressed, I saw Celita in Marie Claire's room making the bed. On the floor was a pail of water and a rag. I knew that Celita would be using these to wash the floor of every room, on her hands and knees. I walked into the room. Celita stopped sweeping and lowered her head.

"How old are you, Celita?" I asked in Creole. She hesitated. I raised her chin to make eye contact.

"Thirteen," she said, but she looked ten or eleven.

"Where's your mother?" I asked.

"In Saint Marc," she said.

"How long have you been staying here?"

"Maybe two years," she said. I recognized the scars on her arms from the tip of a *rigwaz*. My own had faded, but not disappeared. I gave Celita a hug. Tears welled up in my eyes.

"Hug me back," I whispered. "Please." She raised her arms slowly and wrapped them around my waist, and I held her head to my chest. Then I looked at her and smiled. She put her hand over her mouth to keep from smiling.

"You're beautiful. I love you very much. Be strong. You and I are the same. When I was a boy, I stayed in grown-ups' homes. I did everything you're doing now. Do you understand?"

"Oui," she said. Her face was full of life. I handed her twenty dollars. Her eyes widened in disbelief.

"Where could you hide this money?"

"In a cinder block," she said. I recalled that I, too, had hidden my stolen coins in such places when I had been in her situation. I nodded my blessing. She smiled. That smile seemed almost radiant. She put the money in the pocket of her baggy dress and walked outside.

I nosed about the kitchen, looking for the dreaded *rigwaz*, intended of course for one small person in the house. I found it, put the whip under my shirt, walked upstairs, and placed it in my suitcase under my clothes, certain of one thing: They would know who took it. And maybe they would be hesitant about replacing it.

Two days later, Marie-Claire drove me to the airport. She tried to make small talk. My responses were brief, but polite.

As I waited for the flight back to Cincinnati, I found myself still reeling with anger at the situation I had witnessed in the home of Jerome's sister. Why hadn't he told me? By now the anger had turned inward and was mixed with guilt. Why hadn't I confronted Marie-Claire head-on for robbing Celita of her childhood? I had been advocating for eliminating child slavery on a national stage in the United States, and even internationally, in Geneva. But there in my native country, confronted with the real thing, I had been tongue-tied, speechless, emasculated in a way. I had found myself unable to use my considerable persuasive abilities on behalf of one small human being. My rationalization, that by confronting the adults I might have made things worse for the child, no longer convinced me. The fact was: with a *restavek* child staring me in the face, I had blown it.

Not long after returning to Cincinnati, I went to see Jerome at the hospital and found him attached to a dialysis machine.

"How is Haiti?" asked Jerome.

"I don't know. It's not yet a country," I said. Jerome laughed.

I didn't waste a moment in confronting him with the reality that had made my trip almost hellish. "Did you know that Marie-Claire has a thirteen year-old *ti-moun* [child] to carry the load for her entire family?" I asked.

"No, Bobby, I didn't know that," he said.

"Would you have even noticed this child if she had served you water in your sister's house?" I asked.

"Believe me, Bobby. I never saw a *restavek* in her house when I was there." I'm sure he could see that I didn't believe him.

"I'll write to Marie-Claire about it. I promise," he said. A few days later, shortly before he received his bone marrow transplant, Jerome handed me a letter addressed to his sister to mail.

"Can you put postage on this?" he asked, searching my eyes.

After the transplant, Jerome received numerous doses of radiation. I thought they made him smell like creamed corn. I visited Jerome twice a day and spent the night occasionally on a couch in his room. I walked with him daily up and down the hallways of the cancer unit.

When Jerome came home from the hospital, he resumed his dialysis at the clinic, and Social Security continued to provide him with transportation. Weeks later, a copy of Jerome's hospital bill arrived in the mail. He showed it to me. Over a half-million dollars had been paid by Social Security to cover the cost of treating his cancer and dialysis. I told Jerome that he was lucky that a computer, rather than a person, had examined his Social Security record.

After eleven months as a guest in our home, Jerome left for Florida. We stayed in touch by e-mail. Five years after his bone marrow transplant, I learned of his death. His doctor had correctly predicted how long he would live.

Early in 2001, not long after Jerome's departure, I made what amounted to a life-changing move. Unlike so many other such decisions, this one was not made impulsively. I decided to begin the complicated task of setting up a nonprofit foundation. In this way, I hoped to be able to continue my *restavek* advocacy work in a more cost-effective way. This was very new territory for me, requiring a great deal of research and what might best be termed "sweat equity." At one point I chose a name for the nascent foundation: Free the *Restavec* Children, Inc. I listed myself, my wife, Cindy Cadet, and Jerome Laroche as officers. The Ohio Secretary of State's office granted the foundation nonprofit status in May of that year. An existing nonprofit called Free the Slaves, out of Washington, DC, offered to issue tax-exempt receipts, on our behalf, to potential donors. With this arrangement, I hoped to be able to travel to Haiti and work with on-the-ground organizations without relying exclusively on my family's resources. Since I was no longer teaching, Cindy was our lone provider.

That summer, something happened that helped confirm the decision to establish our nonprofit foundation.

The previous fall, I had agreed to an interview for an article that would appear in a major religious magazine. I thought very little of it at the time. At one point they sent a photographer to do some pictures, and I gave them a few of my own photos from Haiti. Nothing happened for many months. Then, in early July, several copies of the latest *St. Anthony Messenger* arrived in our mail. I was that month's cover story for the magazine. I learned that it was the largest circulating Catholic magazine in the country. The article ran five pages. After reading it, I imagined that hundreds of Catholics would start sending letters to the Pope, asking him to address the issue of child slavery in Haiti, a predominantly Catholic country.

I'm not certain whether any such letters were sent, but within days of the magazine's arrival, I began receiving letters from the magazine's subscribers, most containing small donations. One was for five hundred dollars! I answered each letter, expressing my gratitude and promising to keep my new donors updated on the *restavek* issue. The new foundation had taken off!

In the fall of that year, Les Editions du Seuil, a publisher in Paris, published my book in French. I thought that because Haiti was a former colony of France, French citizens, after reading my book, might persuade their government to help Haiti eliminate child slavery. In 1825, the French had forced Haiti, at cannon-point, to compensate former slaveholders for the losses of land and labor that occurred due to the slave revolt. This was in exchange for continued independence and recognition. The repayment terms, huge even in today's dollars, crippled Haiti's economy for more than a century. It was, undoubtedly, the first time in the history of the world that the victor had to compensate the vanquished. The way I saw it, France *owed* Haiti, big time.

In the early summer of 2002, I flew to Paris to promote my book. I was interviewed numerous times in the various media outlets—radio, television, newspapers, and magazines. After several book signings in libraries, I traveled by train to Geneva for more appearances.

One night in Geneva, I addressed a large audience at the International Labor Organization. The next morning, I returned to the ILO and met with Mr. Juan Somavia, the secretary general of the organization. I suggested that the ILO help raise awareness in the hope of changing the Haitian mentality toward children. They opened an office in Port au Prince, but it would be closed because of political violence. By now, I had learned that old societal habits were difficult to break. Because child slavery was so ingrained in Haiti's social fabric, it could not disappear by waving a magic wand. I knew that every group I "evangelized" might be of some assistance in what was more and more clearly becoming my mission in life.

Before I returned to Cincinnati, France-2, a national French TV network in Paris, asked me to join it in putting together a documentary about *restaveks*. I was thrilled and amazed. "The French do care," I thought. I was certain that such a documentary film would hasten the demise of child slavery.

Two months later, I found myself back in Haiti, this time with France-2 Television, assisting in the production of the forty-minute news documentary. In the fall of 2002, the film, *Les Petites Esclaves d'Haiti* (The Little Slaves of Haiti), was aired in every French-speaking country throughout the hemisphere.

For the next few years, I worked part-time as an adjunct professor of American history at Northern Kentucky University. Working part-time gave me the opportunity to continue my stateside advocacy on behalf of the children in Haiti, and of the foundation that Cindy and I had started on their behalf. I took every opportunity to go out to groups in the Cincinnati area and beyond in the hopes of informing them about an issue that usually proved to "blow their minds." My audiences couldn't believe that child slavery still existed in close proximity to our own shores. Sometimes I would tell them that I could not believe it either.

In the spring of 2005, I received an e-mail invitation from the office of the minister of education in the Bahamas to speak in some of their schools. Later, I spoke by phone to the minister's secretary. She said the minister was so touched by my book that he chose it for his book club, which meant it would be read by his staff, Bahamian citizens, and university students. A month later, I flew to the Bahamas and was picked up at the airport by a middle-aged man, a local high school principal named Tom. I was immediately struck by the beautiful hotels and clean roads, and I quickly identified the tourists walking the streets in shorts and sandals as Americans. The land was flat and sandy, with no sign of agriculture.

"When did the Bahamas get its independence from Britain?" I asked Tom.

"In 1973," he said.

"That took a long time," I said.

"Well, we're very proud of our little country."

"And I'm proud that my book will be read by Bahamian students," I said.

"Before we read *Restavec*, we didn't understand why some of our Haitian residents, who had come as undocumented refugees by boat, were sending some of their children to school and keeping others at home. When the police see children walking the streets during school hours, they pick them up and contact their parents. Often, these kids turn out to be Haitians."

"And what happens then?" I asked.

"These Haitians would say the children didn't have the proper documents to be sent to school. Then we'd find out their own children didn't have the proper documentation either. But they still made sure their own children went to school. We didn't know what was going on. Thanks to your book, we now know the real story."

"How does the Bahamian government process these children for school?"

"Their guardians are asked to choose a date of birth, and the government issues them temporary certificates which give these children access to our schools. I don't understand why any adult would keep a child from going to school."

"It's an old Haitian habit. They even have a saying for it: 'When a child is not yours, you give him half a bath,'" I said. Tom laughed.

"The Bahamas seem to be so different from my native island," I said. "Everything here seems so orderly; at least that's my impression."

"Our politicians usually try to do what's best for the country," he said.

"I wish Haitian politicians would come here to take lessons on how to run a country."

"The Organization of American States invited them here for a conference during their last presidential election. When the Haitians were asked about their plans for the future of Haiti, one man pledged not to set fire to his political opponents' homes if they would not kidnap his children." We both laughed.

I spent three days speaking at two different high schools and a university. I was amazed by the maturity and intelligence of the students, who asked many personal and historical questions about child slavery.

"When you were in college, did you think you'd someday speak on behalf of *restavek* children?" a high school girl asked.

"I like your question, and I am so proud of you for asking it," I said. She smiled. "But honestly, I never imagined myself as an ambassador for Haiti's lost children. All I knew was that someday I wanted to show my father that I was worthy of his love."

That afternoon I was interviewed at two Bahamian radio stations, and the next morning I appeared in a television news program. The next evening, a dinner was hosted on my behalf at the Haitian ambassador's residence. Seated on my side were several Bahamian officials. Facing us were the Haitian ambassador and his guests. As soup was being served, a woman sitting beside the Haitian ambassador asked, "Mr. Cadet, how do you like the Bahamas?"

"It's very beautiful here." I couldn't keep myself from adding, "And all Bahamian children go to school." The ambassador picked up on the implied critique.

"Don't forget, Mr. Cadet, that Haiti is a very poor country," said the ambassador. I was angry at the Haitian ambassador for using poverty as an excuse for Haiti's ills. *Poverty is a reality, not an excuse for Haiti to deny children their most basic human rights*, I thought.

"Mr. Ambassador, Haiti can eliminate its poverty. It has more natural resources than the Bahamas. With the sun and the beaches, the Bahamian government creates a tourist industry that's financing public education," I said, perhaps a little too forcefully for the circumstances.

One of my hosts from the minister of education's office, a woman sitting beside me, gently touched my hand and complimented the chef for the delicious vichyssoise. I regained my composure and enjoyed the meal. After dinner, the Haitian ambassador handed each guest a large brown envelope with a gift inside. It was a booklet about the life of Toussaint L'Ouverture, the leader of the Haitian Revolution, who died in a prison in France. "Someday," I said to myself, "maybe he'll have the guts to hand out *Restavec* to his guests."

CHAPTER 16

IN SEPTEMBER OF 2006, I received an e-mail from a French magazine reporter who lived in Paris. He said he had read my book
and requested that I travel to Haiti to help him in writing a story
on *restaveks*. I had made numerous trips to Haiti since 1999, when I
went to find my father and relatives of my late mother. The purpose
of these trips had been to distribute clothes to street boys, support
grassroots organizations working on the *restavek* issue, and observe
the *restavek* culture. I thought it was an opportunity to bring additional international awareness to the plight of these children, and
so I agreed to work with the French reporter. A month later, when a
travel date was set, I phoned a friend in Port-au-Prince and asked him
to try to set up interviews with families who owned child slaves. So I
flew once again to Port-au-Prince, where I met Simon, the reporter
from Paris. He was white, in his thirties.

At this point in time I had begun wondering whether anything
concrete could come of all the money, time, and energy I was invest-
ing in this cause. René Préval, a former vice president under the ex-
priest and ex-president Jean Bertrand Aristide, was now president-
elect. Aristide had been overthrown in February 2004 by former
officers from the Haitian military, and flown to Africa by the United
States. I remembered reading a newspaper article in which Aristide
said he had been kidnapped by US Marines and had no intention of

relinquishing power. If I seem apolitical regarding my native country, it's because I am. My childhood was based on self-preservation. So little ever seemed to change, no matter who was in power. Had I chosen to live in Haiti, no doubt, I would have been more engaged.

When I arrived in Haiti, United Nations troops, in full combat gear, were riding all around the capital in trucks, personnel carriers, and Jeeps, all mounted with machine guns—all this supposedly to help stabilize the situation on the ground for the new government. Their support personnel drove expensive SUVs, and poor Haitians resented them, thinking that they had come to get rich somehow from Haiti's misery.

I was immediately struck by the number of people in the streets speaking on cell phones. Poor people carrying telephones. I shook my head. Digicel, the phone company, sells prepaid minutes on telephone cards wholesale to street vendors, who then resell them retail.

When I arrived, I could see that things were even more neurotic in Haiti than they had been on my most recent trip. Traffic often stood still. Drivers turned on their radios full blast and honked their horns constantly, trying to hurry the cars ahead of them. The streets seemed to belong to men peddling soft drinks, trinkets, and phone cards. All in all, the atmosphere seemed semilawless, worse now than I could even remember.

On my first morning in Haiti, I met up with Simon and my Haitian contact. The three of us drove in a taxi to the nearby town of Santos, where we stopped at a makeshift "people's" restaurant—a tin shack furnished with two benches on which customers could sit. A large woman was cooking rice, red beans, and meat on charcoal stoves. A girl in tattered clothes with a soapy rag in her hand squatted on the ground, washing dishes, pots, cups, and spoons. I could tell from the dried tears on her face that she had been crying. A long switch, freshly cut from a tree, hung on the wall behind her. My Haitian friend introduced Simon and me to the woman and then walked off.

The woman, Antoinette, shook our hands and offered us a seat on one of the benches and then sat down in a chair. A cacophony of street noises filled the shack. The girl looked at us, no doubt the first foreigners to sit down in that shack. Of course she had no idea why we were there. I smiled at her. She lowered her eyes.

"We'd like to ask you a few questions about family life in Port-au-Prince," I said to Antoinette.

"How long have you been in the restaurant business?" Simon asked. I translated his French into Creole.

"Two years," she replied.

"Is business good?"

"Not too bad. Thank God."

"Do you have children?"

"I have two girls, fourteen and sixteen."

"Where are they?"

"They're in school."

"Are you married?"

"Yes, I am."

"How long have you been married?"

"Two years—my second marriage. My first husband died."

"I'm sorry to hear that. What does your husband do?"

"He works in a gas station."

"What's his name?"

"Marcel."

"Who is this girl washing dishes?"

"She's staying with me."

"Where did you find her?"

"My husband's family gave her to me as a wedding gift," she told us, as if she were describing the gift of a CD player or a puppy. Feelings of emptiness came over me. I tried to imagine the girl, nicely dressed, being presented to the woman at her wedding reception, but I knew it didn't happen that way.

"What is her name?" I asked.

"They call her Mimrose."

"How old is she?"

"She's nine or ten years old."

"Why is she not in school?" I asked.

"The business only produces enough to pay my own children's tuition."

"If I were to pay her tuition, would you allow her to go back?" Simon intruded. I translated, and the woman looked at Simon suspiciously.

"Yes, I would," said Antoinette. Mimrose looked at us wide-eyed. I smiled. She lowered her eyes.

"May we come to interview your family this evening?" asked Simon.

"Yes, my husband comes home at five. I'll wait for you here at six."

With my camera, I snapped a picture of Mimrose still washing several large pots and dishes. In a new edition of my book, *Restavec*, that photograph would replace the drawing of a boy, who was supposed to be me, scrubbing floors, that had appeared on the original cover.

We thanked Antoinette and then left with the goal of looking for slave children and taking their pictures. *Restaveks* were easy to find, always wearing tattered clothes, walking children in crisp and colorful uniforms to various schools. There is no such thing as public education in Haiti. Dozens of little, for-profit schools dot every quadrant of Port-au-Prince and most other towns and cities.

"If the school kids are out of uniform, how do you identify a *restavek* from a regular child?" Simon asked.

"It's easy for me, because I was one of them for twelve years. I look for kids with no sparkle in their eyes, kids who are always painfully thin, like the dogs you see walking the streets. If you look carefully, you will see whip marks on their arms and legs. To most people these children are invisible, but I can pick them out from a crowded market.

"A child does not necessarily become a *restavek* just because her parents handed her over to someone. It's the kind of treatment she or he receives from the host family that determines their status," I said. "If, miraculously, a Haitian family takes in a child and treats her like their own, then that child is *pitit kay* [a child of the house]."

When we returned to the little restaurant that evening, Antoinette was waiting to take us to her home.

They lived in a tin-roofed, unpainted, two-room cinder block home with no running water or electricity. In the first room, the family's two daughters shared a double bed. Mimrose, of course, slept on the floor.

Everyone wore clean clothes that night, including Mimrose, whose hair was braided and sporting a red bow. After the interview, I handed Antoinette twenty dollars as a gift. She smiled. "Mèsi," she said.

Days later, I drove Simon to the airport for his flight back to

France. I liked him. He reminded me of my former French professor, Dr. De la Ménardière, who had given me the book *Le Petit Prince*. And that thought gave me an idea, which I decided to act on that very day.

I felt that, perhaps, if Antoinette were to bond with Mimrose, they might become "unique" to each other, as the Little Prince had become "unique" to the fox. I couldn't help fantasizing that Antoinette might eventually see Mimrose as her own daughter rather than her slave. Such hopes and fantasies are usually unfounded in Haiti.

After Simon's flight departed, I returned to the makeshift restaurant and found Mimrose once again washing pots and pans. The customers, all men, sweating heavily, sat on the benches, spooning food from the plates in their laps. The great motivator, the whip, was still hanging there in plain view.

"I have come to register Mimrose in school," I said. Everyone stopped chewing and looked at me. Mimrose raised her head. A hint of a smile seemed to appear on her face. I smiled at her. Antoinette pulled me outside to speak with me in private.

"Did the *blan* send the money?" she whispered, unable to imagine that I, a Haitian, would be paying Mimrose's tuition.

"Yes, but he asked me to personally register Mimrose in school." In truth, Simon had not given me any money for Mimrose's education.

"Is the *blan* coming back?"

"Yes, in a few months. He said that all children are gifts from God and, if you truly love God, you should love Mimrose like your own. The *blan* wants you to divide domestic chores equally among your daughters and Mimrose, and be affectionate to Mimrose and include her in all family activities."

"I understand," Antoinette said somberly, and called Mimrose outside. "She'll go to school in the afternoon from 1:00 to 5:00. I need her here in the morning," she added.

"That will be fine. You'll make the *blan* very happy," I said. Antoinette smiled. I was certain that if Antoinette thought the message and money had come from Simon, her attitude toward Mimrose would improve.

"Go home with Mr. Jean-Robert," Antoinette told the girl. "Put on your clean dress and show him the elementary school."

I took a taxi with Mimrose to Antoinette's house. I sat beside her, holding her hand. Of course, she was scared. She had never been in a taxi before.

"Would you like to go to school?"

"Oui," she said.

"I love you very much. You understand?" I said and kissed her forehead. She couldn't stop smiling.

"What would you like to be when you grow up?"

"I want to be in school."

"No, Mimrose, not where you want to be, but what do you want to be when you grow up?" Mimrose shrugged her shoulders.

"I don't know," she said.

"Why do you want to be in school?"

"I want to learn to read and write." I had never thought of "becoming" anything either. Mimrose's mind was in shackles, just as mine had been when I was her age, expecting to do nothing more than menial jobs the rest of her life. Florence's words echo in my mind to this day: "You'll never be anything but a shoe shiner."

Like Mimrose, I just wanted to be in school, if only to escape the wrath of adults and enjoy a few moments of peace, away from the endless chores. I felt that, influenced by attending a school, Mimrose might recover parts of her childhood. She might be seen differently by other children. Maybe she would even begin to feel good about herself.

At Antoinette's house, Mimrose changed into a clean dress while the taxi waited for us outside. Then we set out for the school Antoinette had suggested. Boys and girls in checkered red and white uniforms walked the streets going to or returning from morning and afternoon classes. The road was unpaved. As we passed them, they disappeared into a thick cloud of dust raised by the cab and other vehicles.

The nearest neighborhood school, an unpainted warehouselike structure, was surrounded by a ten-foot wall. Written on its gate was "Ecole Saint Pierre."

We approached the principal at his desk. Before him, on one of the walls, hung a *rigwaz*.

"Bonsoir," I said, because it was the afternoon hour.

"Bonsoir," he responded.

"I've come to register Mimrose in your school."

As I was paying Mimrose's tuition for the remainder of the year, the students we had passed on the road reappeared at the school's gate. I escorted her to the classroom. The students rose to their feet as we entered, and I signaled them to sit. I could feel the sun's heat radiating from the tin roof. The students didn't seem to mind the heat. Mimrose found a seat in the first row, and I returned to see the principal.

"I would like to ask a favor of you," I said.

"What's that?" he asked.

"I understand it's against the law to whip students. I see a *rigwaz* on your desk. I don't want Mimrose whipped."

"According to the minister of education, we're not to beat students, but sometimes it's necessary," he said.

"I understand, but do you understand my instructions regarding my little friend? I am paying the tuition. I think my request is reasonable."

The man's eyes met mine. He nodded, "Oui, Monsieur, m'komprann [I understand]."

I returned to the makeshift restaurant and gave Antoinette money to buy a school uniform and books for Mimrose.

"The *blan* wants you to send him Mimrose's picture in her uniform and a copy of her report card. Will you do that?" I gave her a card with my address on it.

"Yes, tell the *blan* I will," said Antoinette, excitedly. I sensed that she would not lie to a *blan*.

"Do you have a cell phone?"

"Yes." I wrote down her number. Under the phone system, poor people can receive calls for free. They pay only for their outgoing calls.

The next day I went to the American Airlines office to change my flight. I decided to spend an extra day, observing and speaking with more children trapped in ongoing domestic slavery.

Traffic was crawling on Delmas Street, and the sidewalks were busy with pedestrians and street vendors. The noon sun was pleasant, but exhaust fumes from so many old cars made the air hard to breathe.

I needed to urinate but felt too uncomfortable to do so against electric poles and walls as other men in the Third World often do.

I had truly become Americanized. I found an out-of-the-way place behind the corner of a building. In Haiti, even women can be seen relieving themselves by squatting in gutters and ditches. I began taking a count of small children on the street in tattered clothes carrying five-gallon buckets of water on their heads. There were far too many of them to make an accurate count. No doubt, many of these were *restaveks*. It was so hard for me to imagine how all these children remained "invisible" to the average Haitian, when their plight was so obvious. I reminded myself that average Haitians were the problem. Average Haitians "owned" these threadbare children. Average Haitians were complicit in continuing the practice their ancestors had fought to overthrow.

A skeletal girl with a white plastic bucket caught my eye. Her black dress, wet and muddy, was open in the back for lack of buttons, and I could see welts between her shoulder blades. I guessed her to be seven or eight years old. She was barefoot, struggling with a load too heavy for her small size. I took the bucket from the little girl's head and put it down. She looked up at me.

"Why are you taking my water?" She sounded like a five-year-old. Her eyes were vacant, her face was drawn.

"I want to help you carry it. How far are you going?" I asked.

"Up the road," she said. Since I had always heard Haitian adults say, "I want a child to help me," I wanted the people on the streets to see an adult helping a child. I wished I could have waved a magic wand and instilled the crazy notion in the mind of every Haitian that these children were not beasts of burden. They had feelings. And they had mental, if not physical, breaking points.

"Ki jan'w rele?" (What's your name?)

"M' rele Magalie." (I call myself Magalie.)

"Ki laj ou?" (How old are you?)

"Set an." (Seven.)

As I lifted the bucket to my shoulder, I could see passersby slowing down, looking at me, in sheer disbelief. Then they looked at my companion. For the moment at least, this precious *ti fi* (little girl), whose name was Magalie, aged seven, became visible to them.

We entered a long winding corridor that ended in front of a small cube-shaped cinder block house. I was winded, and my shoulder ached. A large elderly woman was seated in the yard feeding an infant. Both were light-complected.

"Who are you?" she asked, looking surprised.

"They call me Jean-Robert. The bucket is too heavy for Magalie. I carried it for her."

"Are you Haitian?"

"Yes, I am."

"With that accent, I don't believe you're Haitian. You're a *blan*." Haitians often call blacks from outside the country *blans*. Once again, the epithet stung. I didn't want to be spoken of as white, even in Haiti.

"Look at me. I am Haitian, not a *blan*." I spread my arms like Haitians often did to convince her otherwise. A man and a woman came out of the house with a baby.

"Bonjou," I said. "They call me Jean-Robert."

"They call me Thomas," he said.

"They call me Denise," the woman said. I assumed the infant was their child.

"They call me Charité," said the elderly woman.

"What are you to Magalie?" I asked.

"I am her grandmother. Thomas is my son. Denise is my daughter-in-law," said Charité. I was surprised, expecting her to say she was Magalie's "aunt," the name *restaveks* often give the women for whom they slave.

"I am Magalie's uncle," said Thomas. Perhaps Magalie belonged to him, I thought. Likewise, *restaveks* often called the adult man of the house "Uncle."

"Where is Magalie's mother?" I asked.

"Her mother and father died," replied Charité, following this with a brisk order to her resident slave: "Magalie, finish the laundry!"

"Oui." Magalie squatted immediately at a large aluminum basin of wet clothes and began scrubbing them. I noticed that her hands seemed no bigger than tablespoons.

"Does Magalie go to school?" I asked.

"We owe the school. So she got kicked out," said Charité.

"What school?"

"Ecole Saint Vincent, it's a few blocks from here."

"Would you permit me to take her to school and pay the tuition myself?" I offered.

"This child must be the luckiest girl in the world. Go, child! Put on clean clothes," ordered Charité. Magalie ran into the house. A while later, she came out in a pink dress and tennis shoes.

"Is this your grandson?" I asked Charité, as I entertained the infant.

"Yes, this is Leon," she said, and kissed his chest. I was puzzled by Magalie's odd status, a *restavek* among people who were her natural family. *Maybe I can persuade these people that this child Magalie is also worthy of love and affection*, I said to myself.

"I'll see you later," I said, and left taking Magalie by the hand. Once in the street, I immediately began questioning her.

"Is Charité truly your grandmother?"

"Oui."

"Is Thomas truly your uncle?"

"Oui."

"What is your last name?"

"Nicholas."

"What is Charité's last name?"

"Nicholas."

"What is Thomas's last name?"

"Nicholas." I assumed the *restavek* system had become more complex since I was a child.

Are you hungry?

"Oui." From a food vendor I purchased a banana, two boiled eggs, and ice water, which is sold in small plastic bags. After gulping down the food, the child bit a small hole in the bag and squirted water in her mouth and swallowed. I wiped her mouth with my handkerchief. She smiled.

It was past noon when we arrived at the school, a two-story, cinder block house with a tin roof, surrounded by a twelve-foot wall topped with razor wire. "Ecole Saint-Vincent" was written on a sign hanging from a metal post. I pushed open the gate. In the yard was an almond tree. I heard children repeat French phrases in unison after their teacher. We approached a woman on the front porch.

"Bonjour, I am Jean-Robert Cadet, and this is Magalie Nicholas."

"Bonjour, I am Madame Duval. May I help you?"

"Do you know Magalie?"

"Yes, she was expelled months ago. She owes the entrance fee and tuition for September and October."

"What grade was she in?"

"First grade."

"What is Magalie to you?" the woman asked.

"She's my daughter-to-be, and I'd like to pay her tuition from February to June. Will you give me a tour of the school?"

"A tour is not possible."

"Why not?" I asked.

"That's the rule."

"Well, Madame, if I can't see the classrooms, I'll take her to another school."

"Au revoir, Monsieur," the woman said, scowling at us.

"Au revoir, Madame."

Heading back toward the Nicholas home, I noticed a two-story building with a white cross on top. I saw children in uniforms coming out of its gate. "Ecole Chretienne" was written on the wall. We walked in.

The yard was cemented. A man standing on the porch asked to help me.

"I'd like to register my daughter in your school." Magalie smiled. The light that had been turned off in her eyes was suddenly shining brightly.

"Come in," he said, and we followed him to his office.

"I am Jean-Robert Cadet, and this is Magalie Nicholas."

"I am Pierre Louis, the director."

"I removed Magalie from her old school because I was denied a tour of the facilities." Pierre Louis smiled.

"They probably have something to hide. You can visit our school anytime," he said.

"How much is tuition?"

"Two hundred and fifty dollars a year," he said.

"Will you give us a tour?"

"Of course, follow me," said Pierre Louis. The rooms, dark for lack of electricity, were furnished with wooden benches. The walls were bare, and the chalkboards worn. In the backyard were two outhouses. There was no sign of running water.

"You like this school?" I asked Magalie.

"Oui," she said, smiling. We followed Pierre Louis to his office, where he tested Magalie's math skills orally.

"I'll give you fifty dollars and wire the balance when I get home," I said.

"I trust you," he said. He could tell from my accent that I had been living in the States. He wrote the school's address on a sheet of paper and handed it to me.

Magalie and I walked hand in hand back to her home. In the yard I saw a boy and a girl in school uniforms. They, too, were light complected.

"Hello, they call me Jean-Robert."

"They call me Anna."

"They call me Robinson."

"Are you related to Magalie?"

"She's my sister," said Robinson.

"She's my cousin," said Anna.

"You live here?"

"We live next door," said Robinson.

Charité came outside.

"You're back. Did you find the school?" she asked.

"I enrolled Magalie at Ecole Chretienne. It's a lot closer, and she is expected tomorrow."

"Thank you, Monsieur. Now, Magalie, go finish your chores," ordered Charité. Magalie went in, changed into her tattered black dress, and returned. She squatted at the basin, scrubbing the laundry once again, but smiling now.

I took a picture of Magalie and said good-bye to the family, still puzzling over why the girl was her grandmother's slave child.

The next day, before going to the airport for my flight back to Cincinnati, I returned to Charité's home and saw Magalie in her black tattered dress rinsing laundry in the white bucket. Everyone was in the yard speaking to one another excitedly. Magalie kissed me on the cheek, and I held her in my arms.

"She's been telling people you're her papa," said Charité.

"She's a precious child. I don't mind being her papa," I said, hoping to humanize Magalie in her family's eyes.

"I've come to say good-bye. I'll be back in a few weeks with powdered milk, clothes, and vitamins for Magalie and the baby," I said.

"Thank you," said Charité.

"May I have your phone number?" I asked the woman. I put Magalie down, wrote Charité's cell number in my notebook, and left for the airport. I thought perhaps if I continued to show them that Magalie was important to me, they might be more likely to treat her as family. Was I dreaming?

After returning to Cincinnati, I phoned Antoinette. Her tone suggested that she was bonding with Mimrose. So I thanked her for treating Mimrose like her daughter. Then I asked to speak to Mimrose.

"How are you, Mimrose? This is Jean-Robert."

"I am not too bad," she said. I could tell she was smiling. "When are you coming back to see me?"

"Soon," I said. Later I placed a call to Charité.

"This is Jean-Robert. How are you?"

"Not too bad."

"How's Magalie?"

"She's fine."

"May I speak to her?"

"She went to fetch a gallon of water across the street. She'll be back in a minute."

"She's so sweet. God wants us to treat all children well. I'll call back tomorrow." The next day I placed another call to Charité, who handed the phone to Magalie.

"How are you?"

"I am not too bad," she said. But, unlike Mimrose, her tone of voice indicated that things had not improved in the house of her grandmother. I told her I loved her and said goodbye. There was little that I could do until my next trip to Haiti.

Weeks later, Mimrose's picture came in the mail. She wore white ribbons in her hair, a red checkered dress—her school uniform—and a smile. It seemed that Antoinette had kept her promise.

In mid-December 2006, I embarked on yet another trip to Haiti. I had collected toys and supplies from church groups for girls in a privately run shelter. Most of these girls were *restaveks* who had run away from abusive owners. I had also packed some clothes, shoes, toys, underwear, powdered milk, and children's vitamins for my new friends, Mimrose and Magalie.

The girls' shelter was a three-story building in a shantytown called "The City of God." It sat beside a large canal that carried raw sewage to the sea. When I arrived, about fifty girls were on the terrace sitting on benches and waiting for me. I handed out dolls, packages of underwear, socks, dresses, and assorted toys. I noticed several girls with sad faces and approached them.

"What's the matter? Aren't you happy?" I asked.

"M' vle yon poupe blan [I want a white doll]," she whispered in a sad Creole, while trying to push her black doll under my arm. My heart sank. But I understood exactly why they didn't want to play with these dolls. All their lives they had heard and seen Haitians holding whites in high esteem. In their minds and hearts, God, Santa Claus, saints, and angels were white. To them, the Devil was ugly and black, just as I had envisioned him when I was a *restavek*.

Luckily, I remembered that there were several extra white dolls in the bag. I gave them to the two girls. Immediately, they were contented.

Looking at the City of God from the terrace of the school, I saw a long line of white UN trucks and SUVs snarled in the never-ending traffic jam on the road below. Beside the canal, a stone's throw from the road, were naked children, pigs, and skeletal dogs searching for usable/edible scraps among the heaps of mud-coated trash. By turning slightly toward the east, I could see, on the hilltop in the distance, million-dollar homes gleaming like lavish rhinestones.

When it was time for the girls to have lunch, I went into the cafeteria on the second floor. They ate white rice and red beans with fried turkey, served in neon Frisbees. I looked at a Frisbee. It said, "Made in China."

"Where did you get these?" I asked a woman in the cafeteria.

"They were sent from America," she said.

"Do you know what they are?"

"Plates," she replied. *Haiti is still in total darkness*, I thought. I didn't bother to explain to her that the discs were in fact toys, meant to be tossed among the children. She probably wouldn't have believed me.

I stopped at Antoinette's makeshift restaurant to see Mimrose, the child who had been Antoinette's human wedding gift. Mimrose wore a clean dress and a red ribbon in her hair. She was thrilled to see me. I glanced at Antoinette, who had a big grin on her face.

"Did you receive Mimrose's picture?" she asked.

"Yes, I did. Thank you."

"Did the *blan* that paid Mimrose's tuition come with you?"

"No, but he wants to know how you're treating Mimrose."

"Tell him that Mimrose has become my daughter." *Wow! At least one person in all of Haiti has been tamed*, I thought.

"Will the *blan* continue paying for Mimrose to go to school?"

"Yes, he will." I walked with Mimrose to the car so we could have a talk.

"When was the last time Antoinette beat you?"

"She doesn't beat me anymore."

"That's wonderful!" I said. "Now I have another question." She looked at me with bright, expectant eyes.

"What do you want to be when you grow up?" She smiled. She remembered I had asked her that question months earlier.

"I want to be a nurse," she said. Now it was my turn to be thrilled. I could see that her mind was no longer in shackles, that she was no longer living with the shadow of fear hanging over her young life. We walked back to the restaurant. Antoinette was closing up shop. I said my good-byes and then watched as she and Mimrose walked home from the restaurant, hand in hand. For me, this was an incredibly powerful image. In that little moment, my deepest hope was realized: I had determined that the *restavek* system was not an immutable reality for Haiti, nor was it the ugly stepchild of poverty, as so many Haitian officials believe.

I went to upper Delmas to see Magalie. Approaching Charité's house with the supplies, I saw Magalie in a ragged dress, scrubbing laundry. She ran to me. I bent down, and she wrapped her arms around my neck. On her face, arms, and legs were small burn marks. Charité came out of the house, and I shook her hand.

"Magalie has not gained any weight," I said.

"She eats a lot. She's still telling people that you're her father," she reminded me again.

I was angry. "How did she get these scars?"

"She burnt herself lighting the fire. I told her to be careful," said Charité.

"Will you give Magalie a vitamin and a glass of milk before she goes to school each day? Children don't learn much on empty stomachs."

"No problem," Charité said.

I made up a little fib for Charité. "Magalie told me that she wants to take care of you when she grows up." Charité smiled, although she probably knew that Magalie would say no such thing. I was desperately trying to change Charité's heart toward Magalie. Haitian parents make great financial sacrifices to send their children to good schools. In return, they expect their children to care for them in their old age. I hugged Magalie.

"She's a very precious child," I said, and walked away, my heart as heavy as stone inside me.

CHAPTER 17

A FEW WEEKS AFTER my return to Cincinnati, in early January 2007, I received a call from a woman at the Harpo Television Production Studio in Chicago. To say I was overwhelmed when she invited me to be a guest on *The Oprah Winfrey Show* would be a huge understatement. At the time I wrote this chapter (not long before her announced departure from the show), Oprah was the most famous and beloved talk show host in the world. Having "retired" from teaching, I had often enjoyed her programs, including interviews with famous and not-so-famous guests. I had been trying so many different tactics in hopes of securing a humane life for Haiti's *restaveks*. *Maybe*, I thought, *being a guest on* Oprah *will be the thing that finally does the trick.*

As the woman outlined various aspects of my role as a guest on the show, I found myself remembering a dream I had had some time before involving Oprah. In the dream she was driving me through a jungle in an open-top Jeep whose front seat was a couch, like the one she has on her show. She was in jeans and a blouse, and her hair was braided in cornrows. That was all I could remember, but it felt like a positive dream, especially compared to some of my all-too-frequent nightmares.

In short, I was elated to be invited to appear on the show. I recognized that this could be a platform for exposing, to a huge national audience, the issue that had become so central to my life.

Before she hung up, Ms. Robe, the caller, requested three copies of *Restavec*, pictures of Cindy and Adam, and the DVD that had been made of my speeches at the United Nations. I put the receiver down slowly. "This is really happening," I heard myself mumble.

I was bursting to tell this incredible news to someone. I could barely wait for Cindy and Adam to arrive home from school. As she pulled into our driveway, I ran to tell them the news. Cindy was bemused. "I had a feeling something like this would happen," she said.

"That's really cool, Dad," said Adam.

Then I thought of my old friend, Mr. Rabinowitz, who had retired to a senior community in Florida. I placed a call to him.

"Max, guess what? I've been invited to be on *The Oprah Winfrey Show*."

My old teacher nearly jumped through the phone with excitement. He seemed more enthusiastic than even I was. "You're gonna be a star, Jean. And then you'll no longer have time for me."

"It's not that big a deal, Max," I said.

We arrived in Chicago on February 5, Cindy's birthday. *Oprah* paid for our transportation and for all our expenses. The next morning, a limo picked us up and drove us to the Harpo Studios. We met Ms. Robe and followed her through a long hallway decorated with photographs of Oprah with various famous people. One that stood out for me was Nelson Mandela. *Wow! Would I like to meet him*, I said to myself.

Farther down the hall, I was stunned to see an almost life-size, black-and-white photograph of Oprah in jeans and a blouse, with her hair in cornrows. She looked exactly as I had seen her in the dream. I couldn't stop thinking about this weird coincidence. *Could I possibly have seen this photo in some magazine?*

The walls in my dressing room were decorated with pictures of movie stars like Tom Cruise, Will Smith, and others. On a large counter was a tray of sandwiches and cookies of various kinds. A small refrigerator in the corner was stocked with soft drinks.

"Oprah knows how to treat her guests," I said to Cindy. She smiled. Adam and I dove into the hospitality. After our snack, I wandered around the room, investigating every little detail.

"Sit down, Jean," Cindy said. "You're making me nervous, walking around the room like this," Cindy said.

"Me too," Adam said, only to be agreeing with his mom.

"*You're* nervous! I am the one who'll be seen on TV all over the world. How can *you* be nervous?" I asked.

"Sit down. Take some deep breaths, you'll be fine," she assured me.

"You'll be fine, Dad," Adam repeated.

Soon, a woman came in and began applying makeup on my face. I could feel my heart beating. I was really nervous.

We had been told that this particular program would deal with various aspects of modern-day slavery. On the television set in my dressing room, we watched another segment of this show, as it was being taped. Lisa Ling, a reporter who had been in Ghana on assignment, introduced a short documentary on slave boys in a fishing village. The film began with images of boys as young as six years old jumping off canoes to untangle nets stuck on tree branches at the bottom of a lake late in the night. All these children had been sold into slavery by their own mothers and fathers. It was mentioned that some children had drowned doing this work. Watching this sad documentary footage did nothing to ease my nervous agitation. I couldn't help projecting myself into the horror of these young African lives. I knew that these boys could not tell their masters when they were tired, hungry, sleepy, or sick without risk of being punished. Seeing documentary footage of other enslaved children set my mind racing. "Why does the UN allow this to happen?" I said.

Cindy noticed my agitation and did her best to help me focus on the daunting task before me.

At one point, an aide escorted Cindy into the auditorium and gave her a seat in the front row. Adam would watch the taping from the "green room," because no one under eighteen was permitted in the audience.

At some point, a man came into the dressing room and inspected me from head to foot like a drill sergeant. "Take off your shirt. It needs ironing. You know Oprah. She wants everything to be perfect," he said. I wished that he hadn't said that. I followed his orders, and he ironed my shirt. Now I was even more nervous than before.

As I walked onto the set, the audience stood and applauded me. Noticing the couch on the stage, once more I recalled the dream in which Oprah drove me through a jungle in a Jeep with a couch for its seat. Now, having taken my seat on that couch, I saw Oprah in blouse and pants walking toward me, holding her shoes in her hand. *What is that all about?* I wondered. The audience applauded her with a passionate enthusiasm. At that moment, I really couldn't believe this was happening to me. The whole thing seemed over the top. Surreal. *Maybe this is a dream too*, I thought. Oprah sat down next to me, while my heart pounded madly. The applause was dying down. I felt a need to engage her in a brief conversation to relax myself. I leaned over and whispered in her ear: "Oprah, I had a dream about you." I had completely lost track of the fact that I was fitted with a microphone. The audience exploded in laughter, but I had no idea why.

"And what were we doing?" Oprah whispered back to me as she turned her smile toward the audience. The audience roared once again.

"We were traveling," I said. With that, the audience grew quiet. I guess it wasn't what they wanted me to say.

"Dreams can be very significant," Oprah said. She took my hand affectionately, and this gesture calmed me down somewhat.

"For fifteen years my next guest didn't speak a word until someone spoke to him first," she said. As she continued her brief sketch of my life, the video and pictures I had sent were shown to the audience, and all over the country. I was still shaking a bit. Of course, Oprah and I could see the screen also.

"That's okay," she said, comforting me as I fought back tears. There on the screen was a video of Adam and me playing soccer in our backyard, and then of small children in tattered clothes in Haiti carrying buckets of water on their heads. A tiny girl was blowing a condom, her only toy, like a balloon. I was almost ashamed to have the world know that so many children in my country were living in landfills, in filth, and among pigs.

"How does one overcome being a slave who had no name?" Oprah asked. I panicked. I had never been asked that question before.

"I don't think you do, because I believe that your childhood is your foundation," I rambled. Almost simultaneously as I spoke, I thought about what I should be saying. "I don't know what it was like being a child, because I never was one."

"How did you get your freedom?" asked Oprah.

"I was thrown out because I was no longer needed . . ." The right words didn't want to come to me. I was slightly out of control, and was aware of that reality. The bright floodlights illuminating the set made me feel like a deer in the headlights of national television. All I could think of was to say what was most important to me. I had a mission. And so, in the midst of answering one of Oprah's questions, I blurted out my "mission statement."

"I believe that countries that give foreign aid to Haiti should demand that some of it be allocated to eliminate child slavery," I said.

"I agree," Oprah responded, flatly. This was probably not the direction she wanted our conversation to go, but I would not be deterred. I had convinced myself that various world powers would surely address this issue after the show was aired. I guess I was overestimating the power of daytime US television.

The interview lasted nearly forty minutes. After the taping, I was escorted off the stage into a waiting room, while Oprah went into a recording studio. She soon joined Cindy, Adam, and me, and our pictures were taken with her. Afterward I handed Oprah a copy of my book, *Restavec,* in which I had inscribed to her, "My book has given Haiti's 300,000 *restavek* children a voice; now I hope my appearance on your show serves as a doorway to their freedom."

Before we left the studio to catch our flight back home, I went to collect our belongings and saw a woman cleaning the room.

"What are you going to do with the leftover food?" I asked.

"We will get rid of it," she said. For reasons that went back forty years, I hated to see food go to waste, so I asked for a bag. The three of us had a wonderful lunch in the limousine taking us to the airport, thanks to Oprah.

My friends and family and I expected the piece to be aired within days, but that didn't happen.

Four and a half months later, the *restavek* segment was finally aired on *Oprah.* It lasted just ten minutes, and my suggestion that foreign aid be denied to countries where child slavery was practiced had been deleted. However, because of this extraordinary national exposure, many people visited our new foundation's website, and there were many new donations.

One Cincinnati woman who had seen the picture of little Magalie on my website called and asked if she might be able to adopt Magalie. Her name was Shirley. She was married but unable to have children of her own. Days later I met Shirley and her husband, Dan.

"When I saw Magalie's picture, I fell in love with her," Shirley said. "I even had a doll named Magalie when I was a little girl. We'd very much like to adopt her."

"Magalie lives with her grandmother. Her situation is not good, but I don't know if she'd be willing to part with her. I'll be leaving for Haiti soon. I'll ask. That's the best I can do."

A few weeks later, I flew to Florida to spend a few days with Max Rabinowitz and his wife, Phyllis. After I had appeared on Oprah, Max had arranged for me to speak about my book at his retirement community.

Max picked me up from the airport. He had his usual big grin on his face, but what surprised me was his cane. I played it lightly as we walked to his car. "What's up with you, old man?"

"It's just a prop, Jean. I don't really need the damn thing."

"That's good. I just can't picture you getting old, Max."

"Never gonna happen, my friend," he parried. "So what's new with you?"

"Well, funny you ask. After all these years, I went back to my village to see if I could find any relatives and unearth my real date of birth. It was a weird, almost a traumatic experience."

"Good weird or bad weird?"

"Basically good. I think I have more relatives than there are goats in Haiti. But none of them could remember the date. 'Mango season,' they said."

Max chuckled, then told me he was sorry.

"What does it matter?" I reflected. "I'm not the only person in Haiti who has no idea of his birth date."

That evening, after dinner, Max and I sat for a game of Scrabble with his wife and their son, William, who was nearly my age. With one word I scored twenty-five points.

"Wise guy," he said. "I taught you English, and now your vocabulary is better than mine," said Max.

I smiled, "When you called me 'Wise Guy' at Spring Valley High, I thought it was a good name for a person, and wondered if the Guy family would have given me permission to use it." Everyone laughed.

The next day, late in the afternoon, we drove a golf cart to the retirement village community center for my talk. About fifty senior citizens were in attendance. Max stood up to introduce me.

"As many of you know, I am a retired teacher, and I invited our guest speaker to give a talk this evening. In the early seventies, I taught social studies at Spring Valley High School in New York. One day, I saw a black kid sitting in the last row of my history class. He looked withdrawn, sad, and lost," Max said, choking with emotion, tears welling up in his eyes.

He continued, "When I found out he spoke no English and had no friends, I took him under my wing. The kid was amazing. He was a very fast learner." Max choked up again. His voice cracked. He composed himself and said, "Then one day I saw tears running down his face and I asked him what was wrong. He said, in broken English, that he had been thrown out by his host family and was living in a Laundromat." My old teacher then fleshed out a short description of my life in America. "Now, Jean goes to Haiti regularly to help kids in slavery. Here's Jean-Robert Cadet, my hero. I'll let him tell you the rest of his story." As I spoke about my lifelong journey, people cried and laughed. At the conclusion of my talk, the audience applauded, honoring me with a standing ovation. I answered questions about my foundation's goal to free children in domestic servitude through advocacy and education.

In mid-November, I went on yet another trip to Haiti. My plan was to pay school tuition fees for *restavek* children and to participate in a big conference on child slavery. A march would take place on November 18, the National Day of the Child, a symbolic holiday that didn't exist when I was a boy. The events were organized by several grassroots organizations that were working on issues of *dwa timoun* (children's rights).

The first part of the program took place on November 17 at a hotel conference room in Port-au-Prince. I shared a table on a raised platform with seven other speakers. Behind me was a display featuring my book, *Restavec*, which had finally been published in its third language, Haitian Creole. I would be giving copies to the entire audience. Among the participants were a civil rights lawyer, a former *restavek* in her forties, and a government official. Facing us was a large Haitian audience dotted with a few white faces.

When my time came to speak, I was introduced as a former *restavek* and the author of a new book on child slavery. This would be my first public appearance in my old country. Stressful, but nothing compared to *Oprah*. I took a deep breath and stood up. Before I spoke, I spent a long moment attempting to look a number of the gathered Haitians in the eye. Then I began.

"If Toussaint L'Ouverture, our liberator, were alive to see children in tattered clothes walking children in uniform to school, children that are zombified because of emotional and physical abuse, it would break his heart.

"My childhood was stolen in the house where I stayed. To this day, this kind of child slavery continues, and you don't have the will to end it . . ."

After describing a part of my life in the United States, I returned to my primary focus. This time I was determined to speak my mind.

"I wrote this book, *Restavec*, to tell the world of Haiti's shame. How can we, in good conscience, blame the *restavek* system on poverty, when many other nations that are poor don't enslave their children? The Bahamas has far fewer natural resources than Haiti, yet all Bahamian children go to school. Child slavery is destroying our nation's future. To reverse course, all of Haiti's children must be given a full bath." Every Haitian in the audience knew what it meant to give a child "half a bath."

"Naming the airport after Toussaint L'Ouverture was easily done. To truly honor his memory, to really appreciate the sacrifices he made to liberate this nation, you must put an end to child slavery."

I was angry as I sat back down, and the audience knew it. But they applauded loudly, some with tears in their eyes.

I signed copies of my book as gifts for those gathered.

The next morning, the group came together at the Episcopal Cathedrale Sainte Trinité. It was packed with hundreds of children in T-shirts that read: "Yon Ayiti san restavek posib" (A Haiti without the *restavek* children is possible). I sat in the first row listening to sermons from a priest and a pastor.

"Children are gifts from God," said the priest during his sermon. We read the famous prayer attributed to Saint Francis.

These words registered in my mind: "It is in pardoning that we are pardoned and it is in dying that we are born to eternal life." This was a very emotional moment for me, partly because I could not remember ever attending church as a child. Florence didn't permit it. But I had mixed feelings about the Church. It had always seemed too ready to "pardon" the dictators and to focus on eternal life, while ignoring the most vulnerable in Haitian society.

Haiti is still a very Catholic country. The Church is in a position to lead the fight for human rights. Over and over, I've asked myself: *Why doesn't it do it?*

After church, we gathered outside, and I, along with individuals from organizations representing both Haitians and Americans working against child slavery, led some two thousand children on a march to the heart of Port-au-Prince. Traffic stood still. Our banners, as wide as the street, read: "Down with the *restavek* system."

We stopped at the Ministry of Social Affairs and shouted repeatedly in unison, "Make education available to all children." Then we continued a few blocks, faced the National Palace, and sang, "A Haiti without *restaveks* is possible." Finally, we marched to Champs-de-Mars and gathered at the famous statue of Jean-Jacques Dessalines on his horse atop a marble pedestal. From where we stood, I could see the Haitian flag floating proudly in front of the Presidential Palace. I cast my gaze at the hundreds of children before me, sweating in the noon sun, and I knew that children like them had been betrayed by every Haitian president since independence. I hoped that by bringing them into the light, these betrayals would eventually disappear.

That night, I went to visit my little friend, Magalie. I pictured her with Shirley and Dan, the Cincinnati couple who hoped to adopt her. I visualized the new little family coming to visit Cindy and me in our home.

Delmas, the main artery, was dark for lack of street lamps. Feeling my way down the dark corridors that led to Charité's house, I had major doubts that she would turn her granddaughter over to an outsider from the United States. Upon reaching her yard, I saw the light of a gas lamp through cracks in the door and heard Charité talking to another woman. I knocked.

"Who is it?" she said.

"It's Jean-Robert. I've come to see you and Magalie." Charité pushed the door open, and I stepped inside. The other woman disappeared into the next room. The house was hot and stuffy. Magalie, who was bedded in a corner like a puppy, sprang to her feet. I hugged her tightly. She remained beside me in her ragged dress.

"You want to sit a while?" asked Charité.

"Yes, thank you." Magalie read Charité's eyes and returned to her bedding. We sat facing each other, with the lamp between us.

"I'd like to place Magalie in a school across the sea. What do you think?" I didn't want her to know that a white person was interested in adopting Magalie. I thought perhaps she would ask for money because poor Haitians believe, with some validity, that white people are extremely rich. The idea of a couple of Americans paying money for this child seemed too much like doing business in the days of the slave ships.

"Magalie thinks you're her father anyway," the woman responded, shrugging. "Take her. You can have her." More than my feelings of relief and joy, the woman's words stunned me. This was the woman's granddaughter! But there wasn't the thread of an emotional bond between them, just as there had never been any love between Florence and me.

"Does she have a birth certificate?" I asked.

"No, but I let her use my family's name."

"Tell me about her mother and father. How did they die?"

"My son had Magalie outside his marriage. When Magalie was four years old, her mother dropped her off at my door and then disappeared. We don't know where her mother is. As far as I am concerned, she's dead. My son worked at the airport. He was loading a small airplane, and the propeller decapitated him. That was two years ago. The airplane company gave us nothing. He didn't have any insurance, they said. Would you like to see his certificate of death?"

"Yes, it will help with the process," I said. None of this made any sense. Charité and her family had made a slave of their son's child only because she was born out of wedlock.

"Come back tomorrow and I'll give you a copy of the death certificate."

I gave the woman one of the most sincere "thank-yous" of my life.

I approached Magalie, bent down, and kissed her goodnight. She wrapped her arms around my neck.

"Mwen renmin ou anpil" (I love you very much), she whispered. I looked in her eyes. "Mwen renmin'ou anpil tou," I said.

Shirley and Dan were thrilled when I told them that they could have Magalie as their daughter. They hired an attorney to begin the process of bringing Magalie home, where she'd feel safe, loved, and respected. They began traveling to Haiti to bond with Magalie. Dan and Shirley were committed, though they realized that a Haitian adoption could take as long as three years to complete.

A year after Magalie's adoption process began, I met a lovely American couple, Frank and Paula, who were friends with Shirley and Dan. They, too, were childless and wanted very much to bring a child into their home. Like Shirley and Dan, they had fallen in love with a nine-year-old child named Rachelle, whose picture they had seen on the foundation's website. Her situation was much different than Magalie's. She was living with her aunt, Bertha, and Bertha's three biological children, two girls and a boy, in a two-room, cinder block home. Rachelle, whose mother had died, had been abandoned by her father.

Bertha would leave her home at 6:00 a.m. Monday through Saturday to sell used shoes (*pèpè*) at a large market in the heart of Port-au-Prince. Rachelle would stay home with Bertha's children, fetching water and running errands for neighbors until Bertha returned at 7:00 p.m.

On my next trip to Haiti, I went looking for Bertha at her house.

No one was home, but I saw Rachelle sitting on the porch of a neighbor. She was happy to see me. I took her aside for a talk.

"Rachelle, what would you like to be when you grow up?"

"A nurse," she said without hesitation.

"You can become a nurse if you go to a good school."

"I'd like to go to a good school."

"The good school I am thinking about is in America. Would you like to go there?"

"Oui," she said.

"I also know a wonderful family who'd love to adopt you. You'll have your own room with a big bed all to yourself. You'll become their daughter, and I'll be able to see you often. Would you like that?"

"Oui."

"I'll have to convince Bertha to let you come to America. When will she get home?" Since Rachelle wasn't sure, I asked the neighbor, who gave me her own telephone number. "Call me tonight at eight, and I'll hand her the phone," she said.

Hours later, I dialed the neighbor's number. I heard her call Bertha, who soon came to the phone. I told Bertha that I'd like to meet her, and we arranged to meet in the morning. Rachelle, apparently, had told her about our conversation. Early the next day, I went to see Bertha. She was tall, beautiful, majestic, and sported a large straw hat. As we drove to the market, I told her about my plan for Rachelle and promised to bring her bags of Kennedys to sell.

When I returned to Cincinnati, I placed a call to Frank and Paula. "You can adopt Rachelle," I told them. I could tell they were extremely happy about the news. Days later, they began the adoption process to bring her home. The couples would often travel to Haiti to bond with their daughters-to-be.

I recognize that international adoption is not a permanent solution to Haiti's inability to care for all its children. Nevertheless, I see myself in every neglected child, and I yearn to give each one a loving home and freedom from hunger and fear. When the opportunity arises to provide this, I will always act in the best interest of the child because love transcends culture, language, race, and religion.

Since the publication of *Restavec*, I had become known in many circles around Port-au-Prince as "the father of *restaveks*," a title that made me proud in a way. Over the previous years, I had befriended quite a large number of families who held children in servitude. Often I would visit these host families unannounced, bringing small gifts. Knowing that someone cared for these kids, the families treated them more humanely, at least.

I still befriend families and try to improve the situation for children in servitude each time I visit Haiti, but it became clear to me along the way that I could not help Haiti out of the restavek system one child at a time. The problem is deep-rooted in the fabric of society, and thus the change has to be cultural. The hearts and minds of the people of Haiti need to change changes that will not happen in months and maybe not even in a couple of years, but with the gradual sensitizing of the next generation through a national curriculum, songs, and other means of creating a national dialogue about the issue of child slavery.

CHAPTER 18

THESE DAYS, AS I move into middle age, I find that I am more and more reflective about everything: politics, popular culture, religion, relationships, responsibility, life, and love. Probably more than for most people, my thinking often folds back upon my own past, near and distant, and upon those factors, some centuries old, that have shaped me and drawn my life toward its passionate focus.

At this point, I am convinced that colonial slavery did far less damage to its children than does *restavek* servitude today. The colonial slaves in the new world usually had their own communities where children received parental love and lived their childhoods without inordinate fear. Children of slaves knew they were inferior, but not to those who were black like themselves. Like most children, they were disciplined by their parents, but generally not abused. They could be childlike and noisy at times, instead of silent and invisible, like many *restavek* children of today.

I do not exaggerate in asserting that the *restavek* system is destroying Haiti's future and severely limiting the country's potential for development and growth, even its economic well-being. Often *restaveks* grow up to be adults who see no value in other people's lives because their own lives were never valued. They were given nothing, and they have little or nothing to give back, individually, relationally, or in the context of society. Understandably, they are ill-equipped for marriage or parenthood. Many become part of a cynical, hardened criminal caste.

Child slavery perpetuates poverty, illiteracy, and crime. I believe that Haiti, as a nation-state, is severely ill. Every segment of its society is desensitized to the plight of children in *restavek* situations.

Haitian people want their country to be a part of the civilized world, but they refuse to recognize the dark reality that prevents their unlocking the shackles of the past. They are aware that the entire Western Hemisphere looks down on them, and their country, as incapable of growth and forward movement. It is almost as if the slavery paradigm is a nationwide security blanket.

As I reflect on a lifelong journey toward freedom and love, it feels as if my coming to America had been determined long before I was born. Something outside myself seemed to have been protecting me, showing me the way. How else can I explain my moving toward adulthood and modest success without having experienced a moment of parental guidance, a moment of familial love?

Those who have followed my story in the pages of this book can see that I became an adult without ever going through childhood. I hadn't had the slightest notion of how a family functions until Cindy came into my life and, slowly, painstakingly, taught me to be a husband and a dad. Early on, I can see that I had approached marriage with Cindy as if she were a roommate with whom I shared a bed. I could never understand why dinner invitations from her friends were also extended to me, nor could I see why Cindy got upset when I chose not to attend her family events and parties.

I remember the look of disappointment in her face when I told her about a movie I had recently seen at the cinema on a Saturday afternoon. It hadn't entered my mind to take her with me. This happened several times. I just couldn't get it into my head and heart. Allowing myself to be "tamed" was one of the hardest things I ever did. Even now, I'm still working on it.

Here's one final example. I remember vividly the first holiday season Cindy and I spent in our new home. Cindy recalls it almost with horror.

I was determined not to celebrate Christmas, a day that had meant nothing to me in childhood except additional pain and rejection.

Every Christmas as a boy, I had walked the streets in front of Catholic churches carrying water on my head, while the congregation inside sang, "Oh, Holy Night" and other songs. In stores and houses, I heard families laughing and celebrating, their radios blasting songs of *Joyeux Noël*. For me, there was no such thing as "joy" in Christmas. The day was even worse than other days, notable for its absence of joy, its absence of human warmth. On that day I tried to stay numb, like a stone. In all my years in the States, I let Christmas drift by without giving it much of a thought. As far as Christmas was concerned, I could have been a Martian. It was the worst of the holidays for me.

But not for Cindy. She told me she loved Christmas. And she wanted us to have a Christmas tree. *A Christmas tree! Why?* Even the thought of it seemed disgustingly sentimental. To me, the tree was even more ridiculous than Santa. It symbolized everything I had taught myself not to dream of. We argued about it. "No, I don't want a damn tree," I yelled. So Cindy went out and purchased a tree. I felt awful watching her drag it into the house.

Finally, I gave in. I helped fix it in the stand. But I didn't participate in the ritual of decorating it. Cindy did the whole thing. I wouldn't even watch.

When she had finished, she came into the kitchen and took me by the hand and walked me into the living room. "See, Jean, it's only a tree. Don't you see? It's beautiful. A tree can't hurt you," she said. I touched the tree, then its ornaments, and then its lights, staring at it, taking it all in, and trying to understand what it could mean. Standing there, for the first time in my life, I felt a tiny spark of the wonder of this holiday, a hint of the holiness in "Oh, Holy Night."

Gradually, I learned to celebrate Christmas with my wonderful family, who had literally loved me to life.

Perhaps I don't need to remind the reader that this book is a *memoir*, the French word for "memory." In Creole the word is not so different: *memwa*, one of those words derived directly from the French. But there is another word whose origins are not as clear: the word *sonje*, which, as a verb, means "to remember" or "to remind." As a noun, it is one of our words that mean "a dream."

I am not the first to note that looking back on one's life, the act of remembering, is a lot like dreaming. The harder you work at it, the deeper your memory takes you, the more you wind up asking yourself questions like: *Was that real? Could that possibly have happened?* And sometimes, for me, the questions become accusatory of myself: *Could I have been that stupid?* And accusatory of others as well: *Could they possibly have been so cruel and insensitive?* Remembering nightmares is easier than remembering good dreams. This *memwa* has something to do with how, in the right petri dish, a ghastly nightmare can mutate into something much more benign, an almost hopeful dream.

That was what Dr. Martin Luther King Jr. was doing on the steps of the Lincoln Memorial in 1963. He was looking at a historical and ongoing nightmare, and yet choosing to dream in the daylight. "I have a dream," he told us. Thirty-five years ago, I didn't understand that to dream the way King was dreaming meant to *actively* look toward the future, a better future for his country, for all people, for the human race.

At this moment, I too have a dream. Like King's, it is a benign dream, one that *reminds* me of all those hundreds of thousands of children in my native country who live each day without the tiniest stone of hope in their lives. Little boys and little girls in modern slavery (wherever they are), don't dream. Their minds are too busy worrying about their survival and safety. So in a way, I dream for all of them. I dream that one day Haiti will rise from the scourge of child slavery into a sunlit dawn, where all her children have a chance to reach for the golden ring of happiness, as I did. I dream that one day Haiti will back away from government corruption, build infrastructure, and make education a mandated gift to all children. I dream that, one day soon, Haiti's children will no longer be robbed of their childhood and their selfhood.

I am empowered to dream these things because someone like you is reading this book. Because of people like you, the stone of hope is being tossed into the pool of possibility. Who knows what wonderful things will ripple outward?

THE JEAN R. CADET RESTAVEK ORGANIZATION'S CALL TO ACTION

UNIVERSAL EDUCATION IN HAITI

Educated parents have options other than handing over their children to become *restaveks*. They understand the benefit of family planning. Informed farmers avoid deforestation that causes erosion and flooding, which in turn yield poor harvests. A literate Haiti would be inviting for investment that creates employment, generates taxes, and finances infrastructure and education. None of these are reality for Haiti today.

NATIONAL CURRICULUM

A national curriculum that exposes child servitude must be created in consultation with Haitian educators and integrated into primary and secondary schools. This information will change the mentality about acceptance of servitude and influence the next generation.

SPEAKERS' BUREAU

Former *restaveks*, in speaking about their experiences, provide students with powerful firsthand accounts of slavery that are otherwise unavailable to them. Challenged and empowered, the children can plan their own advocacy campaigns, including creating antislavery clubs.

MEDIA

The organization's website and Facebook presence connect activists, network resources, and post updates.

Building on Haiti's strong oral tradition, an annual "Song for Haiti" contest will host Haitian artists who will perform the songs they have written that encourage families to treat children in servitude like their own. The winning songs will be circulated through Haitian radio and TV stations.

To encourage host families to send *restaveks* to school, pro-education and anti-servitude messages will be printed on billboards that show children in rags walking with or carrying children in uniforms to school.

While the culture of *restavek* servitude can be eliminated only by Haitians, who must take ownership of this horrific practice and end its acceptance, its actual elimination requires an international community working toward this goal. Join us so that we can achieve the compulsory education mandated by the Haitian constitution and can unleash the chains of children in servitude. Haiti's children must be freed.

http://www.JeanRCadet.org/